EARLY ELEMENTARY EDUCATION

EARLY ELEMENTARY EDUCATION

Myrtle M. Imhoff

LONG BEACH STATE COLLEGE

FORMERLY SPECIALIST IN EARLY ELEMEN-
TARY EDUCATION, UNITED STATES OFFICE OF
EDUCATION

 New York

APPLETON-
CENTURY-
CROFTS, INC.

*LB
1507
75
1959*

44588

Preface

Our young children are our greatest responsibility and in
them lies our greatest hope for the future.
L. G. Derthick
U. S. Commissioner of Education

Research and studies within the various disciplines concerned with
the development of young children emphasize the influence of the early
years on all later living and achievement. Implications of this knowledge and data have effected increased recognition of the importance of
the early childhood period among both professional and lay persons,
and furthered interest in the provision of well planned, continuous, and
sequential learning experiences for young children under the guidance
of public education as a phase of the elementary school program.

Because of an urgent need for widespread professional and lay
recognition and understanding of the values of early education and
resultant sincere and enthusiastic efforts to provide such opportunities
for *all* our young children, this book was written. It is planned especially
for undergraduate students and teachers interested in early elementary
education; it is designed to give them the understanding and foundation
necessary to work effectively in the field and to further the educational
learning experiences of young children. It can, however, be a functional
help to any group, professional or lay, in their thinking, evaluating, and
planning for early education as a part of our present public responsibility. It is an outgrowth of much study, research, and service in the
field; it is centered in a deep conviction that we are not yet fulfilling
our professional responsibilities toward the young child in his educational needs.

This volume aims to give the teacher candidate for the early elementary field an organized overview of the basic concepts, theory, and

practice of democratic education for young children supported by research and study and supplemented by many illustrations and pictures; it assumes and provides resources for continuing and widening study, research, and understanding as the student advances in the field. Study of the text should be accompanied by observation and participation with young children in classroom and community activities.

The book has been developed in four parts, each planned to further the sound educational thinking basic to a program for early elementary education.

Part One gives a complete overview of the field of early elementary education in its existing programs and as a phase of public elementary education. Detailed study of the young child in his developmental processes and in learning experiences is supplemented by extensive illustration. Part Two, assuming that sound classroom practice is preceded by an intelligent understanding of democratic concepts and values, basic objectives of education, values of early education, and theory of the teaching-learning processes, develops these concepts. Part Three is concerned with practice based on the concepts discussed in Part Two. The organizational patterns of schools and classrooms, the environment and its part in the learning process, the curricula at the nursery school, kindergarten, and primary levels, and the multirole of the teacher are discussed. Illustrations and pictures supplement text. Part Four looks backward to persons, events, and writings of importance for causes of the directions the education of young children has taken in its development, and looks forward in trends in the education of young children and in the educational preparation of teachers for this level. Each chapter includes guides to further study, with functional projects and questions. A general bibliography and selected audiovisual aids are listed in the Appendix.

The writer is indebted to the many who have contributed directly or indirectly to the development of this volume, and especially to her readers, Dr. William H. Burton, Dr. Helen Heffernan, and Dr. Wilhelmina Hill. She wishes to thank the many individuals, school systems, and Teachers Clubs for the use of pictures and materials; and the individuals, professional organizations, and companies who granted permission for the use of quotations.

M.M.I.

Long Beach, California

Contents

Part I

EDUCATION
OF THE YOUNG CHILD

CHAPTER 1

The Field of Early Elementary Education

Today with deepened insight into the importance and influence of guided experiences for the young child, we are continuing to move forward in the planning and practice of education for this level. Significant of the broad and coordinated program emerging for young children is the use of the term early elementary education to indicate the increasing responsibility of public education for the downward extension of the public elementary school to include the kindergarten and the nursery school as an integral part of its program. The kindergarten, the nursery school, and the primary are no longer separate and isolated units but are a phase of the continuous growth and pattern which is the responsibility of the elementary school. It is the responsibility of all concerned to hope and work for this extension which will make guided educational experiences during this important early phase of growth the privilege of all American children.[1]

INTRODUCTION

Early elementary education is one of the most challenging and satisfying fields in the teaching profession! You have decided to take your place among the teachers and administrators who are working with and for young children. Your selection of this educational level should now be followed by serious study and careful evaluation of your interests and abilities, and by an overview of the field.

[1] Myrtle M. Imhoff, "What about . . . THE FUTURE?" *Early Education*, Vol. 2, No. 4 (April, 1957), p. 14.

Your study of early elementary education will be more valuable to you if you have a two-fold approach, that is, both scholastic and practical, the latter being the doing *based on the theory*. Scholastic investigation will give you an understanding of the various programs for young children and a glimpse of future trends within the field; it will reveal the theory and philosophy of elementary education and show you how it is put into actual classroom practice; it will emphasize the important role of the teacher and outline the types of programs for teacher education.

The practical approach, translating the theory into practice, will be a most valuable supplement to your reading and study and will prevent it from being mere "arm-chair" projection. It will involve using every opportunity to get to know, understand, work with, and guide young children. This may include helping in a nursery school, in a child-care center under public school supervision, or in an early elementary level classroom. It may consist of teaching a Sunday school class or tutoring. Or again, it may involve volunteer services in the community, such as helping to guide a Scout or Brownie organization, supervising the activities at a playground and recreation center, or helping with an extended day program. In any event, it will mean that you will avail yourself of every opportunity for *really* getting to know and understand children at various age levels, and for testing yourself to see how effective you are in guiding their play and learning activities. Public school and college staff members are glad to assist in finding such opportunities for prospective teachers and in evaluating with them their abilities and interests for the profession; community agencies welcome capable volunteers.

Your college program may include scheduled observations in early elementary classrooms. These observations are a very important part of your preparation for teaching young children. You should remember that in all instances, however, the children in their learning experiences are the most important consideration, and that your observation of them comes second. Be careful not to disturb the class by your entrance, observation, or leaving, and remain in the background at all times. It is usually best not to show any reaction to the children's behavior, or attempt to speak to the children. Be alert to observe:

4

1. the children in the learning situation, with regard to
    age and growth characteristics and developmental patterns
    responses to ways the teacher guides the learning processes
    thinking and problem solving processes
    individual interests and problems
2. the classroom environment
3. the school: type of building, play space, facilities, room arrangement,
    services, rapport, class size, and program organization
4. the community: socio-economic level, size, relationship to the school
    and use of school building, and facilities.

Further, you should make every effort to become acquainted with publications and research in the elementary and early elementary fields. For this purpose a *Guide to References for Further Study* is listed at the close of each chapter and a *General Bibliography* is supplied at the close of the book. The latter also includes reference guides such as the *Education Index* and the *Encyclopedia of Educational Research* which you will find of much help.

Thus, through reading, study, research, observation, audio-visual helps, and participation, you will prepare for effective service as a teacher in the early elementary education field.

(It is helpful to the student in her later work, student teaching, and beginning teaching if she *begins* at this time to set up a personal file of professional materials. It should be organized according to her individual thinking and use but should contain such materials as the following: reports on observations, annotated bibliographies and summaries of good publications, sources of materials, research data, content information, helps and techniques in teaching the various subject fields, pictures, lists of materials and films for parent's use, sketches and photographs of stimulating room environments, and ideas for units and classroom activities.)

SCOPE OF EARLY ELEMENTARY EDUCATION

Programs for Young Children

Educational programs for young children have existed in various forms since very early times. Study of the history of education and of the classics shows that the great educators of all periods from the early

Early elementary education majors display their files and materials

Greek down to the present time have recognized the importance of early education. (Chapter 11 describes the influence of these early movements on our program today.)

More and more, educators today are recognizing that one of the more important tasks of educating is in the hands of teachers who work with young children. At this early age, where the foundation for all growth and personality is laid, the real challenge to our educational program is made. Experiences of administrators, teachers, and parents, as well as data of research studies, verify the important relationship of adjustment in the early school years to later school success, mental health, and the general well-being of the child. Hence, we are beginning to see the emergence of a broad co-ordinated program of early elementary education extending from the *public* nursery school through the primary level (which usually means the end of the third grade). This newer program concept has its origin in long and varied experience, experimentation, and study in classroom practice founded on research data of the growth and development process and the psychology of learning. It is not just a theory which is first developed and later tried out in classroom teaching.

The recognition of the increasing responsibility of public education for young children and the acceptance of a *real educational* program as a unified, continuous experience based on the developmental growth and maturational pattern of the child have, in turn, effected a change in the term used to designate the program. The terms *nursery school,* *kindergarten,* and *primary* were developed and used to mark off certain grade levels and particular types of programs. Although we continued in the use of independent terms we also moved toward a concept of early childhood education which, while still retaining the separate levels within it, more clearly recognized the bond of continuous growth between the children of the various levels—and that few children matched the "average" as theoretically drawn for the chronological age or grade level. With this increasing understanding of growth processes and the growing acceptance of responsibility by public education, the term now coming into popular usage is that of *early elementary education.* This concept indicates that this period is *one* phase of the *continuous* growth pattern of public elementary education, and implies the downward extension of elementary school responsibility through the four-year-old nursery school level. Within it are included the graded, the block or primary unit, and the multigrade forms of organization. (See Chapter 7.) Designating the end of the primary level as the close of the early elementary education level in no way indicates a break in the continuity of the educational program at the end of the third year or grade. Rather it recognizes the level as one important phase of the developmental pattern of the child within the total pattern of growth.

The terms *nursery school, kindergarten,* and *primary,* used independently, specify particular programs *designed to fit the growth and developmental needs of children of a specific chronological age,* rather than set academic programs. *Preschool* is a term often used to designate the nursery school and kindergarten levels. In that *preschool* implies *before* school entrance, it is an incorrect term. The nursery school and kindergarten programs *are* a part of the total elementary program.

Kindergarten is defined as a program designed for children between four and six years of age but is usually used with reference to five-year-old children. Its purpose is to further the developmental growth of the child in all aspects of personality and to provide experiences which are of immediate help to him, as well as basic for his later learning activities of a more academic nature. *Formal* work in reading and numbers is not justifiably a part of the kindergarten program. In some areas, states, and individual systems the kindergarten is designed to cover the period of one school year while in others it has been extended from a one-year to a two-year period; in still others the program for the four-year-olds has been listed as a nursery school rather than a kindergarten curriculum.

Nursery school is a term which has been widely misused. Correctly applied, the term signifies the downward extension of the educational program in the regular elementary school curriculum to include the child under five years of age (but usually extends in public school practice to only the four-year-olds). This form of early education was introduced in this country in the late 1920's, when it was first brought before the American people by Teachers College, Columbia University. The term *nursery school* needs to be differentiated from that of *nursery, day nursery,* and *child-care center.* The latter programs have their origin in the social work of Oberlin and Owen in an early period of educational history, and were given much emphasis in America

8

through the P.W.A. and F.W.A. programs in the 1940's. With the exception of some child-care centers, these programs are concerned primarily with the physical care and supervision of the child while the parents are employed; health and safety are the major concerns of such programs.

Primary denotes the program designed for the first three grades of school, that is, the first three grades of the graded school, covering the average chronological ages of six to nine. A variation in the organization of the primary program is coming into evidence with the development of a plan in which the teacher remains with the same group for two or three years. In some cases the teacher remains with the group from their entrance into kindergarten through the primary level. Such a plan is an effort to create a learning situation for the young child in which there is opportunity for continuous and all-round development over a period of several years under one teacher. Under this arrangement there is the definite advantage that the teacher is able to know her pupils better; therefore, she can work more effectively with them. (However, remaining for several years under a *poor* teacher could have negative results.) Various names are given to this primary plan of organization; these include the "ungraded primary," "the continuous progress plan," "the pupil progress plan," and other similar titles. Another variation is the multigrade primary class. (Chapter 7 further clarifies and illustrates these plans.)

Programs for young children are found in both public and private schools. Generally, the public school programs tend to be educational programs and are the downward extension of public responsibility for the education of the younger child. Many of the private school and child-care programs are also educational programs, especially in California and New York where much is done to help such schools reach and maintain state standards in teacher certification and programs. The co-operative nursery school program in which parents play a major role is another type of program; where it is developed as part of the Adult Education program, it is usually excellent. However, not all private and co-operative school programs attain acceptable state standards; they vary from simple care and supervision to real education depending on standards, goals, staff qualifications, and supervision.

It is not too important what such educational programs for young children are called. Their real significance lies in the fact that the increasing importance of well-planned programs for young children, organized on sound psychological principles and based on their developmental characteristics and needs, is being recognized more and more by parents and public-school communities as well as by educators, psychologists, social workers, and others who are concerned with the development of young children.

OVERVIEW OF THE FIELD

The major goal of the field of early elementary education is to study and provide for the developmental and personality needs of young children. It involves wide and extended interests and varied abilities. The teacher and administrator working in this field must have:

1. A scientific knowledge and an excellent understanding of the growth and developmental processes of children, and of the psychology of how children learn.

2. An understanding of the place of the school as a social institution in our society, and a working philosophy of education and its objectives as they relate especially to the education of young children.

3. A knowledge of the methods and techniques of organizing and administering the elementary school in general and the early elementary classroom in particular.

4. Academic knowledge and the ability and skills to plan and develop effective learning environments and to guide curricular experiences.

5. An interest and skill in the use of professional organization publications, and in participation in conferences, programs, and workshops.

6. An interest and ability in the development of lay, parent, and community relationships.

7. An understanding of the influence of early educational movements and leaders on the present early elementary education program and on future trends.

A short consideration of each of the above will be given to provide an introduction to the field before considering the topics at length in the remainder of the book.

Developmental Psychology

. . . a scientific knowledge and an excellent understanding of the growth and developmental processes of children, and of the psychology of how children learn.

Change in educational thinking has focused our attention on the total development of the individual child in all the facets of his personality and in his individual potentialities. This means that our schools of today give much attention to the child's physical growth, emotional health, social development, and moral and spiritual growth at the same time that they continue to *retain emphasis* on academic and intellectual achievement. This attention to the continued all-round growth of the child as a whole person has deeply affected the education of young children.

Research in the psychology of growth has shown the facets of personality, namely, physical, mental, social, emotional, and moral, to be closely interrelated in development and function. Isolation of any one facet, such as the physical, is possible for further detailed study, but all personality facets function in dependence on one another. It is recognized that the child will grow, will be happily adjusted, and will be able to undertake successfully and participate fully in the learning experiences of the school most effectively when he has sound physical health. But consideration of his physical health cannot be complete without consideration of his social, emotional, and mental health Likewise, the emotional aspects of growth of the young child have been isolated for further study since this aspect of personality is of much influence and importance, especially in the early years. Young children have two predominant emotional needs: security and affection. It is characteristic of the young child to look to his parents for the satisfaction of these needs, and in the early school years, to his teacher in the school situation. Satisfaction of these basic needs develops good mental health and emotional adjustment; this, in turn, fosters all-round personality growth and makes the child more ready for learning experiences. Difficulties at home or unwise handling of problems in school can prevent the child from being able to profit from even excellent learning situations provided for him. Inept handling of early emotional experiences by parents or teachers can affect the entire later develop-

11

ment of the child academically as well as in personality. Social development is correspondingly important in influencing the growth of the child's personality.

All-round growth is important in the development of young children. We will consider the several facets of personality independently and in their interrelationships in Chapter 3. It is sufficient for our purpose here to realize that the teacher of young children is especially concerned with the growth and development of the child in total personality and *not* alone with helping him to grow mentally and academically. Too, in view of the foundational nature of growth in these early years and its influence on later patterns, it seems justifiable to say that though consideration of whole growth is important at all levels, it is even more important with young children.

Research into how a child learns has paralleled the study of growth; as a result we have developed a more functional approach to teaching. In older educational theory the teacher's main task was the transmission of knowledge, and most often "rote" or memory learning was the method by which this was accomplished. Today, research and experience show that much that is learned "as a lesson" or through rote memory is quickly lost. On the other hand, those experiences that are filled with meaning for us, that are associated with circumstances and things that we know, and that are *used* in our thinking and problem solving are the ones that make lasting impressions and become usable in future experiences. Learning that is used is functional learning. This functional approach to teaching, then, indicates a method which will help make real and purposeful to the child those learning experiences he is having, and will enable him to use such learning in his own thinking and living. Not only does he know facts, but he uses knowledge as the basis of his problem solving, and for critical and creative thinking at his level of maturity—whether he be in kindergarten or in college.

Psychology further enables us to provide increased opportunities for functional learning through understanding of the part played by the various senses (that is, principally, visual, auditory, and kinesthetic and secondarily, taste and smell) in learning. At one time nearly all instruction in the schools was through the visual sense; reading was the primary method of study. Today, we make use of all five sense approaches in learning situations. Each normal child learns through all five sense approaches but usually learns more effectively through one than through the others. Perhaps you find you learn more easily through reading. Another student may learn most quickly through hearing, whereas a third may write notes to best grasp what he is learning. All are learning through all three principal sense approaches, but each finds that the one is most effective and the other two supportive. Classroom methods today make use of all five varied approaches, thereby making all learning more effective for every child.

Studies in psychology and growth give us guides which help us understand the range of differences among children of a specific chronological age in development, needs, abilities, and readiness. Developmental patterns, built on the so-called average or typical child, can be adjusted to the individual and to groups with whom the teacher is working. Psychology, which emphasizes the importance of *readiness* or preparedness to learn, and which teaches that learning experiences based on developmental tasks can provide the best assurance that readiness will develop, outlines these developmental tasks for the various age levels and states their implications for curriculum. Havighurst states:[2]

A developmental task is a task which arises at or about a certain period in the life of the individual, successful achievement of which leads to his happiness and to success with later tasks, while failure leads to unhappiness in the individual, disapproval by the society, and difficulty with later tasks.

Such tasks have their origin in the physical and psychological growth of the individual, in the circumstances and culture in which the individual lives, and in the personality of the individual as it is expressed in terms of his goals and values.[3] For the infant and very young children developmental tasks are largely bio-physical and include learning to walk, talk, and so forth. As children mature, developmental tasks become more concerned with the development of self or personality.[4]

Aydelotte has chartered the developmental tasks outlining specific tasks for each "age group" level. The portion relating to early elementary is cited here.[5]

[2] Robert J. Havighurst, *Developmental Tasks and Education,* rev. ed. (New York, Longmans, Green & Company, 1953), p. 2.
[3] See *Ibid.,* p. 4.
[4] See *Ibid.,* Ch. 2, pp. 6-14.
[5] J. H. Aydelotte, "Developmental Tasks of Children and Youth," in Harold R. Bottrell, *Introduction to Education* (Harrisburg, Pa., The Stackpole Company, 1955), Ch. 6, pp. 145-146.

	Preschool Child Age: 5 (+ or −1)	Early Childhood Age: 6-8 (+ or −1)
Physical Adequacy	Increased muscular controls. Talk, balance, walk, run.	Improve large muscle control. Coordinate large and small muscles.
Affectional Security	Recognize and return affection.	Learn to relate one's self to family and near associates. Learn to give and share affection.
Group Belongingness	Beginnings of social interaction.	Develop ability to interact with age-mates.
Social Competency	Improve speech. Explore local world. Gain simple concepts of physical reality.	Accept adult restrictions and rules in exploring the world. Enormously increase concepts of reality.
Self Concept	Conceive self in relation to some independence from adults.	Increase recognition of independence from adults. Develop sex modesty. Reach intermediate concepts of right and wrong.
Self Adjustment	Attract attention of adult to feelings of need. Accept a time and place schedule of need satisfaction. Reduce responses to feelings of emotion when thwarted. Avoid common dangers.	Accept the authority of adults. Accept and meet the needs for rest, diet, etc. Find both satisfactions and limitations of make-believe. Expect failures as well as successes. Learn that successes are earned by repeated effort. Learn necessity of sharing and cooperating with others.

These developmental tasks, then, have direct implications for classroom planning. They indicate types of experiences and learning for which average children of a given chronological age are ready. Using such tasks as a general guide, and planning in terms of individual variations within her group, the teacher guides the children's development to further growth and readiness for learning.

Philosophy and Objectives

. . . an understanding of the place of the school as a social institution in our society, and a working philosophy of education and its objectives as they relate especially to the education of young children.

As teachers and administrators of programs for young children we must *always* understand and have a solid reason for what we do—especially in those activities that relate to children. Why, then, do we further the type of educational program we have today?

American schools reflect our democratic society and culture. The school is the institution developed to perpetuate the ideals of the society.

Basic to our American society are (*1*) belief in the worth, value, and dignity of each and every individual, and (*2*) recognition of the fundamental need of group interaction. We know that in order to realize and further our goal of democracy each and every individual must be developed through education, and that only through such individual growth will our society continue to advance. Because of this belief our educational program is centered in the all-round growth and development of every child, and at the same time it aims to increase the child's understanding of himself, of others, and of his environment, both immediate and far-reaching.

Accepting this broad foundation of democratic ideals as the basis of all American education, we develop within its framework specific aims for each maturity level in our schools. The early elementary education program has goals specific to it which are planned in terms of democratic ideals and are adapted to its maturity level. These serve as the foundation for continuing growth in the school levels that follow. We will consider in detail the broad objectives of American education and the specific aims basic to the education of young children in Chapter 4.

15

Organization and Administration

. . . a knowledge of the methods and techniques of organizing and administering the elementary school in general and the early elementary classroom in particular.

The educational program in America, as it developed and expanded, became organized into three major divisions. These levels or administrative divisions are: (1) elementary education, including the kindergarten and nursery school; (2) secondary education; and (3) higher education. The major purpose of such division was to further the effective functioning of the school in its development of the child as an individual and as a member of society. These divisions, as part of the whole educational system, offer increased services and resources, better programs, and more effective administration.

Variations are found within our administrative organization of schools, as study of the chart on page 17 will show.[6]

Schools are organized on the graded or year plan. The elementary school may extend only through the sixth grade or year, or it may include the seventh and eighth year. The kindergarten is an integral part of the elementary school in most areas, yet in some parts of the country it still exists as an isolated unit; still other areas may offer no program. Such variations exist not only within the schools in the various states, but even in those within a state, city, or local boundary. The situation with regard to nursery schools is similar to that of the kindergarten. Some few elementary schools extend their program down through the four-year-old nursery school level; many do not include a program for the younger child, while in a few the nursery school and kindergarten form a unit not integrated with the entire elementary school program.

Organization within the individual elementary school may follow one of various plans. The school may be (and usually is) organized on the traditional graded plan with each grade level representing a year of work and subject content. However, more and more we are coming to see the elementary program developed along new lines. One of these involves the establishment of several primary or neighborhood schools

[6] United States Office of Education, *Education in the United States of America,* Special Series No. 3, rev. ed. (Washington, D.C., Government Printing Office, 1955), p. 14.

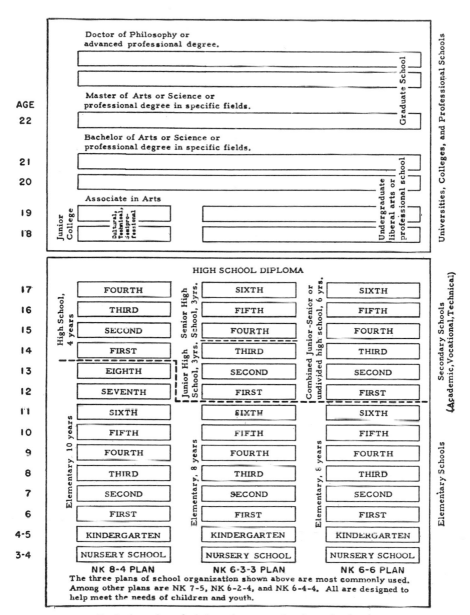

The three plans of school organization shown above are most commonly used. Among other plans are NK 7-5, NK 6-2-4, and NK 6-4-4. All are designed to help meet the needs of children and youth.

Variations in administrative organization of schools

which offer a program extending through the third grade. These several schools, located in the more immediate areas in which the children live, combine their enrollments for completion of the elementary program in one large intermediate-level school. Another variation is the planning of the first two, three, or four years of school as a continuous unit taught under one teacher and referred to as the ungraded primary or the primary unit. The ungraded primary may be found housed in a six- or eight-grade elementary school or in a primary or neighborhood school. A third variation of organization within the elementary school is the multigrade program, which is still largely in the experimental stage. In this plan children of various age levels are grouped into one class unit and the program is adapted to cover the age and grade span. Torrance, California, has recently experimented with this form of classroom organization. (See Chapter 7, p. 136.)

Within the classroom itself various types of organization are used. Classes may be taught as a whole or they may be divided into smaller numbers of children. The purpose of any such plan of grouping is to increase the effectiveness of the learning situation and to further the development of the individual and the group as a whole. Grouping may be done to help some who are slower, to enrich the program for some who are more gifted, to develop or further special interests, and so on. Groups may be planned to include children with a wide range of abilities (called heterogeneous grouping) or to include those of similar abilities (called homogeneous grouping). The *needs* of children are the basis of grouping. (See Chapter 7.)

Learning Environment

. . . Academic knowledge and the ability and skills to plan and develop effective learning environments and to guide curricular experiences.

The learning environment plays a most important role in the educational process of young children. Effective planning and use of the physical and psychological setting are important factors in furthering the development of the child and in guiding and stimulating his development and learning. Herein lies a real challenge for creative teaching.

The physical environment covers (*1*) location of the school, structure of the building, and room facilities, and (2) materials and equipment. In the first group are included location of the playground and of rooms within the building, placement of windows, amount of indoor and outdoor work and play space, toilet facilities, cupboard and storage space, locker space, and bulletin board and display areas. Consideration is given to the factors involved in healthful living such as ventilation, heating, and safety. The second group (materials and equipment) involves furniture (selection of size, kind, and color), rest cots if used, toys, play materials, building blocks of various kinds and sizes, art materials, audio-visual equipment, science materials, musical and rhythmic supplies, and an abundance of free and inexpensive materials.

The psychological aspects of the learning environment concern (*1*) the establishment of rapport and good communication between the teacher and children, and between staff members, and (*2*) stimulation of interest through an extensive use of varied materials.

Curricular experiences are planned in terms of the children's needs at their developmental age level in a learning environment which contains optimum physical and psychological factors. This stimulates growth in all aspects of personality, furthers interest and understanding, and develops skills in problem solving, creative expression, and critical thinking.

Such a learning environment is planned within the framework of the basic objectives and values of the education of the young child. (See Chapter 8.)

Professional Organizations

. . . an interest and skill in the use of professional organization publications and in participation in conferences, programs, and workshops.

The effective teacher finds her participation and interest in professional organizations and their publications one of the most helpful and necessary aids to her continued professional growth. More and more, teachers are turning to professional groups for guidance, stimulation, and for quick, ready data on research studies concerning the teaching-learning process.

The same cause that has influenced the organizing of the school programs for the early years into an early elementary unit, namely, recognition of the continuity of growth patterns and developmental needs of young children, has influenced also the professional thought and organization of teachers and others who work with young children. In the past, independent professional groups organized to work with others teaching at the same level and to consider their common problems. The kindergarten teachers joined together in The International Kindergarten Union (IKU) to study and further the kindergarten. The Primary Council was formed by teachers interested in problems and improvements at the primary school level. The National Association for Nursery School Education organized to improve education at that level. In the beginning each group formed its separate professional programs and assumed that somewhat different problems and approaches characterized their work and interests. In the educational organization of schools at an earlier date the nursery school was a unit separate from the kindergarten, and its program was thought of as distinct from the elementary school as such. Changes in our educational thinking have brought such groups into very close relationships in goals and professional activities, and in some instances have affected the formation of a unified and co-ordinated organization working for the continuous growth of young children from nursery school through primary level. The Association for Childhood Education International is illustrative of this point. During the years 1930-1931 The International Kindergarten Union and the Primary Council united their groups into this new organization, known to professional people as A.C.E.I. The National Association for Nursery School Education, established as a separate group in 1931, became closely allied with the interests and programs of A.C.E.I. and many nursery school teachers became members of both groups. The basic objective of the newly formed A.C.E.I. was to work for young children, and within this goal were opportunities for furtherance of special interests through committees concerned with nursery school education, kindergarten education, and primary education. Greater opportunities for planning for continuous growth of young children were made possible through this step. The A.C.E.I. now includes in its membership teachers of all elementary levels; however, it continues to have the separate nursery school, kindergarten, and primary committees. Very recently the National Education Association has re-established a division for furtherance of interests of teachers of young children in its Kindergarten Primary Department. (See Chapter 11.)

Lay Relationships

. . . an interest and ability in the development of lay, parent, and community relationships.

The responsibility and function of the present-day school is broadening as it becomes more and more a community-centered school, actively planning for and putting forth definite effort to involve lay, parent, and community co-operation.

The school of today is community-centered in three important ways. (*1*) Within the school's major task of responsibility for the educational program, increased opportunity is provided for greater realization of functional learning through reaching out into the community to involve its human and material resources in the school's educational program. (*2*) The school is fast building closer and more effective relationships with parents, lay, and community persons of the area through parent-teacher conferences, committees, commissions, and school building councils, and through bringing lay, parent, and community persons into the school's planning program. (*3*) At the same time the school is increasingly availing itself of the opportunity to serve as a center for the cultural life of the community, both local and world-wide.

We strive in the school program today to plan effective, functional learning situations which will be meaningful. This involves a changing concept of the child growing up in his community, and an extended scope of community understanding of the young child. The program recognizes that the school's expanding environment for education is no longer limited to the classroom but includes enjoyment and appreciation of the outdoors in camp projects and participation in community activities. We have enriched the learning possibilities of our program, especially at the early elementary level, by encompassing and introducing into the school a wide use of all available human and material resources within the community. Concrete experiences are planned. Varied equipment and materials are used. Field trips into the community and visits to the school by persons of the community engaged in many different kinds of work are encouraged. Parent interest and participation in individual child interests and in class activities are invited; parent participation in school and curriculum planning is included in the school scope in some communities.

Thus, today in our functional approach to teaching we have increased the effectiveness and enriched the scope of school activities and learning situations through learning experiences involving the resources of the community. The school has made a definite effort to further lay and parent-teacher education and co-operation and to serve its community. Education, through the school in its community-centered role, has been influenced and changed by its teacher-parent and school-community relationships, methodology and scope, and environmental approach to the learning situation.

Dr. Marion Nesbitt summarizes the concept of the community school fully when she says, "Each time the school serves the community, each time the community serves the school, the threads that bind these two together become stronger, weaving a pattern of warmth and good will."[7] (See Chapter 10.)

History

. . . an understanding of the influence of early educational movements and leaders on the present early elementary education program and on future trends.

One of the fascinating and interesting phases of study of the early elementary education field is the relationship between early educational movements and the works and writings of early educational leaders, and the field as we know it today and as it tends to develop for the future. In the past we find the present reflected and the trends of tomorrow indicated. (See Chapter 11.)

STATUS OF EARLY ELEMENTARY EDUCATION

Study of the widening scope of public education in its downward extension to include the program for younger children shows that today in the majority of the states of our country the kindergarten has become an accepted and integral part of all public school elementary education and that in a few areas the public nursery school is begin-

[7] Marion Nesbitt, *A Public School for Tomorrow* (New York, Harper & Brothers, 1953), pp. 146-147.

ning to become a responsibility of the elementary school. A recent study of the United States Office of Education reports that nineteen states and the Territory of Hawaii contribute from state level to the support of kindergartens in the various school systems within their states or areas. Included in this group are: California, Colorado, Connecticut, Florida, Illinois, Iowa, Maine, Massachusetts, Minnesota, New Hampshire, New Jersey, New York, Ohio, Oregon,[8] Pennsylvania, Rhode Island, Utah, Virginia, Wisconsin, and the territory of Hawaii.[9] In addition, many urban and rural school systems within our country have public school kindergartens established and supported by the local school administration on the same basis as the other levels of the elementary school.

Legally, most states make some provision for the education of young children even if state funds are not provided for this purpose. Such legislation may be *permissive,* that is, it allows that such programs may be established if needed or desired, or it may be *mandatory,* that is, it requires that such programs be established if needed or desired by areas or school systems. Forty-six states have permissive kindergarten legislation and seventeen have permissive nursery school legislation.[10]

Thus, kindergarten education in America is a widespread and accepted part of the public elementary pattern. It is found generally that areas unable to give their young children the advantage of this experience have their reasons in financing and other administrative problems rather than in the non-acceptance of the value of such a program.

Study of the chart[11] reproduced on page 24 gives an excellent overview of the status of early elementary education today, showing the increase in legislation and provisions for the nursery school and kindergarten levels, and indicating the increase in state concern for programs for these levels.

The tables on pages 26-29, prepared on the basis of the most recent data available, reveal a significant cross section of the status of early elementary education as recent as 1955-1956.

[8] Oregon dropped from this list in 1957.

[9] Clayton Hutchins and Albert R. Munse, *Public School Finance Programs of the United States* (Washington, D.C., U.S. Department of Health, Education, and Welfare, Office of Education, 1956), p. 35.

[10] Arch K. Steiner, "A Report on State Laws, Early Elementary Education," *School Life,* Vol. 39, No. 8 (May, 1957), pp. 7-9.

[11] *Ibid.*

STATE	NURSERY SCHOOLS			KINDERGARTENS			TEACHER CERTIFICATION						STATE DEPARTMENT OF EDUCATION	GENERAL SCHOOL ATTENDANCE AGES	
	Authority to establish (permissive or mandatory)	Entrance ages authorized[2]	Method of financing[1]	Authority to establish (permissive or mandatory)	Entrance ages authorized	Method of financing[1]	Degree required	Special certificate for kindergarten	Special certificate for nursery schools and kindergartens	Special certificate for nursery, kindergarten, and primary grades	General certificate with specialization in primary grades	General elementary certificate sufficient	Provides curriculum guides, standards, and general supervision for either nursery schools or kindergartens or both	Permissive (except nursery schools or kindergartens)	Mandatory (ages required to attend)
	1	2	3	4	5	6	7	8	9	10	11	12	13	14	15
Alabama				P[2]	5-8	LF-2								6	7-16
Arizona				P	At least 5.	COMB		X		X			X	6-21	8-16
Arkansas				M	4¾-6.	SA-2	X	X		X[3]		X	X	4¾-6	8-16
California	P				3-6.	SA-2	X	X					X	6	8-16
Colorado														6	8-16
Connecticut				P								X	X	6-21	7-16
Delaware	P	3-9	COMB	P	4-9.	SA-2	X	X	X				X	6-21	7-16
Florida				P		COMB	X					X	X	5¾-21	7-16
Georgia				P	3-6.					X			X	5¾-18	7-16
Idaho		2-6.	PF	M	4-6.	LF-1		X					X	6-21	7-16
Illinois	P		SA-2	P	Under 6.	LF-2		X				X	X	6-21	7-16
Indiana	P			P	At least 5.	SA-2								6	7-16
Iowa				P		COMB								6	7-16
Kansas				P	5-6.	LF-2							X	6-21	7-16
Kentucky				P	4-6.	LF-3	X						X	6	7-16
Louisiana				P	4-6.	COMB		X		X			X	5½-18	7-15
Maine			LF-2	P	At least 4.	LF-2	X	X						5-21	7-15
Maryland				P		LF-2	X					X	X	6-21	7-16
Massachusetts	P	At least 3[7]	COMB	P	(7).	LF-2							X	5	7-16
Michigan	P	(9).	LF-2	P	At least 5.	SA-2		X		X		X		5	6-16
Minnesota				P	4-6.	LF-1	[9]X					X		5-21	(11)
Mississippi			LF-1	P[12]	4-6.	LF-2								6-20	8-16
Missouri	P	Under 4.		P	5-6.	LF-2							X	6	
Montana	P			P	3-6.	COMB				X			X	5-20	8-16
Nebraska				P	4-6.	LF-2	X	X			X		X	6	7-16
Nevada				P	At least 5.	LF-2	X				X		X	5	7-18
New Hampshire				P	At least 5.	SA-1							X	(11)	6-16
New Jersey	P	Under 4.	COMB	P[13]	4-6.	LF-2							X	5-20	6-17
New Mexico	P		COMB	M	5-6.	LF-2	X			X	X	X	X		7-16
New York	P	3-6.	COMB	P	4-6.	COMB				X	X	X	X	4-5-20	7-16
North Carolina	P		LF-1	P[15]	Under 6.	LF-1						X	X	6-21	7-16
North Dakota				M	Under 6.	COMB							X	6-21	7-17
Ohio	P	Under 6.	LF-3	P	Under 6.	LF-3[16]					X	X	X	6-21	6-18
Oklahoma	P	2-6.	PF	M	4-6.	COMB			X			X	X	6-21	7-18
Pennsylvania				P	4-6.	SA-2		X						6-21	8-17
Rhode Island	P	At least 4.	LF-3	P	4-6.	COMB		X			X	X	X	6-21	7-16
South Carolina	P	Under 4.	LF-2	P	At least 5.	LF-2						X	X	6	(11)
South Dakota	P[18]		LF-2	P[19]	Under 6.	LF-3								6	7-16
Tennessee				M	5-7.	LF-1				X		X	X	6-21	7-16
Texas						LF-1	X	X					X		6-18
Utah				P	At least 5.	LF-2	X	X							6-18
Vermont				P	Under 6.	SA-2	X							6-18	7-16
Virginia	P[21]	Under 6.	COMB	P	Under 6.	LF-3	X			X	[20]X		X	6-20	8-16
Washington				P	4-6.	LF-2		X				X	X	6-21	7-16
West Virginia				M	4-6.	COMB		X				X	X	6-20	7-16
Wisconsin	P	Under 4.	LF-3	P[22]		COMB				X			X	6-21	7-16
Wyoming				P	At least 5.	LF-2				X		X	X	6-21	6-21

Legal provisions governing early elementary education in the public schools of the 48 states, as of January 1, 1957

NOTES

[1] The various methods of financing are indicated by symbols as follows:
PF, privately financed by fees and contributions
LF, locally financed:
  1 Special school funds
  2 General school funds
  3 Local funds and/or fees from parents
SA, financed with State aid:
  1 Per pupil formula
  2 In the same manner as other State aid is distributed
COMB, financed by combinations of 2 or more integral parts of PF, LF, or SA.

[2] Authority to establish is limited to independent cities.

[3] Nursery schools not included.

[4] If a child has completed 1 year of kindergarten he may enter the first grade regardless of his age.

[5] Attendance is permitted at discretion of local board.

[6] Local boards may exclude, at beginning of term, all children who will not have reached their 5th birthday by December 31.

[7] School committees may provide extended school services for children aged 3 to 14 who are the dependents of working mothers.

[8] Degree will be required in 1961. Additional training required at each renewal period to meet degree requirement by 1961.

[9] School board determines nursery school ages.

[10] Nursery schools are authorized for separate municipal school districts only.

[11] Mississippi repealed its compulsory attendance law in 1956; South Carolina, in 1955.

[12] Local districts may establish kindergartens only after all other elementary requirements have been met.

[13] Average daily attendance must exceed 15.

[14] Elementary school is a program of 8 grades, exclusive of kindergarten. Maximum compulsory attendance age is 14 in district that does not maintain a high school.

[15] Kindergarten is authorized by voters of the district.

[16] Local boards receive credit for kindergarten equivalent to one-half of an elementary classroom unit from the foundation program.

[17] Includes all elementary grades.

[18] Local boards may operate programs under such regulations as may be prescribed by the State board.

[19] Mandatory in districts with population of 2,000 or more; permissive in others.

[20] Requirements same as in elementary grades, with additional minimum requirement of 3 semester hours in student teaching in kindergarten.

[21] Nursery school program must meet minimum standards established by chief State school officer.

[22] Makes use of weighted pupil formula in regard to ADA enrollment.

CHANGE IN EDUCATION

Change and advancement are characteristic of our American way of life. Our educational process, based on constant study, research, and experimentation, continues to move forward to meet the challenge of the environmental and cultural changes; it aims to better enable the individual to meet and adjust intelligently to the ever-changing situation.

Basic causes of change in education are immediately evident in our everyday environment; they are centered primarily in three major factors. (*1*) An important first cause is the rapid and far-reaching increase in scientific, mechanical, and professional advancement. We see its resulting profound and direct influence in space interests, in automation, in beginnings of the use of atomic energy for peaceful as well as defense purposes, in growing urbanization, in the mobilization of our population, and in the increase in leisure time available to all people. (*2*) A second factor is found in the increasing interrelatedness and interdependence of people which the tremendous scientific progress of recent years has brought about. This has made the average person immediately concerned with world and international issues, with the problems of cultural integration at the local, national, and international levels, and with the problem of the lessened importance of the individual in the move toward greater conformity to group ideas and values. Democracy is centered in growth of individuals as well as in group growth; it loses much if individuality is not given a place. (*3*) A third cause is centered in the extensive professional research within the various disciplines of education, psychology, sociology, anthropology, and social psychology which provides resources for the guidance of the professional staffs working with children in the educational programs of our schools today.

Directions of Change

Education, through research and psychological studies, is meeting the challenge of change. A study of modern education reveals the directions of such educational change. These we could group for our purposes under the following: (*1*) the change of focus from the acquisition of knowledge to functional learning with skills in the processes

ENROLLMENT IN KINDERGARTEN AND IN GRADES 1 THROUGH 3,
AND TOTAL ENROLLMENT IN KINDERGARTEN THROUGH
GRADE 8, IN PUBLIC SCHOOLS, BY STATE: 1955-1956

Region and State	TOTAL K-8	TOTAL K-3	Kinder-garten[1]	First grade	Second grade	Third grade
				Kindergarten through Grade 3		
Continental United States	24,290,257	11,592,540	1,564,396	3,494,997	3,242,407	3,290,740
NORTHEAST	5,166,502	2,490,730	488,439	674,382	642,237	685,672
Connecticut	311,445	154,309	33,970	40,393	39,078	40,868
Maine	140,968	69,180	14,929	17,992	17,802	18,457
Massachusetts	581,895	273,728	41,974	77,413	75,642	78,699
New Hampshire	69,714	32,719	3,578	9,698	9,559	9,884
New Jersey	679,189	338,366	84,069	84,347	82,338	87,612
New York	1,899,194	924,200	222,017	241,757	215,005	245,421
Pennsylvania	1,336,398	629,931	79,000	182,265	183,277	184,849
Rhode Island	91,834	43,757	7,165	12,534	11,828	12,230
Vermont	55,865	25,080	1,737	7,983	7,708	7,652
NORTH CENTRAL	6,765,955	3,383,834	665,763	950,881	875,304	891,886
Illinois	1,141,247	580,482	123,455	163,784	144,680	148,563
Indiana	675,874	324,370	39,761	98,439	92,379	93,791
Iowa	421,300	216,995	46,993	63,768	52,294	53,940
Kansas	335,263	165,042	30,776	45,276	43,707	45,283
Michigan	1,085,118	569,656	150,714	147,038	135,586	136,318
Minnesota	442,930	216,533	44,237	58,918	56,067	57,311
Missouri	574,727	270,696	35,667	80,829	75,953	78,247
Nebraska	196,273	102,175	25,999	25,798	24,815	25,563
North Dakota	96,121	40,932	1,160	13,450	13,007	13,315
Ohio	1,253,518	623,777	102,984	181,215	169,265	170,313
South Dakota	104,598	48,612	6,235	14,970	13,972	13,435
Wisconsin	438,986	224,564	57,782	57,396	53,579	55,807
SOUTH	8,692,569	3,922,972	90,109	1,357,010	1,239,074	1,236,779
Alabama	579,556	255,998	—	90,773	82,181	83,044
Arkansas	325,611	141,159	—	51,197	44,404	45,558
Delaware	51,004	22,939	882	7,757	7,146	7,154
Florida	579,566	255,020	2,477	86,545	83,514	82,484

	(1)	(2)	(3)	(4)	(5)	(6)
Georgia	100,943	101,280	110,958	10,187	323,368	704,993
Kentucky	57,970	66,494	74,031	7,239	215,734	478,413
Louisiana	66,477	67,327	71,594	5,993	211,391	474,444
Maryland	55,672	53,838	54,195	19,457	183,162	393,401
Mississippi	60,188	65,029	86,290	—	211,507	436,433
North Carolina	118,278	115,007	116,604	12,687	349,889	800,874
Oklahoma	45,038	53,052	53,136	—	163,913	373,962
South Carolina	65,390	66,237	73,079		205,706	458,614
Tennessee	85,141	84,150	94,079	—	263,370	597,020
Texas	201,656	199,757	227,640	14,887	643,940	1,387,466
Virginia	89,528	87,647	91,239	6,288	274,702	612,312
West Virginia	49,888	49,726	54,199	—	153,813	351,904
District of Columbia	11,370	12,285	13,694	10,012	47,361	86,996
WEST	476,403	485,792	512,724	320,085	1,795,004	3,665,231
Arizona	24,186	24,839	30,163	4,759	83,947	177,310
California	233,744	248,748	264,463	230,650	977,605	1,942,128
Colorado	34,767	34,231	36,037	21,839	126,874	257,072
Idaho	15,626	15,277	16,005	—	46,908	107,942
Montana	13,587	13,795	14,370	2,609	44,361	97,023
Nevada	5,782	5,484	5,798	4,116	21,180	41,767
New Mexico	20,546	21,182	20,546	6,372	68,646	146,307
Oregon	36,950	34,919	35,836	8,790	116,505	255,826
Utah	21,199	20,255	20,329	10,413	72,196	151,317
Washington	62,571	59,657	61,601	26,626	210,455	434,716
Wyoming	7,435	7,405	7,576	3,911	26,327	53,823
Outlying parts of the U. S.						
Alaska	3,945	4,208	4,349	2,013	14,515	27,437
American Samoa	877	516	544		1,937	4,586
Canal Zone	1,324	1,217	1,201	885	4,627	9,263
Guam	1,473	1,856	1,803	—	5,132	9,679
Hawaii	—	—	—		—	—
Puerto Rico	82,999	74,154	75,712		232,865	477,701
Virgin Islands	663	602	670	338	2,273	5,005

¹ Includes enrollment in nursery schools.

Based on advance data from forthcoming Chapter 2, 1954-56 Biennial Survey of Education, Office of Education, Washington, D.C.

PERCENTAGE DISTRIBUTION ENROLLMENTS IN KINDERGARTEN AND GRADES 1-3, AND KINDERGARTEN ENROLLMENT AS A PERCENTAGE OF TOTAL ELEMENTARY ENROLLMENT IN KINDERGARTEN THROUGH GRADE 8, IN PUBLIC SCHOOLS, BY STATE: 1955-1956

Region and State	Percentage distribution of total enrollment in kindergarten through grade 3, by grade				Kindergarten enrollment as a percentage of total enrollment, Kgn. through grade 8
	Kgn.	Grade 1	Grade 2	Grade 3	
Continental United States	13.49	30.15	27.98	28.39	6.44
NORTHEAST	19.61	27.08	25.79	27.13	9.45
Connecticut	22.01	26.18	25.32	26.48	10.91
Maine	21.58	26.01	25.73	26.68	10.59
Massachusetts	15.33	28.28	27.63	28.75	7.21
New Hampshire	10.94	29.37	29.22	30.21	5.13
New Jersey	24.85	24.93	24.33	25.89	12.38
New York	24.02	26.16	23.26	26.55	11.69
Pennsylvania	12.54	28.93	29.09	29.28	5.91
Rhode Island	16.37	28.64	27.03	27.95	7.80
Vermont	6.93	31.83	30.73	30.51	3.10
NORTH CENTRAL	19.67	28.10	25.87	26.36	9.84
Illinois	21.27	28.22	24.92	25.59	10.82
Indiana	12.26	30.35	28.48	28.91	5.88
Iowa	21.66	29.39	24.10	24.85	11.15
Kansas	18.65	27.67	26.48	27.44	9.18
Michigan	26.46	25.81	23.80	23.93	13.89
Minnesota	20.43	27.21	25.89	26.47	10.00
Missouri	13.18	29.86	28.06	28.91	6.20
Nebraska	25.45	25.25	24.29	25.02	13.25
North Dakota	2.83	32.86	31.78	32.53	1.21
Ohio	16.51	29.05	27.14	27.30	8.22
South Dakota	12.83	30.79	28.74	27.64	5.96
Wisconsin	27.73	25.56	23.86	24.85	13.16

SOUTH	2.30	34.59	31.59	31.53	1.03
Alabama		35.46	32.10	32.24	
Arkansas	3.84	36.27	31.46	32.27	1.73
Delaware	.97	33.82	31.15	31.19	.42
Florida	3.15	33.94	32.75	32.34	1.44
Georgia	3.36	34.31	31.32	31.22	1.51
Kentucky	2.84	34.32	30.82	31.51	1.26
Louisiana	10.62	33.87	31.85	31.48	4.95
Maryland		29.59	29.39	30.40	
Mississippi		40.80	30.75	28.46	
North Carolina	7.74	33.33	32.87	33.80	3.39
Oklahoma		32.42	32.37	27.48	
South Carolina		35.53	32.20	32.27	
Tennessee		35.72	31.95	32.33	
Texas	2.30	35.35	31.21	31.31	1.07
Virginia	2.30	33.21	31.91	32.59	1.03
West Virginia		35.24	32.33	32.43	
District of Columbia	21.14	28.91	25.94	24.01	11.51
WEST	17.83	28.56	27.06	26.54	8.73
Arizona	5.67	35.93	29.59	28.81	2.68
California	23.59	27.05	25.44	23.91	11.88
Colorado	17.21	28.40	26.98	27.40	8.50
Idaho		34.12	32.57	33.31	
Montana	5.88	32.39	31.10	31.07	2.69
Nevada	19.43	27.34	25.89	27.30	9.85
New Mexico	9.28	29.93	30.86	29.92	4.36
Oregon	7.54	30.76	29.97	31.72	3.44
Utah	14.42	28.15	28.06	29.36	6.88
Washington	12.65	29.27	28.35	29.73	5.12
Wyoming	14.86	28.78	28.13	28.24	7.27
Outlying parts of the U. S.					
Alaska	13.87	29.96	28.99	27.28	7.34
American Samoa		28.08	26.64	45.28	
Canal Zone	19.13	25.96	26.30	28.61	9.55
Guam		35.13	36.17	28.70	
Hawaii (not reported)					
Puerto Rico		32.51	31.84	35.64	
Virgin Islands	14.87	30.35	26.48	29.17	6.75

(Based or advance data from forthcoming Chapter 2, 1954-56 Biennial Survey of Education, Office of Education, Washington, D.C.).

of thinking; (2) the planning for child development through curriculum and learning experiences based on developmental psychology, and (3) the growing development of the community-centered school. A brief consideration of each of these factors follows.

Focus on Functional Learning and the Process Skills. There was a time in educational history when the major function of the school was considered to be the transmission of knowledge to the young of the society mainly through rote memorization. It was assumed that when children reached maturity they would use such knowledge effectively in their lives. It was assumed, too, that it was possible for the school to give the child a fair cross section of the information and skills that he would need—and so education was looked upon as a preparation for life. Today, research is rapidly deepening and broadening the intensity and scope of knowledge in many fields, especially in that of science, to the point where it is increasingly difficult to acquire a broad foundation in many fields along with specialization in one. As we continue to progress this will become even more true. Nor can we, in terms of our rapid scientific progress, foretell with fine accuracy what living will be like in the next decades or in the year 2000, when many of the children currently enrolled in early elementary education programs will be in the prime of their lives.

Psychology and education indicate an answer to this problem. The school must teach the child skills in processes of how to think and how to solve problems *using* knowledge. The school, centering its focus on the development of the child in the skills of the psychological processes of problem solving, critical thinking, and creative expression can enable him to meet "the existing situation" more intelligently, whether that situation occurs at the present time or some later date. Through skill in these processes the child will be enabled to continue to meet situations effectively as society and scientific knowledge advance, for he will know how to use data to work out and think through situations and problems. The school will have given him a basic technique along with functional knowledge, rather than just a fund of knowledge that may or may not become obsolete in part. This means that the modern school must continue to do all that it has begun in the way of developing the child in all the facets of his growth by making learning functional, and that, through the development of thinking skills in children, it must give them the ability to continue to live effectively. The process skills are implied in democratic living which requires the individual to analyze situations and problems, to gather and use facts and knowledge relating to these problems, to evaluate critically such data, and then to develop the answer or solution that best fits the situation. The process skills are timeless -the knowledge involved will change as society continues to develop and as science continues to advance. Education at all levels, and beginning with the young child's program, should develop these process skills.

An excellent professional reference on the philosophy, form, and place of the processes in education has been developed by Dr. David Russell in his book, *Children's Thinking*. In our text we are concerned with developing young children's programs within this framework of knowledge and processes.

Child Development. An important emphasis of the present educational program is on guiding and planning for the learning and development of the child as a total personality, giving attention to his physical, emotional, social, and moral as well as intellectual development, along with *retained emphasis* on academic achievement (as noted above, pp. 11-15). This trend is turning from total stress on academic and intellectual achievement as they are measured in terms of grade standards alone. It has made possible more effective learning and fuller development of the child through recognition of the interrelatedness of the personality facets. It is sufficient to note here that academic success has been shown by research studies to be directly related to growth and developmental factors. The child who has a physical handicap of sight or hearing is unable to work to full capacity until the difficulty is corrected. The child who is shy and unable to establish rapport with his peers or teachers is obviously handicapped in communication, while the child who has an emotional block or upset is unable to focus full attention on learning. Again, no one of these facets of personality affects the child independently. The child who is ill is affected emotionally and socially; the child who is emotionally upset has problems in social relationships with his peers and adults and has physical reactions to his emotional difficulties. All affect academic achievement. The curriculum which is planned in terms of data from scientific research in child study reaches far beyond academic achieve-

31

ment. While the child learns subject matter he becomes a wholesome, adjusted individual, and his needs for security and recognition, self-direction, affection, extended social skills, communication with others, growing independence, and creative expression are being met.

The teacher working in this educational program must have more than a wide knowledge of academic subject matter. She must have, in addition, a scientific and thorough understanding of the growth and development process, and must know how to give effective attention to individual and group needs. She must give consideration to the child's physical development and health, to his social adjustment to peers and adults, to his emotional and mental health, and to his sensitivity to values—all as an intrinsic part of his acquisition of a solid foundation in the culture, knowledge, and skills which are basically the responsibility of the school. This implies an understanding of how the child learns at the different age levels and what the developmental task patterns are for the various phases of growth. Further, it requires that the teacher be able to recognize and help children in their varying abilities, needs, and rates of maturation.

Community-Centered School. The school is becoming a community-centered institution in a real sense because of the changes which are occurring in our society (as noted above, pp. 21-22). As our society continues to develop, the school promises to become more and more the force for greater understanding and advancement in the community.

Change in Early Elementary Education

Evidences of change in the form of American education are present to some degree in all school levels, but recognition and acceptance of the directions of change in our educational thinking are influencing in particular the thinking within the field of elementary and early elementary education. In these programs there is leadership for and greater freedom in introducing into classroom procedures the educational helps based on experimentally tried and validated scientific and action (or curriculum)[12] research in the psychology of learning and the developmental growth pattern. At the same time many educators are

[12] See M. Stephen Corey, *Action Research to Improve School Practices* (New York, Bureau of Publications, Teachers College, Columbia University, 1957).

coming to recognize that one of the most important tasks of educating is in the hands of teachers who work with the young child. The foundation for personality growth laid at this level has significant influence on later learning and living.

THE FIELD OF EARLY ELEMENTARY EDUCATION

The program in early elementary education is the foundation and core of the programs at all levels in our educational system. It is a program that is moving rapidly from subject-learning emphasis alone to attention to whole child growth. It strives to deepen and widen the child's understanding of himself and of others, and of the world in which he lives. It is founded on valid research drawn from all disciplines touching on the child as a personality, including psychology, pediatrics, study of mental health, anthropology, and sociology as well as education. Its foundations are the principles of democracy which accept and respect each child as an individual and give attention to his growth as a member of the group. It sees early elementary education as a real and functional part of the dynamic process of living —as a vital learning phase of the continuous life cycle, with its key words being "continuity" and "democracy."

PROJECTS AND QUESTIONS

1. Scan recent copies of *Time, Newsweek, Harpers, Saturday Review,* and other current publications. List five major problems and interests in current society, and show: (1) their relation to education, and (2) implications for our responsibility as professional educators.
2. Evaluate your daily use of skills in problem solving. Illustrate. Recall your experiences as you came through the elementary school, and weigh rote learning against problem-solving experiences. Support your thinking through actual incidents and experiences.
3. What teaching of problem-solving skills and attention to individual whole growth of children have you observed in your school visitations? Be specific.
4. Illustrate one learning experience you have observed or read that could be related to each developmental task listed in the chart on page 14.

5. Describe and evaluate the *types* of programs provided for young children in your immediate community.
6. Explain the early elementary field to a lay person.

GUIDE TO REFERENCES FOR FURTHER STUDY

ALMY, Millie C., "Programs for Young Children," *Educational Leadership,* Vol. 8 (February, 1951), pp. 270-275.

———, "Are They Too Young for Problem Solving?," *Progressive Education,* Vol. 27 (March, 1950), pp. 143-148.

———, "Principles and Practices of Nursery Education," *Exceptional Children,* Vol. 21 (October, 1954), pp. 18-21.

American Association of School Administrators, *The Expanding Role of Education,* 26th Yearbook (Washington, D.C., The Association, 1948).

Association for Supervision and Curriculum Development, *Forces Affecting American Education,* 1953 Yearbook (Washington, D.C., The Association, 1953).

———, *Organizing the Elementary School for Living and Learning,* 1947 Yearbook (Washington, D.C., The Association, 1947).

BOTTRELL, Harold K., ed., *Introduction to Education* (Harrisburg, Pa., The Stackpole Company, 1955).

California Elementary School Administrators Association, *The Elementary School at Mid-Century,* 23rd Yearbook (San Francisco, The Association, 1951).

COUNTS, George S., *Education and American Civilization* (New York, Bureau of Publications, Teachers College, Columbia University, 1952).

Department of Elementary School Principals, *Contemporary Society— Background for the Instructional Program* (Washington, D.C., The Department, 1957).

Educational Policies Commission, *Education for All American Children* (Washington, D.C., The Commission, 1948).

HAVIGHURST, R. J., *Developmental Tasks and Education* (New York, Longmans, Green & Company, 1953).

———, *Human Development and Education* (New York, Longmans, Green & Company, 1953).

———, and NEUGARTEN, Bernice L., *Society and Education* (Boston, Allyn and Bacon, Inc., 1957).

HILDRETH, Gertrude H., *Child Growth Through Education* (New York, The Ronald Press Company, 1948).

HYMES, James L., Jr., *A Child Development Point of View* (Englewood Cliffs, N.J., Prentice-Hall, Inc., 1955).

MEAD, Margaret, *The School in American Culture* (Cambridge, Mass., Harvard University Press, 1951).

NESBITT, Marion, *A Public School for Tomorrow* (New York, Harper & Brothers, 1953).

RUSSELL, David H., *Children's Thinking* (Boston, Ginn & Company, 1956).

STRATEMEYER, Florence, and others, *Guides to a Curriculum for Modern Living* (New York, Bureau of Publications, Teachers College, Columbia University, 1952).

See *General Bibliography*.

CHAPTER 2

The Young Child in School

*Only as he successfully passes through one stage will
he be able to adjust to the next one with confidence and
thus, stage by stage, successfully reach the final one of
mature adulthood.*[1]

INTRODUCTION

All contact with and planning for young children must begin with a
knowledge and understanding of the child himself. This is where any
introduction to the field should begin. How better can one begin to
know and understand young children than by visits to early elementary
classrooms?

Children in the various levels of the early elementary education program differ considerably. Rapid growth during the early years causes
the children to change in basic developmental patterns and tasks even
within a year span. Four-year-old children seem much less mature and
developed than those who are five; the fives, while mature compared to
the four-year-old group, appear quite young when their typical pattern
is looked at from the primary level. Within the primary there are
marked differences in growth at six and at eight.

Each of the years of this early period is marked by distinctive growth
characteristics based on the average or typical child of that age; hence,
variations in the school program are designed in general to meet the
immediate needs of the age level for which the learning experiences are

[1] Henry F. Helmholz, M.D., *The Function of the P.T.A. in Continued Health
Supervision of Children* (Chicago, National Congress of Parents and Teachers,
February, 1957), p. 1.

36

planned. You must keep in mind, however, that while all normal children follow a general basic pattern, individual children differ widely in their rates of growth and in their backgrounds, abilities, and experiences. Hence, the study and observation of young children should be approached from a noting of the typical or average range and pattern of development of a group of children (based on cross-section studies of many children and called *status* study) and of an individual child (based on a long period study of the growth and personality of one child and termed *longitudinal* study).

Within this chapter we describe and illustrate different and varied learning experiences for young children; this will enable you to observe the developmental age span and some of the program activities of early elementary education. Included are learning experiences for four-year-old children (nursery school), five-year-old children (kindergarten), and children six to nine years of age (primary). If at all possible, you should make classroom visits in your community school and begin your actual contact with and observation of young children at this time.

Your observations at this beginning stage should be centered in two purposes: (*1*) to become acquainted with the different developmental patterns of children four to nine in general, and to note evident differences in children in height, weight, maturity, social adjustment, and emotional control; and (*2*) to observe the types of environment and learning experiences teachers use to meet the needs of the young children with whom they are working. General guides for observations were given in Chapter 1, pp. 1-5.

In many school systems children are given some introduction to the school before they are actually enrolled. A review of the readiness-for-school-entrance program, and actual classroom programs follows.

READINESS FOR SCHOOL ENTRANCE

The Preschool Roundup

When the young child is ready to enter under the supervision of the public school, whether in the nursery school, the kindergarten, or even in the first grade in those areas where no kindergartens are maintained, the school usually takes the initiative in helping prepare him for the experience. Some guidance is given the parents and some school experience given the child. In some areas, children are invited to visit in the nursery school or kindergarten during the semester prior to their enrollment; in others, some activity such as the preschool roundup is held.

Though schools vary in their approach to developing parent and child readiness for the child's entrance into school, the preschool roundup is one of the major techniques used by many systems. It offers the parent guidance in how to help prepare his child for school, and gives him an understanding of the school program and its purposes; at the same time it provides the school a means of becoming acquainted with the child and of examining him in his growth and development, especially with regard to physical factors. In this program, parents who have a child eligible for school entrance during the next session are advised through school bulletins, newspaper notices, and letters to the home that a preschool roundup will be held on a certain date. This advance publicity includes information regarding the nature of the roundup activities, the schedule and program for the date set, and the entrance age requirements for enrollment. It also gives the parent information regarding the type of data he must bring to the meeting, such as the child's birth certificate, and a statement of vaccination.

Parents report to the school at the scheduled roundup program time. The programs vary according to the different localities where they are held, but basically they are designed to acquaint the parent with the nature of the curriculum and to give the school a beginning knowledge of the individual child. Information regarding the child's health history and his family data is recorded, and a file of information (called a cumulative record) helpful to the school in guiding the child's progress is begun. The director of instruction or the superintendent of schools meets with the parents as a group and answers questions, outlines the work and goals of the school and the place of the kindergarten program in the elementary school program as a whole, and urges parent interest in the school and in the Parent Teacher Association. The parent then has an opportunity to meet and talk with the kindergarten teacher who will have his child in her class. In some schools the school doctors and nurses are present and a medical examination of each child

38

is made at this time. If any problems or difficulties appear in the child's health the parents are advised; this permits attention to the problem before the child's school entrance. In other areas, it is recommended to the parent that a health examination be made by the family physician before the opening of school and a report of this examination be made to the school doctor on a regular school health form which is provided. In some systems, the dentist is also a member of the medical team at the roundup.

Usually a small mimeographed or published handbook of information is distributed to parents during the roundup meeting. This handbook is a written record of the detailed information which the parents should have concerning the program, schedules, regulations, and procedures of the school. The following list is representative of good public school parent handbooks:

"In the Kindergarten"	Baltimore Public Schools, Maryland
"Going to Kindergarten"	Cincinnati Public Schools, Ohio
"Going to First Grade"	Cincinnati Public Schools, Ohio
"School Days Are Happy Days"	Chicago Public Schools, Illinois
"Welcome to Kindergarten"	Glencoe Public Schools, Illinois
"Your Child Goes to Kindergarten"	Hawaii Department of Education, Honolulu, Hawaii
"Happy Journey"	National Education Association, Washington, D.C.
"A Good Start"	Pittsburgh Public Schools, Pennsylvania
"In Our Kindergarten"	San Diego County Schools, California
"A Day at Nursery School"	Kansas State Teachers College, Emporia, Kansas

The preschool roundup gives much attention to the child's physical health since it is basic to school adjustment and readiness to learn. Parents need and are increasingly taking advantage of this help.

P.T.A. Health Supervision

Recognition of the importance of the health aspect of growth in the young child and its close interrelationship with the other facets of the child's personality is seen in the recent action of the National Congress of Parents and Teachers. In May, 1956, the Board of Managers of this group adopted a statement, prepared by its National Health Chairman,

Dr. Henry F. Helmholz, approving continued health supervision of children through periodic health examinations of well children from birth through high school. Because of the significance of this plan in its forward look, and its recognition of the interrelatedness of facets of growth in the young child, excerpts from it are quoted below:[2]

The objectives set by the National Congress of Parents and Teachers might be all summed up in one sentence: Our objective is to make mature adults out of our growing children. We aim to help each child to pass successfully through the various stages of growing up. Only as he successfully passes through one stage will he be able to adjust to the next one with confidence and thus, stage by stage, successfully reach the final one of mature adulthood. Personality growth begins with the infant's developing a sense of trust in his surroundings, a sense of security based on learning that his wants are taken care of. Failure to develop a sense of trust makes it extremely difficult to develop successfully each of the following stages. Because this experience occurs in the first three years of life, the damage done at this time can be repaired only with the greatest difficulty in later years. Our work for the good of the child must start with the newborn infants. In fact, it should start even earlier—with the infant's parents— to be sure that they are mature adults who recognize their child's need for help in growing up.

This over-all objective . . . points up the importance of having our expanded health program start at birth. An infant's feelings of trust and security depend in no small measure on his physical health and well being. And so, throughout the years of development, even the purely physical aspects of health—good sight, good hearing, a well nourished body—are of vital importance in this process of passing successfully through the stages of growing up. Unless physical defects, however minor, are quickly identified and remedied to the fullest extent possible, children will be handicapped in their passage from one stage of their growth to the next. Even when no defects are present, both the child himself and his parents need to be assured that he does have good health, a fact that we have kept in mind while urging the periodic health appraisal of the *well* child, not merely the one who is known to be ill.

Those who have worked with the Summer Round-Up of the Children, our earlier project for health examinations of children about to enter school, are already familiar with the values of thorough physical checkups by competent physicians. The expanded program is a recognition of the fact that the needs met by the Summer Round-Up neither begin nor cease upon entrance to school but continue throughout the child's life. . . .

[2] *Ibid.,* pp. 1-2.

LEARNING EXPERIENCES FOR CHILDREN FOUR TO NINE

Outdoor activities develop growth and muscular co-ordination.

**Environment should be spacious, stimulating,
and informal.**

The young child derives pleasure from outdoor activities.

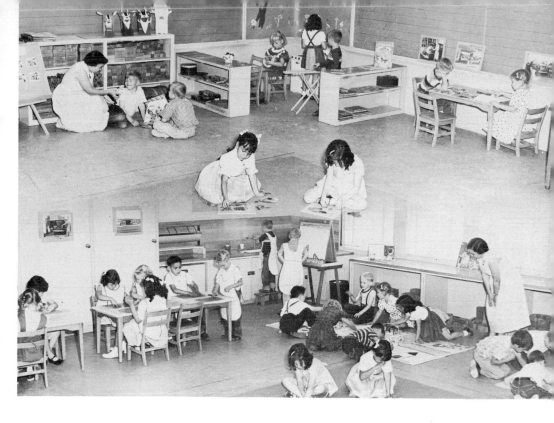

A well planned room environment stimulates enriched learning experiences.

Loving, observing, and caring for pets and living things is important.

**Learning experiences begin with what the
child knows and loves.**

Family life is a major interest of the young child.

Through dramatic play we learn about our environment.

Interest in environment widens.

We plan, discuss, and evaluate together.

Learning experiences develop skills in the processes of thinking and problem solving.

The young child learns by doing.

We learn to listen and to enjoy.

Learning experiences develop skills in communication: listening, reading, speaking, and writing.

Books are fun. They help us learn about the world around us.

We read under teacher guidance.

We read in peer groups.

Number concepts are related to concrete objects and social usage.

Learning experiences develop skills in quantitative concepts.

Cut-outs show fractional values and relations.

*Learning experiences develop
expression and creativity.*

To create is fun! Shall we tell you the story of what we've made?

Music—singing, rhythms, instruments—encourages expression and gives emotional release.

The very young child
likes solo play.

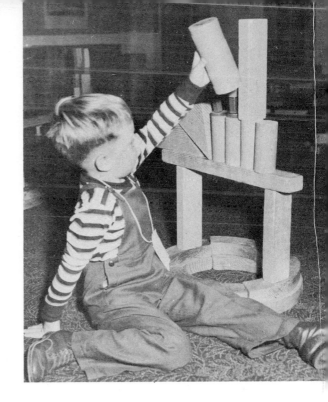

Learning experiences foster growth in social skills.

He also likes parallel
play and work.

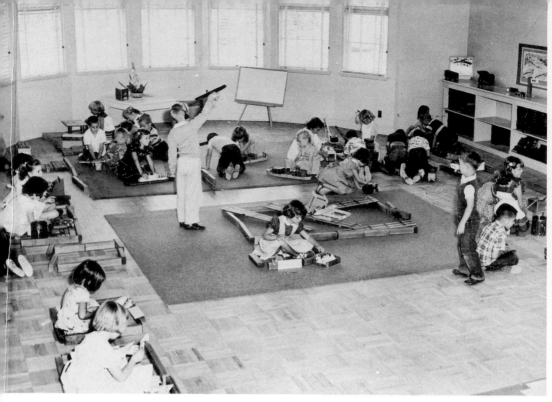

At five we see some solo play and work, some parallel play and work, and some co-operative play and work.

Group activity is important for primary children

Learning experiences are planned In a rhythm
of quiet and active periods.

**Learning experiences develop independence,
responsibility, and care and use
of materials**

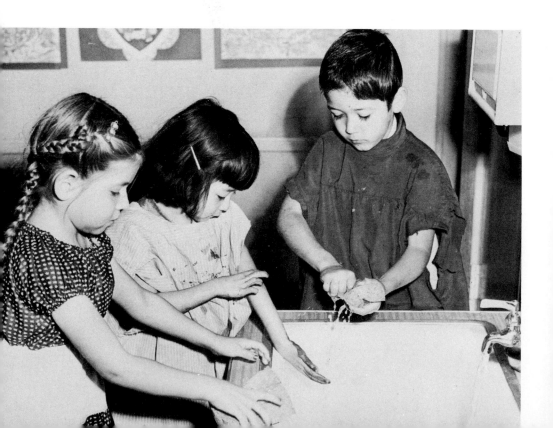

Such a program insures a better health foundation for the child's growth and learning and would prove a valuable supplement to the increased attention to health as a facet of growth in our early elementary programs.

EARLY ELEMENTARY PROGRAMS

The illustrated outlines of programs at the nursery school, kindergarten, and primary age levels are general in nature. They will, however, give a basic understanding of the continuity and variations in these various phases of the whole early elementary program. The chapter on curriculum (Chapter 9) will develop and illustrate the individual nursery school, kindergarten, and primary programs.

PROJECTS AND QUESTIONS

1. Identify from the illustrated programs in this chapter and from your classroom observations the similarities, differences, and evidences of continuity in the various phases of the early elementary education program.

EARLY ELEMENTARY EDUCATION

Programs:	Nursery School	Kindergarten	Primary
Similarities:			
Differences:			
Evidences of Continuity:			

2. Where in the early elementary program do you see opportunity for:
   a. teacher-pupil planning?
   b. teacher-pupil evaluation?
   c. development of communication skills?
   d. development of problem solving and thinking skills?
   e. development of social growth?
   f. provision for growth needs?

    g. attention to individual needs? interests? problems?

    h. attention to the psychology of how young children learn?

3. On the basis of the illustrated programs and your observations illustrate the influence of:

    a. the immediate community and environment on the programs.

    b. the kindergarten program on the primary program.

GUIDE TO REFERENCES FOR FURTHER STUDY

ALMY, Millie C., "Programs for Young Children," *Educational Leadership,* Vol. 8 (February, 1951), pp. 270-275.

Association for Childhood Education International, *Kindergarten Teacher's Portfolio* (Washington, D.C., The Association, 1951).

————, *Nursery School Portfolio* (Washington, D.C., The Association, 1953).

————, *Primary School Portfolio* (Washington, D.C., The Association, 1956).

BARNETT, Glenn E., "The Educational Setting of Early Childhood Education," *California Journal of Elementary Education,* Vol. 17 (February, 1949), pp. 134-138.

California State Department of Education, *A Teacher's Guide to Education in Early Childhood* (Sacramento, The Department, 1956).

————, The Kindergarten Issue, *California Journal of Elementary Education* (August, 1955).

California State Supervisors Association, Helen Heffernan, ed., rev. ed. *Guiding the Young Child* (Boston, D. C. Heath & Company, 1958).

CULKIN, Mabel L., *Teaching the Youngest* (New York, The Macmillan Company, 1949).

GANS, Roma, and others, *Teaching Young Children* (Yonkers, N.Y., World Book Company, 1952).

HAGGARD, Ernest A., "Learning: A Process of Change," *Educational Leadership,* Vol. 18 (December, 1955), pp. 149-156.

HARTLEY, R. E. and others, *Understanding Children's Play* (New York, Columbia University Press, 1952).

HAVIGHURST, Robert J., *Human Development and Education* (New York, Longmans, Green & Company, 1953).

HILDRETH, Gertrude H., *Child Growth Through Education* (New York, The Ronald Press Company, 1948).

KELLOGG, Rhoda, *Nursery School Guide* (Boston, Houghton Mifflin Company, 1949).

LAMBERT, Hazel M., *Teaching the Kindergarten Child* (New York, Harcourt, Brace & Company, 1958).

LEE, J. Murray, and LEE, Dorris May, *The Child and His Development* (New York, Appleton-Century-Crofts, Inc., 1958).

MOUSTAKAS, Clark E., and BENSON, Minnie P., *The Young Child in School* (New York, Whiteside, Inc. and William Morrow & Company, 1956).

READ, Katherine, *The Nursery School: A Human Relations Laboratory* (Philadelphia, W. B. Saunders Company, 1950).

SCHERER, Lorraine, and others, *How Good Is Our Kindergarten?* (Washington, D.C., Association for Childhood Education International, 1958).

SHEEHY, Emma D., *The Fives and Sixes Go to School* (New York, Henry Holt & Company, Inc., 1954).

WILLCOCKSON, Mary, ed., *Social Education for Young Children* (Washington, D.C., National Council for the Social Studies, National Education Association, 1956).

WILLS, Clarice D., and STEGEMAN, William H., *Living in the Kindergarten* (Chicago, Follett Publishing Company, 1956).

————, *Living in the Primary Grades* (Chicago, Follett Publishing Company, 1956).

CHAPTER **3**

The Child Four to Nine

INTRODUCTION

Good teaching has its foundation in a real love and understanding of each boy and each girl in the class group, and of the group as a whole in its age characteristics. This means the teacher must have scientific knowledge and understanding of the developmental growth pattern of young children and an appreciation of each individual within the group as a unique person, but it also means she must know the spirit and intangible qualities of the young personality. The following readings on "What Is a Boy?" and "What Is a Girl?" define these qualities in an unforgettable way and with deep insight; they have a place in furthering our understanding of children along with the scientific and scholastic research and data that follow in the remainder of this chapter. For this reason we quote them below.

WHAT IS A BOY?[1]

Between the innocence of babyhood and the dignity of manhood we find a delightful creature called a boy. Boys come in assorted sizes, weights, and colors, but all boys have the same creed: To enjoy every second of every minute of every hour of every day and to protest with noise (their only weapon) when their last minute is finished and the adult males pack them off to bed at night.

Boys are found everywhere—on top of, underneath, inside of, climbing on, swinging from, running around, or jumping to. Mothers love them, little girls hate them, older sisters and brothers tolerate them, adults ignore them, and Heaven protects them. A boy is Truth with dirt on its face,

[1] Alan Beck, *What Is a Boy?* (Boston, New England Mutual Life Insurance Company, 1950). Quoted by permission.

Beauty with a cut on its finger, Wisdom with bubble gum in its hair, and the Hope of the future with a frog in its pocket.

When you are busy, a boy is an inconsiderate, bothersome, intruding jangle of noise. When you want him to make a good impression, his brain turns to jelly or else he becomes a savage, sadistic, jungle creature bent on destroying the world and himself with it.

A boy is a composite—he has the appetite of a horse, the digestion of a sword swallower, the energy of a pocket-size atomic bomb, the curiosity of a cat, the lungs of a dictator, the imagination of a Paul Bunyan, the

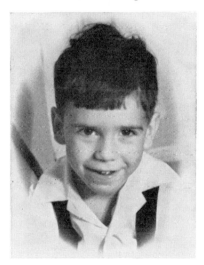

shyness of a violet, the audacity of a steel trap, the enthusiasm of a fire cracker, and when he makes something he has five thumbs on each hand.

He likes ice cream, knives, saws, Christmas, comic books, the boy across the street, woods, water (in its natural habitat), large animals, Dad, trains, Saturday mornings, and fire engines. He is not much for Sunday School, company, schools, books without pictures, music lessons, neckties, barbers, girls, overcoats, adults, or bedtime.

Nobody else is so early to rise, or so late to supper. Nobody else gets so much fun out of trees, dogs, and breezes. Nobody else can cram into one pocket a rusty knife, a half-eaten apple, 3 feet of string, an empty Bull Durham sack, 2 gum drops, 6 cents, a sling shot, a chunk of unknown substance, and a genuine super-sonic code ring with a secret compartment.

A boy is a magical creature—you can lock him out of your work shop, but you can't lock him out of your heart. You can get him out of your study, but you can't get him out of your mind. Might as well give up—he is your captor, your jailer, your boss, and your master—a freckled-face, pint-sized, cat-chasing, bundle of noise. But when you come home at night with only the shattered pieces of your hopes and dreams, he can mend them like new with the two magic words—"Hi Dad!"

WHAT IS A GIRL?[2]

Little girls are the nicest things that happen to people. They are born with a little bit of angel-shine about them and though it wears thin sometimes, there is always enough left to lasso your heart—even when they are sitting in the mud, or crying temperamental tears, or parading up the street in mother's best clothes.

A little girl can be sweeter (and badder) oftener than anyone else in the world. She can jitter around, and stomp, and make funny noises that frazzle your nerves, yet just when you open your mouth, she stands there demure

with that special look in her eyes. A girl is Innocence playing in the mud, Beauty standing on its head, and Motherhood dragging a doll by the foot.

Girls are available in five colors—black, white, red, yellow, or brown, yet Mother Nature always manages to select your favorite color when you place your order. They disprove the law of supply and demand—there are millions of little girls, but each is as precious as rubies.

God borrows from many creatures to make a little girl. He uses the song of a bird, the squeal of a pig, the stubbornness of a mule, the antics of a monkey, the spryness of a grasshopper, the curiosity of a cat, the speed of a gazelle, the slyness of a fox, the softness of a kitten, and to top it all off He adds the mysterious mind of a woman.

A little girl likes new shoes, party dresses, small animals, first grade, noise makers, the girl next door, dolls, make-believe, dancing lessons, ice cream, kitchens, coloring books, make-up, cans of water, going visiting, tea parties, and one boy. She doesn't care so much for visitors, boys in

[2] Alan Beck, *What Is a Girl?* (Boston, New England Mutual Life Insurance Company, 1950). Quoted by permission.

46

general, large dogs, hand-me-downs, straight chairs, vegetables, snow suits, or staying in the front yard. She is loudest when you are thinking, the prettiest when she has provoked you, the busiest at bedtime, the quietest when you want to show her off, and the most flirtatious when she absolutely must not get the best of you again.

Who else can cause you more grief, joy, irritation, satisfaction, embarrassment, and genuine delight than this combination of Eve, Salome, and Florence Nightingale? She can muss up your home, your hair, and your dignity—spend your money, your time, and your temper—then just when your patience is ready to crack, her sunshine peeks through and you've lost again.

Yes, she is a nerve-racking nuisance, just a noisy bundle of mischief. But when your dreams tumble down and the world is a mess—when it seems you are pretty much of a fool after all—she can make you a king when she climbs on your knee and whispers, "I love you best of all!"

NEEDS OF YOUNG CHILDREN

In stressing the important and vital need for educational opportunities for young children, the American Association of School Administration stated that a well planned program satisfies such basic needs as follows:[3]

1. *Children need to grow up:* they need to become independent of adult help and guidance, gradually but steadily; to learn to share possessions, to control anger; and to accept responsibility as leader and as follower.
2. *Children need to develop the inner self:* they should have ample opportunity to express their thoughts and feelings, to exercise their creative powers, and to preserve their curiosity and spirit of wonder through varied experiences with art, music, literature, nature and games.
3. *Children need affection:* they must be loved, appreciated and wanted by those closest and most important to them. Children need to grow up in an atmosphere of happiness, warmth and security.
4. *Children need to learn to live with others than members of their own families:* they should be able to live, work and play acceptably with other children their own age. They should develop a sense of belonging which affords them ample security with older and younger chil-

[3] American Association of School Administrators, *Expanding Role of Education,* 26th Yearbook (Washington, D.C., The Association, 1948), pp. 34-35.

dren, with adults, and eventually, with all kinds of people in all walks of life.

5. *Children need adult guidance:* the sympathetic understanding guidance of happy, well adjusted adults helps children to develop the confidence, insight, skills, and attitudes they need to make them feel at home in their ever enlarging world.

6. *Children need freedom to play:* they should be able to give a natural and free expression to their energies in surroundings that are clean, healthful, and reasonably safe from the serious accident hazards so commonly found in uncontrolled environments.

7. *Children need a rich, challenging environment:* the child's environment should offer both indoor and outdoor space. Many materials should be at hand for his use, and there should be constant opportunity for him to do things; to construct, to explore, and to experiment in his own childish way and on his own developmental level . . . with satisfying results.

8. *Children need a balanced day and life:* the child's schedule should give him time and opportunity for rest, work and play. It must include those eating, sleeping, washing, dressing and toileting experiences so essential during early childhood to establish sound habits.

GROWTH AS CURRICULUM BASIS

Using the developmental growth pattern of children as the basis of curricular and learning experiences in planning for the group and for individuals within the group is termed the child development approach to curriculum.

This approach, founded on developmental psychology, gives much attention to the whole personality growth of the child in all its facets and interrelationships, and at the same time provides for the development of each individual child in his various needs and abilities. Hence, its primary focus is on the child and social processes rather than on subject content; the latter becomes the means for growth rather than an end in itself.

In accepting the child in all his relationships as the center of all planning for learning experiences, this curricular approach reaches far beyond the scope of the immediate classroom; it concerns itself with the child's home life, parent and sibling relationships, his out-of-school living, his play and recreation, his community contacts, and all forces that have an influence on his life and growth, as well as his peer and

Children of the same chronological age may vary greatly in growth and development, as this picture of a group of five-year-old children shows

other relationships within the immediate group in which he is placed in school. Too, in acceptance of the child development approach, the school and its staff recognize that they are a part of the total environment which influences the child, rather than the only force effective in his growth. The following charts give a beginning study of growth and development characteristics as curriculum basis. In the use of these charts and all comparable data and materials showing the *average* or typical characteristics of a chronological age, there must be recognition of the fact that no real *average child* exists; that such a portrayal of average is a listing of the characteristics most commonly found in children of a particular age through cross-sectional studies (status studies) of many children. Each child, however, according to his individual developmental pattern differs from the *average* or *norm* in varying degrees for each characteristic. Too, as a whole individual, the child's *total* personality is unique to himself; he will differ from all other children even though he may be one within the *average* group.

49

The following charts have been developed from the materials and data in Arnold Gesell and Frances L. Ilg, *Child Development,* I and II (New York, Harper & Brothers, 1949), and from observation. They are meant as a beginning study for student research, not as a completed compilation.

AT FOUR

Developmental Growth Pattern

Height and weight growth rates slow down
Boys and girls are similar in height and weight
Full night rest and an afternoon nap are needed
Large muscles are developing (small are undeveloped)
Motor co-ordination and control are improving
Energy and drive are abundant
Activities (as eating and talking) can be combined
Fatigue comes quickly
Assertiveness is strong
Boasting, bragging, name calling, and showing off are common
Questioning is centered in "how" and "why"
Attention span is lengthening
Oral expression is fluent
Sentences and longer phrases are used

50

Different rhyming, silly, or nonsense words are liked
Imaginative power is vivid
Speech and actions are exaggerated
Some sharing is begun
Social growth is rapid (likes and wants to be with peers)
Few special friends are developed
Play is more with own sex
Play is with a few at a time, solo, or parallel
Independence is growing in toilet habits, self dressing
Independence is growing in relations with parents and peers
Affection is shown toward family, teacher, and peers
Sibling relations may be poor
Humor is beginning to be enjoyed
Fears of animals and strangers exist
Death causes curiosity but isn't understood
Inconsistency is typical
Drawings and paintings are made without plan or details

Implications for the Teacher—Provision for:

An informal program
Low level of organization of activities
Close home-school relationships
Rhythm of activities of play, work, and rest
Long rest periods
Daily health inspection
Excursions and firsthand experiences
Strenuous indoor and outdoor activities
Much free choice and variety in materials
Activities for furthering large muscle and motor growth and co-ordination
   as play on bicycles, wagons, playground apparatus, running, climbing,
   hopping, jumping, cutting with scissors, sawing, painting, dancing, block
   building
Creative expression in paint, clay, finger paint, drawing, singing, rhythms,
   dramatic play
Much oral communication
Independence in dressing and toilet habits
Social and motor skills in eating (snack time)
Free choice of friends in work and play
Social skills of sharing and co-operation
Materials, lockers, and shelves low enough for child use and care
Solo, parallel, small group, and co-operative play as fits children's needs
Construction and block work and play
Quiet-play activities

51

Nature interests and activities
Basic pattern of routines
Guidance and control of activities
Satisfaction of the "why" and "how"
Attention to individual needs and differences
Song and rhythmic expression
Preparation of child for baby in the family
Situations and interest developing co-operative play
Free and stimulating emotional climate encouraging expression
Observation of pets and nature
Socially acceptable behavior
Attention to birthdays and holidays
Time and space to do
Environmental concepts through dramatic play, stories, and excursions

NOW FIVE

Developmental Growth Pattern

Uniqueness of personality is evidenced
Individual differences are more evident
Figure is more compact
Stability is achieved
Growth rate slows down
Health is good but communicable diseases are contracted easily
Good postural control is developed
Personality is more poised, calm, and well organized
Large muscles are developed (small still undeveloped)
Co-ordinated skills are increased
Activity is excessive
Tires easily but need for long afternoon rest is lessened
First lower teeth are being lost
Vision is far sighted causing difficulty in close focusing
Handedness is definitely established
Eye and hand co-ordination are improving
Girls begin to mature more rapidly than boys
Attention span is lengthening
Emotional balance is improved (less crying, showing off)
Security and affection are major needs
Home and family (especially mother) are center of interest
Self reliance and self dependence are growing
Self interest is strong
Self criticism is begun
Adult help and guidance are wanted

Conformity is accepted
Routines are important
Co-operation and sharing are begun
Co-operative play is limited to small groups
Boys and girls interplay freely
Thinking is factual and concrete
Meaning is centered in experience and the present
Reality and imagination begin to be differentiated
Plans can be made; activity has direction

Tasks need completion for satisfaction
Fears are few because thinking is reality-centered
Praise is needed
Humor and repetition are enjoyed
Oral communication increases (2000 or more words)

Implications for the Teacher—Provision for:

An informal program
Environment rich in varied materials, centers of interest, and stimulating
    activities
Group approval and acceptance of all children
Group activities and beginning peer interaction

Much freedom for children to "do"
Flexible time schedule
Large work and play space areas
Free and directed group experiences
Rhythm of change in work, play, and rest
Established routines
Praise and encouragement
Special interests, abilities, and needs met
Activities and information centered in the family and immediate experiences
Opportunity to learn by doing
Firsthand experiences and observations
Health and safety development through rest and snack periods, and health inspections
Development of large muscles through climbing, hopping, skipping, jumping, hollow block play, indoor block play, large bells, rhythms, and playground apparatus
Development of smaller muscles and co-ordination through wood work, cutting, paper tearing, easel painting, finger painting, clay, and puzzles
Development of vocabulary and communication skills through firsthand experiences, stories, language arts, pictures, picture books, poetry, dramatic play, and free discussion
Planning, discussing, and evaluating individual and group activities
Time to complete what is done
Timing in activities
Solo, parallel, and co-operative play as needed
Widened attention span and interest activities
Accepted social ways of acting and behaving
Child responsibility in materials and activities
Readiness for academic activities through incidental teaching of numbers, activities, story sequences, dramatic play, and observations
Control through interest and re-direction of interests and a positive approach
Attention, respect, and praise for the individual and the group

AT SIX

Developmental Growth Pattern

Period is one of growth and developmental change
First teeth are being lost
First permanent molars are appearing
Leg growth is rapid
Contagious diseases are more liable
Thought and action are inconsistent; may move to and from extremes

54

Indecision is characteristic
Choices are difficult
Behavior is varying and vacillating
Integration is lessened
Social relations are often difficult
Peer acceptance is necessary
Extreme activity is evident
Large and small muscles are used (large most easily)
Reactions involve the whole organism

Routine is liked and desired
Dramatic self activation is a means of growth and learning
Tensions are caused by the developmental process
Intellectual processes are concrete
Magic is liked
Dramatic self-projectiveness is significant
Basis for self evaluation and appraisal is laid
Democratic social rights and values are being learned
Attention span continues to increase
Many fears exist
Self is all important
Interest is in activity more than in results
God and prayer become real and important
Death is feelingly related to self and family

Interests are widening
Acceptance of family baby must be guided by parents
Parent moods and emotions affect the six

Implications for the Teacher—Provision for:

Foundation in familiar school experiences and readiness
Emotional climate of security and freedom
Experiences fostering integrative growth emotionally and mentally
Mental health attitudes
Preventive discipline
Activity programs
Self activity for the child
Creative rather than rote learning
Stress on process skills (plan, activity, evaluation)
Dramatic expression for self expression
Socially acceptable behavior concepts
Humor in everyday living together
Rhythm of rest, play, work, and change
Large materials and equipment supplemented by some involving smaller
  muscle co-ordination
Repetition in program (providing for illness absences and re-teaching
  needs)
Experiences of doing, exploring, and manipulating
Emphasis on processes rather than products
Observation and discrimination
Systematic reading readiness and beginning reading activities
Development of number concepts
Widened community understanding
Gradual adjustment to organized school activities
Individual development (leadership, ability, needs, etc.)
Social skills in co-operative group work and interaction

THEN SEVEN

Developmental Growth Pattern

Calmness and self absorption are characteristic
Assimilation of subjective experiences is occurring
Period is one of inner tensions
Growth is slow but steady
Posture is unilateral
Large muscles are well controlled
Small muscle control is increasing
Sensitiveness to others is increasing

Personal social relations are more intense and necessary
Independence is increased
Thinking is personal-social
Play is still individual and not highly organized
Group co-operation is improving
Personal rapport with teacher is needed
Variability is still evidenced
Retreat and withdrawal are used
Concepts of ethical values are beginning to develop
Truth and property rights still cause some difficulties

Reasonableness and critical abilities are developing
Sense of perfection is strong
Perseverance is characteristic
Thinking is centered in the widening community
Orientation in time and space is developing
Conditions and causes stimulate thought
Praise and acceptance are important and needed
Some control of fears is begun
Interest in family group is strong
God becomes an interest of greater concern
Death concepts become more detailed and realistic
Self awareness is increased
Goals are set beyond own abilities
Attention span continues to lengthen

Opposite sex is less favored
Dramatic play interest is high
More complex planning is possible

Implications for the Teacher—Provision for:

Individual rapport with each child and the group
Firsthand experiences and study trips
Background experiences and vicarious experiences
Self responsibility for use of time
Orientation in time and distance
Timing of activities considering readiness
Rhythmic change of quiet and active periods
Activities for increasing motor control
Mental health attitudes
Process teaching
Construction, manipulation, and outdoor activities
Group acceptance and praise of each individual child
Dramatic play interest
Creative expression through art, music, dance, and stories
Much use of literature, stories, and poems
Guidance in behavior evaluation
Attention to special abilities, interests, and needs
Widened community knowledge and understanding
Increased quantitative concepts
Widening scope of interests and skills

NOW EIGHT

Developmental Growth Pattern

General health is improved
Bodily movements are poised
Small motor co-ordination has developed
Personality is more outgoing and extrovertive
Eyes function well in near and far vision
Actions are characterized by speed and eagerness
Maturity is beginning to be evidenced
Intellect is broadening and maturing
Sexes are tending to segregate
Sex differentiations are increasing
Interest in all human relations is strong
Contact with environment is positive and outgoing
Self awareness is increased

Status relationships are constantly changing and maturing
Parental affection and admiration are strong
Independence of the teacher is growing
Participation in group control and discipline is beginning
Age groups are capable of some independent action
Peer judgment is more important than adult
A best friend is desired
Sense of ethics and justice is appearing

Property sense is keen now
Urge to collect is high
Sensitiveness to criticism is keen
Dramatic interest continues
Flexibility in role playing is strong
Money, property, ownership, and possessiveness are very important
Sympathy and insight into other cultures are shown
Sense of orderliness exceeds ability to be orderly
Some exaggeration is expressed in speech and feeling
Individual differences continue to widen
Fears are minimized
Relationship of school and home interests is more involved
Deprivation is effective discipline
Basis of adult maturity is laid

Implications for the Teacher—Provision for:

Well organized and stimulating program
Wholesome emotional classroom environment
Child leadership and responsibility growth
Respect for child's maturity
Attention to individual abilities and needs
Natural grouping of children by children
Opportunity for much movement and activity
Longer periods of work and activity
Independent self direction
Much teacher-pupil planning and evaluation
Allegiance to peer group a discipline aid
Praise and encouragement
Child development in self criticism
Little need of direct discipline
Expression and creativeness in activities and materials
Increased technical knowledge and skills
Small muscle co-ordination as in pen writing
Increased oral communication skills
Group activities and clubs to further interests
Near and far vision activities
Brief, clear directions
Wide individual reading interests
Enjoyment of activity rather than victory
Extended day interests and activities
Widening interests in community
Deepened quantitative concepts and understandings
Process skills in problem solving, creative expression, and critical thinking
Mental health attitudes

Basic Implications for the Early Elementary Program

Emphasis on whole personality growth
Rhythm of activities of work, play, and rest or change
Timing of learning experiences in terms of the child's readiness, needs, interests, and maturity
Attention to the individual as an individual personality
Opportunity for firsthand experiences
Space, freedom, and time for the child "to do" and "be"
Establishment of routines
Emphasis on security and affection needs
Wholesome and stimulating emotional and learning climate
Development of process skills

Continuity in development

Foundations in academic learning concepts

UNDERSTANDING OF CHILDREN

Throughout this chapter we have been concerned with developing an understanding of children. Just what is implied in this? The Commission on Teacher Education best defined what it means for a teacher to understand a child in terms of the growth and development process in its publication, *Helping Teachers Understand Children*. It stated:[4]

We believe . . . that teachers who understand children think of their behavior as being caused. They see a youngster's present actions as based upon his past experience, as shaped by his present situation, and as influenced by his desires and hopes for the future . . . It also implies that every boy and girl is educable, that unacceptable behavior can be changed, and that desirable and effective action can be evoked. This, we think, can be accomplished by arranging conditions and situations that are appropriate to the child's developmental level, capacities, and personal needs; by maintaining relationships with him that are supporting and reassuring; and by providing him with experiences that help him to understand the world and people around him, and that indicate effective ways of acting which he himself can perfect. . . .

A second characteristic . . . is that they are able to accept all children emotionally, that they reject no child as hopeless or unworthy. . . . It is the obligation of teachers to accept every child as having intrinsic worth, no matter what his capabilities or behavior . . . and the further obligation to assist every pupil in realizing his potentialities.

. . . teachers who understand children invariably recognize that each one is unique.

. . . the various sciences concerned with human growth and behavior have demonstrated that young people, during the several phases of their development, face a series of common "developmental tasks" . . . Understanding teachers know what these tasks are; their sequence and timing in relation to physical, social, and mental maturity; what complications often arise as persons with different characteristics and backgrounds work at them; and what conditions, relationships, and experiences are most helpful to children in mastering each of them.

[4] Commission on Teacher Education, *Helping Teachers Understand Children* (Washington, D.C., American Council on Education, 1945), pp. 8-12.

. . . they know the more important scientific facts that describe and explain the forces that regulate human growth, development, motivation, learning, and behavior . . . The child lives and acts as an indivisible unit and understanding teachers study him as such; so their interpretive generalizations also have to be knit together into a synthetic whole that will show the interdependence and interaction between different aspects of growth, development, and behavior.

. . . the understanding teacher habitually uses scientific methods in making judgments about any particular boy or girl. . . .

To sum up, our definition of understanding a child includes contrasting subjective and objective elements . . . it calls for the subjective acceptance and valuing of individual boys and girls emotionally and philosophically rooted and serving to reassure and afford security to all children, even when they misbehave . . . it also implies objectivity in the use of sound procedures and knowledge to interpret the causes of a child's acts, to appraise his adjustment problems and personal needs, and to work out practical ways of helping him master his developmental tasks. . . .

PROJECTS AND QUESTIONS

1. In a classroom visit observe the physical and other personality characteristics of the five-year-old children (or any one of the early elementary levels). How does your observation list of traits compare with that made from book study concerning the same age children? You saw no "average child." Of what value, then, are the concepts of "the average child" for any chronological age?
2. Collect pictures and illustrations of young children. Classify them into groups according to your decision of the age of the child, basing your judgment on child growth and development study.
3. List evidence of individual differences and teacher attention to them in your observations.
4. Describe problems in development that you had to overcome. How would you help a child in your classes meet and overcome the same problems?
5. What evidence have you from observations and growth and development study that the nursery school and kindergarten are not just "play" and "baby sitting" sessions?
6. You have visited classrooms with nice, even pattern drawings and paintings; you have also visited classrooms where paintings and drawings were freehand and sometimes only slightly resembled the object. Evaluate; give reasons.

7. How would an "understanding teacher" handle:
   a. an awkward child?
   b. an aggressive child?
   c. a withdrawn child?
   d. a child emotionally upset by a broken or disturbed home?

GUIDE TO REFERENCES FOR FURTHER STUDY

ALMY, Millie C., *Child Development* (New York, Henry Holt & Company, 1955).

AMES, L. B., "The Sense of Self in Nursery School Children as Manifested by Their Verbal Behavior," *Journal of Genetic Psychology,* Vol. 81, (1952), pp. 193-232.

BALDWIN, A. L., *Behavior and Development in Childhood* (New York, Henry Holt & Company, Inc., 1955).

BARKER, R. G., KOUNIN, J., and WRIGHT, H., *Child Behavior and Development* (New York, McGraw-Hill Book Company, Inc., 1943).

BOSSARD, James H. S., *The Sociology of Child Development* (New York, Harper & Brothers, 1954).

CARMICHAEL, L., ed., *Manual of Child Psychology* (New York, John Wiley & Sons, Inc., 1954).

D'EVELYN, Katherine, *Meeting Children's Emotional Needs* (Englewood Cliffs, N. J., Prentice-Hall, Inc., 1957).

GESELL, Arnold, and ILG, Frances L., *Child Development* (New York, Harper & Brothers, 1949).

HARTLEY, R. E., and others, *Understanding Children's Play* (New York, Columbia University Press, 1952).

HAVIGHURST, Robert J., *Human Development and Education* (New York, Longmans, Green & Company, 1953).

HURLOCK, Elizabeth, *Developmental Psychology* (New York, McGraw-Hill Book Company, Inc., 1953).

Institute of Child Study, University of Maryland, "Child Growth and Development," *National Education Association Journal,* Vol. 47 (December, 1957), pp. 571-580.

ISAACS, Susan, *Social Development in Young Children* (New York, Harper & Brothers, 1946).

JENKINS, Gladys, SCHACTER, Helen, and BAUER, William, *These Are Your Children,* Rev. ed. (Chicago, Scott, Foresman & Company, 1953).

JERSILD, Arthur T., *Child Development and the Curriculum* (New York, Bureau of Publications, Teachers College, Columbia University, 1956).

———, *Child Psychology* (Englewood Cliffs, N. J., Prentice-Hall, Inc., 1954).

LEE, J. Murray, and LEE, Dorris May, *The Child and His Development* (New York, Appleton-Century-Crofts, Inc., 1958).

MARTIN, William E., and STENDLER, Celia Burns, eds., *Readings in Child Development* (New York, Harcourt, Brace & Company, 1954).

MEEK, Lois H., *Your Child's Development and Guidance Told in Pictures* (Philadelphia, J. B. Lippincott Company, 1951).

MERRY, Frieda K., and MERRY, Ralph, *The First Two Decades of Life* (New York, Harper & Brothers, 1950).

MILLARD, Cecil V., *Child Growth and Development in the Elementary School Years* (Boston, D. C. Heath & Company, 1951).

MURPHY, L. B., *Social Behavior and Child Personality* (New York, Columbia University Press, 1937).

Ohio State University School Staff, *How Children Develop,* University School Series, No. 3 (Columbus, Ohio State University, 1949).

PECK, Leigh, *Child Psychology* (Boston, D. C. Heath & Company, 1953).

RAND, Winifred, SWEENEY, Mary E. and VINCENT, E. Lee, *Growth and Development of the Young Child* (Philadelphia, W. B. Saunders Company, 1953).

STERN, C., and GOULD, T., *Early Years of Childhood* (New York, Harper & Brothers, 1955).

STONE, Joseph, and CHURCH, Joseph, *Childhood and Adolescence* (New York, Random House, Inc., 1957).

STRAUSS, A. L., "The Development of Conceptions of Rules in Children," *Child Development,* Vol. 25 (1954), pp. 193-208.

WOLF, Anna, and SZASZ, Suzanne, *Your Child's Emotional Growth* (New York, Doubleday & Company, Inc., 1954).

WOLFF, Werner, *The Personality of the Preschool Child* (New York, Grune & Stratton, Inc., 1946).

Part II

PHILOSOPHY AND THEORY

CHAPTER 4

Democratic Education Guidelines

The governing purpose of education in a democratic society is to support, perpetuate, enlarge, and strengthen the democratic way of life.[1]

INTRODUCTION

We have looked briefly at the field of early elementary education and at changes in educational thinking and practice. We have related these changes in a general way to the teaching of young children. Such changes, however, are the result of gradual growth, progress, and research; they are centered within the stable framework of the foundation and objectives of education in our American society. What is the foundation of our educational system? What are the objectives of American education? What specifically are the objectives of education as applied to elementary and early elementary education?

EDUCATION REFLECTS AND AFFECTS THE SOCIETY

Even a brief glance into comparative education will show us that the educational system in any country is a reflection of the philosophy and society of that country at the same time that the school is one of the social institutions which a society develops as a means of continuing and furthering its culture and ideals. Study of the people and ideals of a country reflects the type of educational philosophy and curriculum that one may expect to find.

[1] James L. Mursell, *Principles of Democratic Education* (New York, W. W. Norton & Company, Inc., 1955), p. 3.

Russia

Illustration of how the educational philosophy and the school curriculum are related to and dependent on the society in which they exist is seen in the contrast of Russian and American education. A recent study of the Office of Education, reporting on education in Russia, states:[2]

Soviet policy precisely enunciates the function of education in the USSR; to serve the needs of the State. The State is preeminent. To its full development every person is expected to contribute his best efforts as his primary obligation. The growth and development of his own individuality are of secondary importance. . . .

Soviet education aims at education for excellence with freedom of choice resting with the State to the end that the State may be developed to the optimum. By contrast, education in the US aims to give every individual the right of free choice to the end that each may have opportunity to develop his individual capacities to the optimum consonant with his abilities and his desires. . . .

Schools are opened, approved, and run by the State. The State determines the curriculum and methods of instruction to insure that education is in line with Party and State policy and that it can be planned and directed for the Nation as a whole. . . .

The State system of education covers all levels—from preschool through the university . . . .

America

American schools reflect the democratic nature of our society and of our heritage of individual and group co-operative living as expressed in our Declaration of Independence, the American Constitution, and in the privileges of free speech and free worship, the use of methods of discussion and arbitration, the power to vote, and faith in group efforts to further individual and group living. Basic to our democratic concept are (1) the maximum development of the individual as an individual, and (2) the maximum development of the society in which he lives. The core of the American concept of democracy is the recognition of the worth and dignity of each person as an individual. Our society regards individual development as its foremost task and privilege. It

---

[2] Office of Education, Division of International Education, International Educational Relations Branch, *Education in the USSR,* Bulletin 14 (Washington, D.C., Government Printing Office, 1957), pp. 14-15.

effects as far as possible the fullest realization of personal potentialities. This, in turn, leads to the development of the individual as a contributing member of his group and of society, and fosters effective citizenship and the continuation and improvement of co-operative democratic processes.

How is this basic democratic concept translated into practice in our society? It necessitates that as far as possible we must help every individual to develop so that he can (1) choose and set for himself worthwhile goals for living, (2) determine purposes that give direction to his actions, and (3) plan and carry out actions that enable him to realize his purposes. Evaluation of his actions by the individual in terms of the purposes he sets must follow; this evaluation, in turn, helps determine his future actions. Do you not set purposes and goals for yourself? Effective teaching is a major goal in your thinking! Then are your goals not set on purposes? Aren't you planning and carrying through the means to realize this goal? Evaluation of action helps you build more constructively and purposefully toward your goal. Such a democratic process requires critical and creative thinking; it requires conditions and opportunities for the fullest development of each and every individual according to his gifts, abilities, and situations. At the same time it places on each individual an obligation to give and to do his best; it relates directly to individual and group welfare; and it establishes belief in the wonderful possibilities for the growth, development, and improvement of both the individual and our society.

American education is thus guided by our concept of democracy, which has been defined in terms of its purpose as "so to organize society that each member may develop his personality primarily through activities designed for the well-being of his fellow members and of society as a whole."[3]

AMERICAN DEMOCRATIC EDUCATION

The American education program expresses our concern and respect for and confidence in our children. It is a program that is centered in the child and his growing understanding of himself and his environ-

[3] United States Bureau of Education, *Cardinal Principles of Secondary Education*, Bulletin No. 35 (Washington, D.C., Government Printing Office, 1918), p. 9.

ment as he moves from knowledge of his home, school, neighborhood, community, state, and world to full maturity. It is designed to fit the pattern of democratic living and to ensure its continuation and improvement.

Control

To understand our system of education we must take into account two basic facts. (*1*) Since there is no national pattern of education under national control in our country as there is in most of the countries of the world, the curricula of the various schools are developed generally on the basic objectives of American education, and specifically on the requirements of their respective school systems which are under state and local control; and, therefore, these curricula may vary in the way in which they realize the major objectives of education in terms of the immediate needs of their area or locale. (*2*) However, since the curricula of the various school systems are developed within the framework of the American culture, they do follow common basic guidelines in terms of democratic education.

Guidelines

The basic guidelines for democratic education are evident in the above discussion. (*1*) There is respect for each individual as a person. Curricula, therefore, must be flexible and dynamic; they must be built on the needs and interests of the child at the different developmental age levels and must provide for individual growth in all the facets of personality, that is, physical, mental, social, emotional, and moral as well as intellectual. (*2*) The second basic guideline is the development of social competencies of the individual as a member of groups, and of society as a whole.

These guidelines, translated into a program at the early elementary education level, do *not* in any sense mean that the school for the young child is not a place where skills and knowledge are developed. Rather, it emphasizes that the subject matter skills and knowledge and basic processes be stressed in guided learning situations meaningful to the child. Teachers today make full use of a variety of materials and activities planned to increase the child's understanding of himself and of the world in which he lives, to further his social competencies in group

living and adjustment, and to strengthen his peer and o¹
ships.

In order to realize our goal of democracy, then, we be
and every individual must be given the opportunity fc
through education, and that through such individual growth ᵤ᷈
as a whole will continue to advance. Hence, we may state the purpose
and function of American education as follows:[4]

1. The public schools are our chief and most effective means of develop-
    ing free men capable of solving problems and governing themselves
    successfully.
2. In a democracy, society has an obligation to provide free and equal
    educational opportunities for all children and youth, and the learner,
    according to his ability, has an obligation to take advantage of the
    educational opportunities offered.
3. The main purpose of the American schools is to provide for the fullest
    possible development of each learner for living *morally,* creatively,
    and productively in a democratic society.

Implied in this statement are: (*1*) attention to individual needs, and
(*2*) provision of experiences in the processes of thinking and in
methods of living and doing which will give the individual skill and
understanding in everyday living situations.

Objectives of American Education

General Objectives. The major purpose of our educational program
as stated above has been resolved into a more detailed and specific
statement at various times in our educational history. This has facili-
tated the translation of the major goal into secondary and curriculum
goals related to specific content, child development, and social processes. Understanding of the basic goal *is essential* for the professional
person in the classroom, but that goal *must also be analyzed and related in a specific way* to the immediate needs and tasks of the classroom.

A significant development of the purposes of American education
into a fuller statement was made in 1918 by the Commission on the
Reorganization of Secondary Education and published in the *Cardinal
Principles of Secondary Education;* the statement was made for all

[4] Association for Supervision and Curriculum Development, "Platform of Belief,"
News Exchange (April, 1956), p. 4.

.evels of American education including the elementary. This first important formulation of objectives is sometimes referred to as the "Seven Cardinal Objectives of Education." The objectives listed were:[5]

1. health
2. command of fundamental processes
3. worthy home membership
4. vocation
5. citizenship
6. worthy use of leisure time
7. ethical character.

In 1938, the Educational Policies Commission of the National Education Association restudied the objectives of democratic education and decided that the objectives should be stated in terms of individual behavior. They listed four objectives; these have been and continue to be a major force in educational thinking. Because of their importance these objectives are listed here for study.[6]

1. The objectives of self-realization

The inquiring mind. The educated person has an appetite for learning.
Speech. The educated person can speak the mother tongue clearly.
Reading. The educated person reads the mother tongue efficiently.
Writing. The educated person writes the mother tongue effectively.
Number. The educated person solves his problems of counting and calculating.
Sight and hearing. The educated person is skilled in listening and observing.
Health knowledge. The educated person understands the basic facts concerning health and disease.
Health habits. The educated person protects his own health and that of his dependents.
Public health. The educated person works to improve the health of the community.
Recreation. The educated person is participant and spectator in many sports and other pastimes.
Intellectual interests. The educated person has mental resources for the use of leisure.

[5] United States Bureau of Education, *op. cit.*, pp. 10-11.
[6] Educational Policies Commission, *The Purposes of Education in American Democracy* (Washington, D.C., National Education Association, 1938), pp. 50, 72, 90, 108.

2. The objectives of human relationships

Respect for humanity. The educated person puts human relationships first.

Friendships. The educated person enjoys a rich, sincere, and varied social life.

Cooperation. The educated person can work and play with others.

Courtesy. The educated person observes the amenities of social behavior.

Appreciation of the home. The educated person appreciates the family as a social institution.

Conservation of the home. The educated person conserves family ideals.

Homemaking. The educated person is skilled in homemaking.

Democracy in the home. The educated person maintains democratic family relationships.

3. The objectives of economic efficiency

Work. The educated producer knows the satisfaction of good workmanship.

Occupational information. The educated producer understands the requirements and opportunities for various jobs.

Occupational choice. The educated person has selected his occupation.

Occupational efficiency. The educated producer succeeds in his chosen vocation.

Occupational adjustment. The educated producer maintains and improves his efficiency.

Occupational appreciation. The educated producer appreciates the social value of his work.

Personal economics. The educated consumer plans the economics of his own life.

Consumer judgment. The educated consumer develops standards for guiding his expenditures.

Efficiency in buying. The educated consumer is an informed and skillful buyer.

Consumer protection. The educated consumer takes appropriate measures to safeguard his interests.

4. The objectives of civic responsibility

Social justice. The educated person is sensitive to the disparities of human circumstance.

Social activity. The educated citizen acts to correct unsatisfactory conditions.

Social understanding. The educated citizen seeks to understand social structures and social processes.

Critical judgment. The educated citizen has defenses against propaganda.

Tolerance. The educated citizen respects honest differences of opinion.

Conservation. The educated citizen has a regard for the nation's resources.

Social application of science. The educated citizen measures scientific advance by its contribution to the general welfare.

World citizenship. The educated citizen is a cooperating member of the world community.

Law observance. The educated citizen respects the law.

Economic literacy. The educated citizen is economically literate.

Political citizenship. The educated person accepts his civic duties.

Devotion to democracy. The educated citizen acts upon an unswerving loyalty to democratic ideals.

Elementary Education Objectives. From time to time other statements of the objectives implied in the major purpose of democratic education have been made. Of immediate interest to us in the elementary field is the statement of elementary school objectives prepared by the Mid-Century Committee on Outcomes in Elementary Education, and published by the Russell Sage Foundation in 1953. After much research and study by an outstanding group of educators, the following list of objectives was drawn up as a statement of the goals of democratic education in the elementary school. Since understanding of such a guide is an invaluable and essential basis for all teaching processes, the objectives are quoted here at length for detailed consideration and study.

In the Russell Sage Foundation publication of the elementary school objectives (edited by Nolan C. Kearney), characteristics of the recommended goals are discussed. These include "broad scope and rich variety," "a sound core of knowledge, understanding, skill, and competence," "development of interests, attitudes, and ideals that are wholesome in terms of our democratic ideology and rich cultural tradition," "evidence . . . of the effects on the tasks of education of social conditions in the home, in the community, and in the school," . . . "of the effects of the child's physical development toward maturity and of the physiological background of his learning and his personality."[7]

[7] Nolan C. Kearney, ed., *Elementary School Objectives* (New York, Russell Sage Foundation, 1953), pp. 43-44. (By permission of Russell Sage Foundation.)

It is further noted that the objectives include both "fundamentals" or "subject matter content" and "broad generalizations, understandings, habits of work, social attitudes, and others of a like kind." Attention is given to "development of the capacities and potentialities of the child as an individual," and to "social or group skills."[8]

In reviewing and studying these objectives the reader should keep in mind the democratic foundation of American education, the realization that we work with the child as a total personality made up of closely interrelated physical, mental, social, emotional, and moral facets, the range of individual differences, and the place of the family and community in all living and learning.

The educators who outlined the goals accepted four basic concepts. They are:[9]

. . . [1] There is an ever-widening environment in which the child grows. [2] There are fundamental organic and social needs to be met if the child is to mature and develop properly. [3] Within limits, this growth and development of children follows certain patterns. [4] There is an intrinsic logic in the nature of many of the "subjects" that children study.

[It is to be noted in point four above that, while subject fields have a logical sequence, this does not mean teaching such fields per se. "There is a good deal of evidence to indicate individual differences among children as to what is best to learn 'next', and that initial learning is not necessarily best when constrained to any logical pattern."[10] This statement is to be understood, then, from the developmental point of view.]

A summary of the nine objectives listed in the study includes:

1. Physical development, health, and body care

    This goal involves health and safety. It includes consideration of individual health and of elementary public health, and involves physical education, personal grooming, safety, sportsmanship, and an understanding of growth and maturation.

2. Individual social and emotional development

    The fostering of mental health, emotional stability, and growth of personality is the aim of this objective. The school, while using every possible means to further wholesome growth, recognizes that all the child's learning experiences, in and out of school, are of influence.

[8] *Ibid.*, p. 45.
[9] *Ibid.*, p. 131.
[10] *Ibid.*, p. 132.

3. Ethical behavior, standards, and values

Development of personal and social values and behavior in the cultural pattern of our society is necessary for the individual's satisfactory and happy adjustment in daily living. This objective purposes such development and is closely related to the development of the individual in his social and emotional aspects and in his social relations.

4. Social relations

This objective is concerned with the development of the child in his personal-social relationships in the family, school, and widening community. Herein attention is focused on the child.

5. The social world

Not only must the child develop in his personal-social relations but also in the broader social environment. This goal, focused in terms of the form and mores of our democratic society, the physical environment, and the world community, sets necessary avenues of development for the child as a member of the community, nation, and world.

6. The physical world

The educative process strives to orient the child in the physical world and in scientific advancement, and to develop him in the use of the scientific method of thinking in his daily living.

7. Esthetic development

Intellectual, emotional, and moral aspects of esthetic appreciation and expression in the fields of art, music, and crafts are important in child development.

8. Communication

The means of expression and impression by which individuals and groups communicate, including reading, writing, composition, correct usage, spelling, speaking and listening and their implied skills of library work, group participation, and so on, are of basic importance in all education.

9. Quantitative relationships

The child must develop in knowledge and understanding of quantitative measure and competence in its use.

In its excellent outline of goals the Committee (*1*) developed each goal with regard to (*a*) knowledge and understanding, (*b*) skill and competence, (*c*) attitude and interest, (*d*) action pattern, and (*e*) determining conditions; and (*2*) aimed for realization of the goal in the (a) primary level, (b) intermediate level, and (c) upper-grade period of the elementary school.

In our study of these recommended goals we will be concerned with them only as they relate to the *primary* period. All items listed relate to the child at the end of third grade, or about nine years of age.

OUTLINE OF THE RECOMMENDED GOALS[11]

1. Physical development, health, and body care

   a. Knowledge and understanding

   The child knows that there is value in our air, good food, proper exercise, clean hands, good health habits, adequate sleep, simple preventive medication. He knows how and when to brush his teeth and has some knowledge of how infections are spread. He practices safe behavior in crossing streets, and in using fire, knives, machinery. He knows that animals and plants provide foods for man. He is aware of the dangers of strange dogs, animals in the zoo, unknown growing vegetables and berries. He knows that medicines, the unknown contents of bottles, or things that look edible may be poisonous. He knows the meaning of the skull and crossbones on bottles and boxes.

   b. Skill and competence

   In his play the child can skip, hop on one foot, climb, descend, jump, jump rope, suspend from bars, run with ease, and perform stunts appropriate for his age and grade. He identifies and can perform various steps in folk dances, imitative play, circle games, and other group games. He skips to music in unison with others. He tries to use hands skillfully and to develop eye-hand co-ordination. He can throw and catch a large softball; build boats and houses of blocks; handle pencils and paint brushes; use hammer, saw, screw driver, broom, mop, dust brush, dust cloth. When climbing he hangs on "tight." He cares for his own person: hair, teeth, nails, and skin. He dresses himself, managing shoelaces, buttons, zippers, and fasteners. He eats without undue spilling of food.

   c. Attitude and interest

   The child shows interest in his own growth and development; begins to accept his own physical and intellectual limitations, including handicaps that cannot be corrected. He is eager to learn new games and try them out, and plays games without fear. He

[11] See *Ibid.*, pp. 52-120.

has a broad and generalized eagerness to learn about the many interesting and stimulating things that concern his adjustment to life around him.

d. Action pattern

The child is becoming used to washing his hands before eating and after going to the toilet. He is growing in habitual attention to personal cleanliness; covers nose and mouth with handkerchief when sneezing or coughing, keeps hands and objects out of mouth, uses only his own towels, toothbrush, and other personal articles. He eats wholesome food, chews it well, and accepts it in some variety. Although he ordinarily does not require a nap during the day, he rests when tired, engages in quiet activities right after eating, and gets adequate sleep according to his needs. He habitually engages in active play. He stays away from other people when he or they have communicable diseases, and has no undue fear of a doctor, dentist, or nurse. He shows some concern for proper room temperature, good light for reading, and safety conditions where playing or working. He practices safety behavior with fire, tools, with sharp objects, with matches, and with traffic, traffic signals, traffic regulations, bicycles, and public vehicles.

e. Determining conditions

Increasingly our school systems feel responsible for providing conditions under which simple health rules can be learned at school in the early schools years—often through the offices of the school nurse or doctor, but also in connection with the provision and use of equipment and facilities for play and rest, for sports and games, for nutrition and cleanliness, and so on. At the same time it must be remembered that the foundation for most of the patterns of behavior in caring for the body are established by family training in the earlier years.

Many of our outcomes are limited by the natural sequences in the development of the child's body, such as those that tend to establish hand-eye dominance, the need or lack of need for sleep during the day, and the need for an enjoyment of food.

Increasingly our society tries to see that children have no remediable physical or mental defects. This effort will and should be intensified.

2. Individual social and emotional development

a. Knowledge and understanding

The child begins to understand some of his strengths and some of his weaknesses, what he does well, and what he does not do so

78

well. He knows that not everything that he sees and hears is accurate or true. He begins to understand that he is an individual who must think and act for himself and assume individual responsibility as rapidly as he can and as freedom is given him to do so. He understands that his actions will affect the response of others to him.

b. Skill and competence

The child is able to make oral announcements on his own, to give simple directions clearly, to work alone for a period of time, to work out some of his problems independently, to recognize the most obvious of jokes, and to have some capacity to be a good sport when defeated. He can carry out brief, individual assignments in school without supervision.

He has enough social tolerance to be able to accept differences in manners, speech, and in grooming. He is able to be friendly and easy with members of other ethnic and class groups. He can arrange classroom furniture for effective group work and communication. He helps to put away materials and equipment after use. He is able to travel alone on streetcars, buses, and other public conveyances for short distances.

c. Attitude and interest

The child shows pride in completing his share of a class project by calling the attention of others to it, wanting to take it home, and so on. He shows pride in the growth of his skills and has a desire to be adequate in the situation at hand. He feels a sense of personal worth and esteem. He is developing the attitudes that allow him to face difficulties frankly and realistically, to deal with his feelings of anger and hostility, to want to be trusted, to want less adult supervision in his play. He shows an interest in his own physical and mental limitations and those of others, and experiences a minimum of disturbance at handicaps that cannot be corrected. He accepts his own sex and sex role. He eagerly seeks school experiences despite the necessary limitations of school routine. He has a favorable attitude toward parents, teachers, and peers—he appreciates their contributions, reacts to their disapproval with some slight signs of independence and to their approval without prolonged elation. He is openly disappointed with his failure in school work. He tends to become increasingly critical of himself and less critical of others. He has an interest in animals as pets, and an affectionate interest in babies. He identifies himself with one or more glamorous persons (for instance, Hopalong

79

Cassidy). He has a collection hobby; he enjoys active play. He is developing the ability to accept manners, speech, grooming, and behavior that are different from his own or those of his family or neighbors. His attitudes towards his brothers and sisters are fairly free from hostility.

d. Action pattern

The child acts within a pattern of positive self-expression and increasing individual integrity. This involves some rebelliousness and some questioning of the complete validity of statements by older children and adults. It also involves self-assertion, the making of minor choices, and the committing of some errors. He thinks more for himself, makes more of his own decisions, appraises his own performance, entertains himself when alone, goes on errands and to and from school by himself, defends himself, makes some independent choices in eating.

When interested, he will sometimes work for an hour or more at a single task. He tries to finish the work he has begun and, since he can sustain his attention for a longer period, frequently succeeds in controlling his behavior to reach certain goals or to handle increasingly difficult situations. When he has finished one piece of work, he tends to find something else worthwhile to do. He selects and takes part in various games and recreational activities suitable to his age and grade. He seeks vicarious adventure through books, radio, movies, and television. He encounters mild physical injuries or accidents to property with brief and not intense grimacing and crying. While failure at school work sometimes elicits an openly disappointed reaction, there is some indication of renewed effort toward accomplishment and of growth in ability to receive and act on criticisms without feeling hurt. Failures in social relations are met with a willingness to discuss the problem with the teacher (when she takes the initiative). There is a tendency to compete (in school work and in behavior) with others for the teacher's approval. He is able to control his behavior so as not to lose the love of persons important to him. He refrains from hasty judgments of others. He usually handles feelings of anger by channeling them into some constructive activity, rather than by hurting persons, destroying property, or bottling up his emotions.

e. Determining conditions

During these years, and to a certain extent thereafter, the child is highly dependent on adults for all sorts of decisions—where to go and when, what to wear, and so forth. For example, his attitudes (mentioned above) toward failure in school will be greatly influenced by his teacher's attitude or his parent's attitude toward that failure. His sex role, whether masculine or feminine, is set for him by his culture and his social class, and is very different at age nine from that at age twelve or fifteen. It has little relationship at this age to physical maturity, except in cases of extremely early or retarded maturation.

3. Ethical behavior, standards, values

   a. Knowledge and understanding

   The child knows the basic rules in such concepts as the ownership of property, trespassing, theft, and the responsibility of the finder of lost articles. He recognizes the rights of weaker persons to freedom from unprovoked aggression and bullying. He begins to realize that freedoms and privileges involve responsibilities. He can distinguish his property from the property of other individuals and groups. He can differentiate between truth and falsehood on an elementary level. He is beginning to develop a sense of fair play. He is beginning to understand the purpose of the school. He differentiates between aggression that merely produces pain and aggression that produces bodily injury. He is forming religious ideas, such as an idea of God. He sees the simple morals in narratives and in such materials as the easiest of *Aesop's Fables.* He knows that people approve of efforts to make the world "better."

   b. Skill and competence

   The child is developing skill and competence in expressing values. This is usually done in absolute terms and is generally limited to classifying as "good" or "bad," particularly when the values refer to human behavior. He has learned to handle some of his own disputes without adult assistance and to make some of his own simple rules. He knows how to take turns at games, sports, talking, and in the use of supplies and facilities.

   c. Attitude and interest

   The child is friendly toward other people. He reacts to his associates in accord with his assessment of their personal qualities, but without regard to their race, religion, or national origin. He is aware of the interdependence of all members of the community, is concerned with maintaining his and their health, safety, and happiness. He disapproves of stealing, and has a "hands off" attitude toward the property of others. He respects the rights and individuality of others. He is developing a sense of fair play and honesty. He has sympathy for those who are ill or in trouble.

He has a keen sense of wonder about the unseen world. His attitude toward school, teachers, aggression, and moral behavior can be moderately identified with parental values, but he cannot yet discuss these values much beyond the repeating of parental opinions.

d. Action pattern

The child is acquiring a set of values and an ethical system as a guide for his behavior. At this stage he can help to make rules of behavior for his group involving the rights, the property, and the personalities of his peers, or the use of school equipment and materials for the playing of games. He tends to obey school rules that he has participated in discussing or establishing or that he has accepted. He has a keen sense or fairness in applying group standards to his peers, and adult standards to adults, but is not acute in applying these standards to himself. However, he abides by them most of the time.

e. Determining conditions

At this stage the standards of politeness, of honesty, of correct or moral behavior that are shown by children, especially in any situation that is encountered for the first time in school, are largely the result of family and home environment. The child's belief about good and bad, right and wrong are laid down in his early years in the context of his family. These early formulations, carried into the wider interaction of the school, enable him to act more and more consistently as an honest, responsible, and loyal person in a variety of situations if his home background has been good. If not, the school is faced with increased responsibilities. His ethical code also develops in the give-and-take of games and other activities with his peer group. This new code is more flexible and modifiable than the code taken uncritically from the parents. These ethical ideas are in a gradual state of development. As the child approaches adolescence, his code of personal behavior enables him to make increasingly specific and valid personal judgments on questions of honesty, loyalty, responsibility, consideration for others.

4. Social relations

a. Knowledge and understanding

The child begins to realize that freedoms and privileges involve responsibility. He shows growing understanding of why other children and adults behave as they do. He knows about the more familiar occupations of various persons in his community. He understands generally the process of electing officers of his group. He knows the rules of the team games he plays. He understands that there are harmonious ways to get along with many different kinds of people, including "difficult" people.

b. Skill and competence

The child is able to participate in group discussion of plans for future group action, a play, a trip to a factory or a picnic, and decisions governing the group's behavior in very simple matters, such as whether the class should have an outdoor picnic or an indoor party. In participation of this type, he knows how to listen to what others say, take his turn in suggesting activities or in giving directions to others, carry on a friendly conversation, assume group leadership on occasions, participate with others in group meetings, work on a cooperative project, share information with others, recognize and introduce visitors hospitably, and behave appropriately when differences of opinion occur.

In strictly peer relationships, he is able to enter into play situations with others, follow the rules of the game, introduce and lead, or accept and follow in new games and dances. He is able to find his way around the neighborhood.

c. Attitude and interest

The child is willing to be of service to the group of which he is a member. He enjoys team games and group games and is beginning to be interested in organized games; plays regularly and eagerly, though often separately, with from one to three children of the same sex. He is irritated when deprived of opportunity to play with his peers. While he chooses the same sex for ordinary play, he shows no resentment when working with the opposite sex in semi-formal situations, as in a class project.

He begins to show interest in joining others in clubs, tree houses, and other groups in and out of school. He shows a developing 'we' feeling in eagerly seeking social experiences and in recognizing and respecting the rights of others. He feels himself a part of such large school concerns as safety at crossings, clean playgrounds, and orderly halls. He is pleased when visitors come. He begins to develop "pals"—"bosom friends." He shows interest in stories about other children, their adventures and their pets. In an interview, his responses show generally a favorable attitude toward parents, teachers, and peers; he has relatively few complaints about them. He competes with his classmates for the teacher's approval of the quality of his work. He appreciates his parents and does not wish to hurt them. He is becoming more critical of himself and less critical of others.

d. Action pattern

The child shows acceptance of the roles played by different people in his group, and shows ability to shift his own role, for example, from chairman to simple member. He is able to accept group decisions that he has opposed, without prolonged argument or refusal to conform. In games or play sessions, he follows pupil leadership, abides by rules, rarely fights, defends himself when necessary, shows increased sympathy and understanding of why others behave as they do, and begins to appreciate the abilities of other children. He treats handicapped children constructively. In the classroom he helps with planning under the guidance of the teacher, reacts thoughtfully to discussions, and abides by decisions. He helps put away supplies, to care for equipment, and so on. In small groups he shares toys, tools, and materials with others. He waits his turn in using equipment, being leader, and so on. He helps others and assumes increasing social responsibility. He generally has several friends with whom he works and plays. He may belong to a club—formal or informal. He extends common courtesies to visitors or guests. He performs his proper duties and chores, and shares in the responsibilities of the family.

In his social group he really discovers and learns his social personality—his social stimulus—value to others and theirs to him. He begins to develop abilities and attitudes to use in approaching people, in avoiding them, in conversing with them, and in being sympathetic with them. He develops constructive relationships with those about him. To some degree he accepts and makes use of the intellectual, physical, and racial differences found among his classmates.

e. Determining conditions

In getting along with age-mates in a constructive pattern of social interaction, the peer group provides an important milieu for personal and social development. It seems to fulfill some needs and perform some functions which no other setting provides. In the peer group a child can work out a conception of himself and arrive at some estimation of how his contemporaries regard him. In such a setting it is possible to develop the idea of having co-equals to an extent that is seldom achieved when children are trying to relate to the always more powerful and wiser adults. A sense of personal worth is partly developed through being able to make realistic comparisons of one's own abilities, talents, and accomplishments with those of persons at the same point of development. That is to say, the child must "try his muscles" (physically, emotionally, intellectually) against those of peers— not evaluate himself against those much further advanced or retarded. It seems that few children develop into happy, successful, well-adjusted people in later life unless they have been able to engage in continuing, positive, well-knit interaction with a peer group during these years of growth.

5. The social world

   a. Knowledge and understanding

   The child should understand the roles of teachers, principal, other school adults, members of the family, and public servants in the community—policeman, fireman, postman, garbage collector, and others—as they affect his life and the lives of others.
   The child should know and understand many facts about his neighborhood and city, particularly those that bear upon the lives of children. He should know something about important men and events in his community, in his country, and in other countries. He should know something of the way of living in early days in his community, in his country, and in other lands. He should begin to understand how man has adapted himself to his environment by contrasting the ways of living of various primitive people, of early shepherds and farmers, of colonizers and pioneers, with present modes of living. He should know something about the life and culture of the American Indian, the Eskimo. He should understand the relationship between seasonal changes and the way people live and dress.
   In this area he should have a growing geographical vocabulary and a reading recognition of simple, basic words, such as country, state, president, court, Indian.

   b. Skill and competence

   The child should be able to read a map of his city or town and to find his own home, school, and church on it. On larger maps he should be able to indicate some points of interest and to chart some imaginary travels. He should be able to contrast the ways of doing work with tools and with machines. He should be able to classify the vocational activities of various people under such major headings as building homes, getting food, making clothes, trading. He sees that people in one vocation or occupation are dependent on many others in other occupations. He should be able to take part in dramatizing short scenes and historical occurrences and in reading stories about child-life among other people.

He is moving away from a pattern in which nearly all rules of behavior come from stronger persons, and tends to conform not because he is restrained but because he consents.

He develops an appropriate sex role (this may vary from one social class to another) and adopts the social convention of sex modesty.

c. Attitude and interest

The child is learning an appropriate set of social attitudes toward institutions and social groups and toward members of other racial, religious, or socio-economic groups. He shows an interest in needy children in other parts of the world. He should be interested in "once upon a time" stories about important persons in the past, some of which will be related to the observance of holidays and special days. He is interested in primitive peoples and prehistoric times. He has a friendly attitude toward the various people in the community who serve him—policemen, firemen, mailman, and others.

d. Action pattern

The child's patterns of action in his social world are determined by a well-developed curiosity about various facets of life. He possesses a sense of humor that enables him to take a joke or two on himself. He shows a tendency to defend others who are wronged or injured.

He increasingly tends to be able to use the printed word for obtaining information about the social studies.

While becoming a bit less dependent on adults, he still needs and seeks their suggestions and approval. He may develop an affectionate, constructive relationship with at least one adult outside his family group. He cooperates in a friendly manner with public servants—policemen, postmen, teachers, garbage collectors, and others, with whom he comes in contact, accepting them as agents of the community.

e. Determining conditions

In his early years the child learns an appropriate set of social attitudes within the structure of his social groups. He learns these

86

attitudes largely as they originate in the family, but the influence of his peer group may change their direction tone, and intensity to a moderate degree. He is influenced greatly during the early school years by his experience with public servants of all kinds—teachers, policemen, mailman, playground director, fireman. He is greatly influenced by people in his religious world, by people he meets who have other racial or cultural backgrounds, and by businessmen. The school should provide a setting in which all these experiences may contribute to the central ideal of democracy.

6. The physical world

   a. Knowledge and understanding

   The child knows the names of the common pets and farm animals. He knows the names of many of the common local plants: garden plants, flowers and crops. He knows about the foods of different animals and the products that animals provide man in the way of food, clothing, and shelter. He is familiar with some of the animal and insect pests. He knows of the use of trees for providing fruit, shade, and lumber and for beauty.
   He is able to read and understand simple maps of his neighborhood, his city, and his expanding community of interest. He is aware of the world as a globe, has some preliminary understanding of its main divisions and regions, and its relationship in space to the sun, the moon, and the stars. He begins to be acquainted with simple natural features, such as mountains, lakes, islands, oceans, rivers, and streams—particularly if these are found in his immediate environment. He begins to learn about simple machines, the elemental scientific background to transportation and communication.
   He is able to generalize in simple terms about seasonal changes; their effect upon the way people live, dress, and eat; and their effect upon plant and animal life. He has some elementary knowledge of the fundamental processes of nature, their influence on man's way of living and his adaptations to them. He knows little stories about a few of the great men of science and something about some of the new developments in science. The child should be able to answer such questions as: What happens to water when it freezes? What makes the rain fall? Why do we have dew in the morning? He acquires a vocabulary to match his knowledge in all these areas. His knowledge is reflected in his art work, his writing, and other areas. He finds understandable answers to his questions about sex and human reproduction.

b. Skill and competence

The child has a beginning skill in using maps, locating places, and routing actual or imaginary trips. He uses many of our simple tools correctly. He is able to measure accurately with rulers and perhaps with some other simple measuring instruments available in the school, to use patterns, and make minor repairs and adjustments on such objects as wagons, bicycles, and flashlights. He has skill with such things as Tinker Toys, and Lincoln Logs. In terms of his community and socio-economic status, he should be able to operate a radio and television set, ride a bicycle, row a boat, and swim. He should be careful in crossing streets, should play safely, and know how to deal with fire. He should have skill in reporting his own observations of animals, plants, and physical science phenomena.

c. Attitude and interest

The child shows a desire for information about such matters as transportation, construction, techniques of warfare, astronomy, industrial processes. His interest and curiosity begin to develop in the form of a somewhat generalized inquisitiveness about the weather, the sky, the earth, living things, machines, transportation and communication, and the natural world about him. He shows interest in science stories, pictures of animals and plants from various regions, conservation, protecting birds and bird nests, and making science collections. He begins to develop pride in good workmanship, in planning work, and in finishing things well; thus, he becomes critical of his own work and makes greater effort to improve.

d. Action pattern

The child actively seeks information to satisfy his curiosity. He brings science materials to school to share with others. He helps to plan and set up procedures for the cooperative solution of problems, and also tries to solve problems individually. He has an appreciation of his surroundings and uses his senses to learn about his environment and to report on simple observations. He habitually asks sensible questions to satisfy his curiosity about scientific matters. He tends to differentiate between fact and fancy, and to make the best hypotheses within the limits of his ability. He employs experimental procedures in solving practical problems, such as the best way of raising plants, caring for animals, making an aquarium or terrarium, finding out what makes a cool jar "sweat" or the temperature of boiling water. He assumes responsibility for the care of plants, animals and science materials in the schoolroom and for the care of pets, shrubs, gardens, and lawns at home and in the community. He practices rules of conservation in regard to the natural world about him, and in saving essential materials in the school and in the home. He frequently develops skill in constructive science hobbies.

e. Determining conditions

Many of the specific outcomes mentioned under the child's physical world are highly dependent on socio-economic status and geographic locale. Conditions in the home and in the community are very important in this respect. Such factors must be taken into account by teachers because no child will do all these things. For example, a child in the slums of some cities (or in rural sections of Nevada or Texas) would have little interest in knowing how to row a boat, nor would he need such knowledge. Again, some children have erector sets, electric and steam trains, and similar toys in great profusion from infancy, while others never see them except in store windows. Traffic safety is very different in Lame Deer, Montana, from that on Clark Street in Chicago.

A child's background of folklore or superstition in some cases affects his scientific attitudes, particularly in the lower grades. A child's early experiences in obtaining answers to his "why" questions may be an important factor in his early school learning about the physical world. His opportunities to explore, be they such things as the countryside while at camp, or the continent of Asia through movies and books, are very important.

7. Esthetic development

a. Knowledge and understanding

The child becomes conscious of color, form arrangement, and design in the objects and structures about him, and of descriptive or symbolic representations of people, things, and situations. He recognizes some of the primary and secondary colors, bright and dull colors, gay and drab colors, warm and cool colors. He knows the use of pencils, chalk, crayons, water colors, finger paints. He knows that color hues and tones can be changed by mixing or applying one over the other. He can distinguish pictures of various types; landscapes, portraits, storytelling, imaginary people, animals. He is able to recognize some of the world's great paintings. He knows the joy of using clay to express form and shape.

He knows the use of simple rhythm instruments, recognizes

rhythms that are similar, and distinguishes those that are different. He is able to count time and sometimes to recognize measure and accent and repeated rhythmic pattern when listening to music. With the school *and the home* as factors, he may have some knowledge of the notes of the scale and recognize bars, the key of C, the key of F, and perhaps the staff, the whole note, the half note, and the quarter note. He can recognize some musical instruments by sound as well as by sight and recognize some of the world's masterpieces by sound, if not by name and composer. He sees the colors and hears the music in nature about him.

b. Skill and competence

He knows how to use simple rhythm instruments. He can skip to music in unison with others, clap hands to the rhythmic patterns of a new song, keep step to music, interpret rhythm through bodily movements, quickly grasp the melody of a song, sing in tune without the piano, discover new tunes and patterns in music, and sing a few songs if provided with the words.

He is able to draw and paint, with some realism and detail, but— more important—with satisfaction to himself, the simple things that strike his fancy, such as trees, animals, and human figures. He uses pencils, crayons, paints, finger paints. He can create simple designs or reproduce them from memory. He can use margins in mounting, in writing papers, and so on. He can use clay in simple pottery forms. He can weave simple mats and make simple constructions with paper, cardboard, metal.

He can listen to and observe, or plan to take part in, a dramatization. He can detect rhythms in poetry. He can derive meaning from poems concerning child life. He is developing skill in using his small muscles in the arts and crafts.

c. Attitude and interest

The child enjoys listening to music, poetry, stories. He enjoys taking part in and attaining skill in dramatizations, singing, and work in graphic arts and crafts. He finds pleasure in color, sound, and form. He enjoys familiar songs either as listener or as a producer. He enjoys expressing himself through rhythm and through all the artistic media. He tends to be critical of his own performances at the same time that he acquires some judgment of quality and an appreciation of beauty.

d. Action pattern

The child tends to seek vicarious adventure through books, radio, movies, and television, and to relieve his feelings and tensions through these media as well as through art, music, and other creative work. He frequently looks at picture-books and magazines, and occasionally reads brief stories not directly related to his school work. The stories sometimes deal with primitive ways of producing music and graphic art, of writing, of reading and communications, of calculating, and of producing and using utensils and tools. He tends to carry over his school esthetic experiences into life outside school.

e. Determining conditions

Not all children possess the talent for artistic expression that is of importance to some, but it seems clear that creative activity may play an important role in personal development. By the third grade, each child should have had experience and guidance with a variety of media for this purpose. It is probably not worthwhile, with the devices currently available, to attempt the measurement of personal gains achieved through creative work nor the excellence of artistic judgment. It is, however, possible to record interest and participation. The difficulty of measurement should not lead us to underestimate the importance of this sphere of development.

8. Communication

a. Knowledge and understanding

The child should be able to recognize at once the words that are part of his basic reading sight-vocabulary, and to define many common words that he uses orally, including common abstract terms. He knows how to read the period at the end of sentences (and some children will read quotation marks around direct quotations, question marks, and exclamation marks). He should understand that many words "pair off" as opposites. He should be able to distinguish between the names of persons and things and the action words. Basic to his understanding of communication is his growing recognition that words and sentences are useful only as they have meaning for him.

He should be able to name and recognize all the letters of the alphabet in random order and to repeat the alphabet. He should be able to spell from dictation 7 out of 10 unfamiliar one-syllable words if they are completely phonetic. He should be able to spell from 500 to 700 of the most commonly used words. Children should know the common sounds (in words) that go with the letters that represent them. They should recognize simple phonetic clues in spelling and use simple word-analysis techniques as an

91

aid in spelling. They should know the standards for letter formation, spacing and alignment, in manuscript or cursive form.

b. Skill and competence

(Reading). The child does assigned reading by himself. He reads, first, to get the whole story, anticipates the story from its title, picks out the chief sentences, and is able to tell what each says. He reads to find answers—what, where, when, why. He can recall the sequence of a story or the facts read in a story. He can read a simple narrative of ten pages with comprehension and pleasure, if there are but few unfamiliar words. He can indicate the interesting features of a book by describing or dramatizing them. He can distinguish the chief elements of a story and repeat them. He can repeat the narrative of a story for children in the language of the author. He reads simple informational material with comprehension. He handles second-grade material in silent or oral reading easily, reading or pronouncing most of the words accurately. In third-grade material, he reads with a comprehension score of 80 per cent. He can read 7 out of 10 paragraphs of third-grade material and recognize many of the main ideas. Silent-reading rate should be between 95 and 120 words a minute; not over 30 regressions per 100 words of easy material; not over 140 fixations per 100 words of easy reading material. He makes but few reversals on letter forms, as "b" for "d," and rarely does he reverse letter sequence, writing "not" for "ton." He has a recognition span of at least four-letter words, such as "come" or "hand." He reads with rhythmic eye movement, and without lip movements or whispering.

(Word Study). He recognizes and produces the individual letter signs for the common blends. He can fuse two- or three-letter sounds into a single word and can recognize letters by their sound. He can recite the alphabet. He can sound out 6 out of 10 completely phonetic unfamiliar words. He grows in skill in attacking unfamiliar words; picks out new words in a story, notes how they differ from similar words, and notes context in an effort to find meanings.

(Book and Library Skills). He handles books properly, begins to use the index and table of contents in his search for information, and uses a children's dictionary or a picture dictionary to locate words or to find their spelling and meaning.

(Speaking). He converses easily, fearlessly, confidently, and fluently, with children and with adults. He gives simple oral directions clearly, makes telephone calls efficiently and courteously, gives interesting reports on personal and group experiences, choosing interesting incidents to relate.

He contributes to group sessions and enterprises by sharing his experiences, giving directions to others, suggesting activities, and arranging classroom furniture for effective work and communication. He suggests reasonable solutions to immediate problems of group behavior.

He can plan a short talk, can make oral announcements, give clear directions, describe and discuss ideas obtained from reading, motion pictures, and the like. He can present short reports on trips, interviews, books. He can dramatize stories, impersonate characters, develop dialogue, and pronounce correctly the words he uses. He speaks with sufficient volume and clarity and does not use baby-talk or show evidence of avoidable speech defects. In speaking, he avoids errors that are not common in his home or community.

(Spelling). He can spell 400 common one- or two-syllable words. He uses simple generalizations and some knowledge of phonetics, consonants, and vowel sounds as aids in spelling. He knows how to use an apostrophe in a few simple words such as "don't." He is able to form simple plurals.

(Handwriting). He can write legibly with a pencil and perhaps with a ball-point or fountain pen (either manuscript or cursive writing). He keeps a reasonably even margin, and is able to form most capital and small letters correctly if given time. He writes his own name well, maintains good posture in writing, and can write legibly 40 letters a minute or 60 letters a minute if the material is repetitive (quality of 50 on Ayres scale is sometimes recommended). Not more than 3 out of 25 of his written words should require study before they can be read. He should be able to form the letters of the alphabet in their correct proportions, and to space properly above and below the base line.

(Composition). He is acquiring a "sentence sense." He uses capitals to begin sentences and for proper names, uses a period at the end of sentences, and groups together two or more sentences that follow each other easily.

He is able to compose and write simple letters independently with at least a realization that there should be a heading, salutation, message, complimentary close, and signature. He should be able to copy forms for writing friendly notes, letters of thanks, letters of request, and letters of invitation. He should be able to write notes to parents about school events.

He should be able to write a one-paragraph story, using some descriptive words about people. He should be able to write his street address (city, state, and country) and the date.

(Listening). He listens carefully in order to comprehend simple statements in direct conversation or in audiences, and puts in writing ideas that concern him. He is able to remember a series of three or more steps when listening to directions, and can write a short sentence from dictation.

c. Attitude and interest

The child likes to write short friendly notes, to read for recreation or information, to talk and listen to others respectfully and thoughtfully, to recite poems, and to retell favorite stories. He is interested in the sounds of words in word-families, in rhymes, in secret languages and codes. He characterizes his efforts in absolute terms of good and bad. He begins to develop attitudes toward radio and television programs.

d. Action pattern

The child habitually listens to others while they talk or give reports and he waits until they have finished or for an appropriate opportunity to speak. He finds good reading materials and shares them with others, both through reading aloud and through recommending poems, stories, plays, and news items. He habitually reads to others to inform, to help solve a group problem, and to entertain. He reads more rapidly silently than orally. He looks for information in books and reads for meaning. He voluntarily reads magazines and newspapers and books designed for children, and reads poetry and stories for personal pleasure.

He uses the picture dictionary in the library, and habitually studies new words and words he is uncertain about spelling. He writes occasional brief stories for fun. He contributes to class discussions at least briefly each day, and asks questions about topics that interest him. He tries to establish habits of correct usage in oral communication.

e. Determining conditions

A nine-year-old child is maturing and his span of attention is lengthening to the extent that he can sustain it for a period of twenty minutes or longer.

In our culture the middle-class child is under tremendous pressure from his home to learn to read and to master the other verbal skills. Care must be taken that the schools do not increase these pressures unduly. Lower-class children do not feel the same pressures outside of school and, hence, may lack motivation for the mastery of many of the verbal skills. Thus, the determining conditions differ greatly from child to child. The child shows high identification with parental values, such as attitudes toward the school and teacher, aggression, religion, and moral behavior, though he cannot discuss these matters much beyond expressing parental opinions.

9. Quantitative relationships

   a. Knowledge and understanding

   The child understands, reads, and writes three or four place numbers. He understands some of the simple similarities between modern modes of counting and calculating and those used by peoples in earlier times. He understands that to have meaning numbers must apply to a quantity of something. With his home and his community as factors, he is able to apply numbers to the months in a year, eggs in a dozen, pennies in a dime, quarter, or dollar, minutes in an hour, inches in a foot, feet in a yard, and pints in a quart (as these are within the range of child's experiences). He understands the common liquid and dry measures, weights, the calendar and the clock, United States coinage. He understands addition and subtraction, division and multiplication. He understands the concept but not necessarily the symbol of the common fraction. He understands arithmetic symbols such as plus, minus, multiplied by, divided by, equals, dollar sign. He can read Roman numerals up to X. He knows the abbreviations for the common units of money and of time. He understands general quantitative words, such as many, seldom, often, much, little. He masters the simple combinations in addition, subtraction, and multiplication with high accuracy.

   b. Skill and competence

   He knows the correct answers to most of the fundamental combinations and can solve simple one-step problems in which the words are within the pupil's reading vocabulary, and the subject matter is within the child's experience. He can count by 2's, 3's, 4's, 5's, and 10's up to 50 or 100. Sometimes he learns to count backward in the same way. He can master such tasks as tallying votes in a class election. He follows the principle that we deal with tens in combinations the same way we deal with ones, using the position of the numerals to keep the answers clear. He is able to bridge the tens. He is able to write the digits from zero to nine correctly. He can add, subtract, multiply, and divide in the ones and tens and can "carry" in each process. He can multiply with a one-figure multiplier and a multiplicand not exceeding three digits. He can demonstrate simple fraction problems with concrete materials, dividing them into halves, thirds, and fourths.

He can handle simple problems arising in his everyday life. He can tell time, using minutes, quarter hours, and hours. He can use units of money, such as a penny, nickel, dime, quarter, when shown the coins, and can make change from a dime and a quarter with accuracy.

c. Attitude and interest

The child has a respectful attitude toward the usefulness of arithmetic and its practical and scientific applications.

d. Action pattern

The child habitually regards arithmetic examples and problems as questions. He tends to consider quantities in terms of their excess or deficiency in relation to other quantities. He thinks in terms of measurable amounts or countable units, such as inches, pints, minutes, and cents. In descriptions or discussions of events or situations, he habitually looks for the statements that contain numbers. He does not try to add unlike quantities such as pencils and marbles.

He is able to handle his own financial transactions. He reads and writes three- and four-place numbers. He can derive division combinations from multiplication, can use numerals in asking and answering questions, and can apply numbers in keeping game scores, marketing, and so forth. He is able to read dates, sizes in shoes and clothing, radio and television dials, book page numbers, house numbers, serial numbers, his own weight on the scales. He is able to measure the dimensions of objects, mark off a sheet of paper with a ruler into square inches, and measure the quantities of liquids with a measuring receptacle.

e. Determining conditions

Young children come to grips with numbers in much the same way that they learn by experience in other areas. Quantity as it involves size in space, existence in time, appearance in terms of distance must be encountered successfully before the growing infant can learn to manipulate his own body and his simple utensils and toys with more than random effect. At the time of entering school, the child has had much experience with quantity. The main problems of the early school involve two tasks: (1) to further enrich quantitative experience, and (2) to provide spoken and written symbols with which to think and communicate quantitatively. (Remember that thinking, even on this level, involves generalizing in a simple way.)

There will be great individual differences in children in innate ability and in early quantitative experiences. Respect or disrespect for numbers and the extent of the desire to learn arithmetic will be affected by family background.

How are such objectives realized by the teacher in classroom situations? Planning the curriculum or learning experiences for any maturational level from the kindergarten through the college *must* begin with an overview and understanding of basic goals and objectives.

Each fall at the beginning of the school year the teacher should reconsider the basic goals of education and the total picture of the educational program; within this framework she then should outline the year's goals and purposes for her specific teaching level. With this foundation she considers the maturity level, the needs, and the readiness of the immediate group or class that she will teach, and then plans in detail. The teacher should never begin her planning with just the *specific* year or subject to which she is assigned; nor should she plan independently of other educational levels, subject content, and the maturity and needs of her specific group. Such over-all planning makes for finer and more professional teaching. Units for the specific year are planned and developed with regard for continuity and sequence within the whole-year plan, which is developed, in turn, within the framework of the total educational goal.

(Goals for the early elementary educational level are basically the same as those for the other levels of our educational program. However, the specific way in which the goals are realized differs for each of the maturational levels; in this respect the goals of the early elementary period differ from those of more mature levels. For example, the basic contribution of the Language Arts, which includes reading, writing, speaking, literature, and spelling, is skill in communication. This goal extends over all levels of the school program. In the kindergarten this goal is specifically the development of oral expression and readiness for reading. In the first grade it involves more advanced communication skills, such as further development in oral speech and

97

FRAMEWORK FOR EFFECTIVE CLASSROOM PLANNING

Major Objective of Education

maximum growth of the child as an individual and as a member of society

Secondary Objectives of Education

self-realization, civic responsibility,
human relationships, economic efficiency

Elementary Education Objectives

individual social and emotional development; physical development; health and body care; ethical behavior, standards, and values; awareness of quantitative relationships; knowledge of the physical world; knowledge of the social world; esthetic development; communication skills

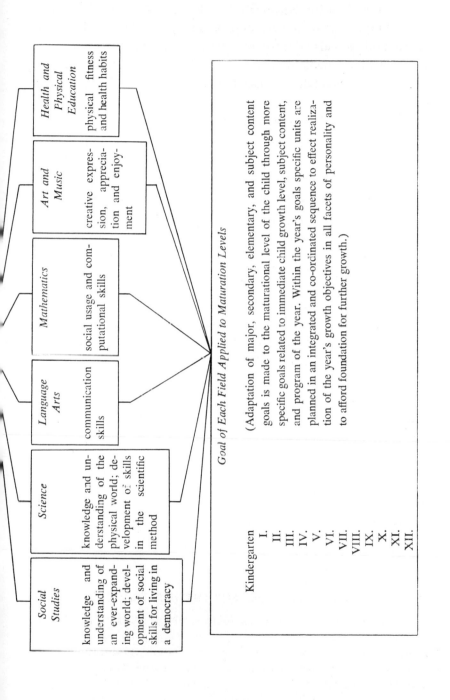

Social Studies	Science	Language Arts	Mathematics	Art and Music	Health and Physical Education
knowledge and understanding of an ever-expanding world; development of social skills for living in a democracy	knowledge and understanding of the physical world; development of skills in the scientific method	communication skills	social usage and computational skills	creative expression, appreciation and enjoyment	physical fitness and health habits

Goal of Each Field Applied to Maturation Levels

Kindergarten	(Adaptation of major, secondary, elementary, and subject content goals is made to the maturational level of the child through more specific goals related to immediate child growth level, subject content, and program of the year. Within the year's goals specific units are planned in an integrated and co-ordinated sequence to effect realization of the year's growth objectives in all facets of personality and to afford foundation for further growth.)
I.	
II.	
III.	
IV.	
V.	
VI.	
VII.	
VIII.	
IX.	
X.	
XI.	
XII.	

beginning reading. In the Social Studies field the basic goal is giving the child a knowledge of society and of the world about him. In the kindergarten this is realized through widening and enriching the child's knowledge of his immediate environment, family, home, school, and neighborhood. As the child matures the scope of the goal and content widen correspondingly.

The chart on page 98-99 graphically presents this concept.

Thus, while the objectives of education cover the whole period of an individual's growth, both within and outside the school, there are within these objectives implications specific to the field of early elementary education. In view of the maturational level of the young child, the appearance of specific developmental characteristics, needs, and tasks, and of the percept-concept level, certain emphases are desirable in the adaptation and realization of phases of the general objectives to the education of young children.

PROJECTS AND QUESTIONS

1. The statement was made recently that the teaching of democratic ideals and values is possible beginning only in the intermediate level of the elementary school. Cite five illustrations from your observation to disprove this statement.
2. Democratic philosophy of education must be the foundation and guide of American education at *all* levels. Practice based on such guidelines is developed in accord with scientific research. Evaluate the following practices in terms of this view.
   a. workbooks
   b. ability grouping
   c. celebration of holidays
   d. memorization
   e. exclusion of anything offensive to a minority
   f. study of community
   g. student council for grades 1-8
   h. handwork and construction activities

GUIDE TO REFERENCES FOR FURTHER STUDY

ADAMS, Fay, *Educating America's Children* (New York, The Ronald Press Company, 1954).

American Educational Research Association, National Education Association, *Social Framework of Education* (Washington, D.C., The Association, December, 1955).

COUNTS, George S., *Education and American Civilization* (New York, Bureau of Publications, Teachers College, Columbia University, 1952).

CREMIN, L., and BORROWMAN, M., *Public Schools in Our Democracy* (New York, The Macmillan Company, 1956).

Educational Policies Commission, National Education Association, *Education for All American Children* (Washington, D.C., The Commission, 1948).

GRIEDER, C., and ROMAINE, S., *American Public Education: An Introduction* (New York, The Ronald Press Company, 1955).

HAVIGHURST, Robert J., and NEUGARTEN, Bernice L., *Society and Education* (New York, Allyn and Bacon, Inc., 1957).

HOPKINS, L. T., *Interaction: The Democratic Process* (Boston, D. C. Heath & Company, 1941).

LANE, Howard A., and BEAUCHAMP, Mary, *Human Relations in Teaching* (Englewood Cliffs, N. J., Prentice-Hall, Inc., 1955).

LINDBERG, Lucile, *The Democratic Classroom: A Guide for Teachers* (New York, Bureau of Publications, Teachers College, Columbia University, 1955).

MURSELL, James L., *Principles of Democratic Education* (New York, W. W. Norton & Company, Inc., 1955).

CHAPTER 5

Basic Values of Early Education

The school provides the opportunity for the young child to emerge from his original egocentricity and learn to identify his welfare with that of the larger group to which he belongs.[1]

INTRODUCTION

Progress in the downward extension of public education to include younger children is more dependent on an increased and widespread *knowledge* and *recognition* of the values and effects of such a program by both professional and lay persons than on a need for a determination of such values and effects. The basic philosophy of American education has shown the values. Research studies and practice have given valid evidence of effects. Objective recognition of such values and effects through the universal establishment of programs for young children, though justified and necessary, has not followed. Unfortunately, in some situations the cost of providing the extra year or two of guided educational learning experiences for young children is given more consideration than the deep and far-reaching returns of such a program to the child and his parents, and eventually to society.

The kindergarten is rather generally accepted in American education, though it still lacks *state* support in almost two-thirds of the states in our country. (See pp. 22-24.) However, it is widely established and supported by local and regional school system administra-

---

[1] California State Department of Education, Bureau of Elementary Education, *Teachers Guide to Education in Early Childhood* (Sacramento, The Department, 1956), p. 15.

tions and communities. The nursery school is much less accepted as a part of public education in our country. Where these programs do exist, they are usually accepted for intrinsically sound and valid reasons, not because custom or some similar reason demands.

Nor should the programs for four- and five-year-old children be isolated from the rest of the elementary program. The study of growth and development has shown us that children grow and mature in a continuous pattern. Educational programs must parallel this growth pattern to be effective. Continuous learning experiences should be provided for children from four years of age on as a phase of the total elementary program under the supervision of the public elementary school. Based on needs and maturity, these experiences should follow the developmental sequences natural to children. The program of guided experiences for young children with provision for social and growth needs continues through a smooth and gradual transition into the program of the primary level with its more formal activities *if* the total learning experiences are patterned on the development natural to the child at the different age levels. Both the early program and the primary program lose much of their effectiveness if they are considered as separate levels. Too, if they are not developed on the bases of children's needs, they defeat the purposes for which they are planned. This was brought out vividly recently when a member of our profession phrased his concept of the kindergarten as "a time to get in the reading and numbers you're supposed to start in the first grade because there's just too much for that first-year level." Academic work per se in a kindergarten defeats the value of the program and may even result in harmful and negative effects. No program at all is better than one which develops negative effects! The true nursery school and kindergarten are a logical part of any educational program that aids in the child's growth and develops his personality along with his academic abilities—not only in the 3 R's but in all subjects.

The acceptance of the program for younger children as a part of the total elementary program is not a new concept. As early as 1919 Dr. Samuel Chester Parker of the University of Chicago, collaborating with Miss Alice Temple, Head of the Department of Kindergarten-Primary Education of the same University, stated in his preface to a text on methods in the elementary school, "The kindergarten is treated in this book as the first regular grade of the elementary school, as is now the case in the better public schools."[2]

A New Charter for Young Children, presented by Dr. Roman Gans and her associates in their 1952 publication,[3] expresses clearly the present concept of professional and public responsibility for continuous early elementary education. Excerpts from it follow:

Specialists in the fields of health, welfare, sociology, anthropology, law, and education have shown that the personality of the child is developed in the early years of life. What happens to the young child, in the home, in the neighborhood, and in the community, will largely shape his chances for a wholesome and satisfying life. Consequently, what he experiences in his first years in school has more influence on him than any later education . . . With the help of data from many related fields, it is possible to develop a clear picture of children in the schools as we find them today. Professional people, as well as other spirited citizens, are demonstrating a greater concern for children and a clearer understanding of their needs.

    II. Young children should have as their right group experience in good nursery schools, kindergartens, and primary grades. This experience should begin at the age of three for some, at four for the majority, and should be available for all from the age of five through eight.

    III. Young children should have as their right an acceptance as individuals by every adult who helps to guide and foster them.

    IV. Young children should have as their right an educational program that guides them in the light of their individual needs toward moral, constructive living in a world of fellow men.

Organized Learning Experiences for Young Children

Little doubt exists today concerning the validity of the statement that the experiences and environment of the early years exert a deep and lasting influence on the child's personality, behavior, and achievement. Yet, we hesitate to move forward in providing professional guidance for young children through our public schools. *Why?*

Evaluation of the values and benefits of an educational program must be made in terms of the objectives of such a program. The learn-

[2] Samuel Chester Parker, *General Methods of Teaching in Elementary Schools,* rev. ed. (Boston, Ginn & Company, 1922), p. 11.

[3] Roma Gans, Celia Burns Stendler, and Millie Almy, *Teaching Young Children* (Yonkers, N.Y., World Book Company, 1952), pp. 44-45.

ing experiences designed for four- and five-year-old children are not planned to assist first grade work. Rather, they are planned to meet the scientifically determined needs of young children in their developmental growth in our social culture. Emphasis in the program for young children is on good social adjustment and living as a foundation for all later development of personality and as a foundation of readiness for all later formal learning experiences.

The learning experiences of the early period, then, do differ from those of the primary and elementary programs. This is logical and necessary. The interests of the children at this age are still deeply home-centered. Their maturity calls for an organized program that develops without demanding, for a teacher who guides but who can still function as a parent when need arises, and for opportunity for development through play, the child's natural way of learning and working.

Dr. Parker directed attention to this explanation of the function and purpose of the kindergarten long ago when he stated:[4]

An ordinary observer in a modern kindergarten may see the children engaged in such activities . . . (playing house; a play project: band and bandstand; etc.). To such an observer the children seem to be merely playing—playing house, playing store, playing with dolls, running, skipping, dancing, singing, etc. The kindergartener, however, will tell you that while it is merely play for the children, they are being trained in "community life, industrial and fine arts, language, music, physical education, nature study, and number work." She may tell you that the purposes of the play activities are represented in the following impressive terms:

1. *Social or moral purposes:* for example, teaching non-interference with other children; self-control, as in keeping quiet when someone else is speaking; order, as in putting the doll's clothes away; working for some definite end, as in procuring the seeds and preparing the soil for planting; obedience, as in following promptly the teacher's directions.

2. *Training in reflective thinking, in problem solving:* for example, in devising by experimental folding a paper basket that will hold the seeds that are to be planted; in devising a slanting roof to be built on a toy barn; in devising a bridge of blocks to cross an imaginary stream that has been marked with chalk on the floor; in choosing colors for various decorative purposes, etc.

[4] Parker, *op. cit.,* pp. 18-19.

3. *Training in expression:* for example, in drawing and coloring when the children use colored crayons to represent a flowering plant; in oral expression, when they tell about their toys at home or their field trip to the grocery store.

4. *Training in aesthetic enjoyment:* for example, in fundamental, rhythms, as in clapping, skipping, and dancing; also in music, drawing, painting, designing, and story telling.

5. *Training in manual skills:* for example, in piling blocks, in cutting with scissors, in modeling with plasticine, in throwing and catching a ball.

From the beginning, programs for young children have been planned on values and benefits specific to their maturity level. An examination of values in our present programs for four- and five-year-old children follows.

Values and Benefits

Public education for young children is an important and effective supplement to the child's home life. It is not meant in any interpretation of program to be a replacement for the home.

The UNESCO report[5] of a group studying the value of true educational programs for young children[6] stated:

there comes a time in the young child's life when the family—at any rate as it exists in urban life—cannot provide all that is needed to stimulate and aid in the development of the child's potentialities. . . . More and more they (mothers) recognize that the nursery school can act as a bridge to help the child to pass from an intimate and exclusive relationship to the mother to the wider relationship between individual and society.

The true nursery school . . . aims to extend and supplement the work of the mother in making the full development of the child possible.

Moreover, the program for four- and five-year-old children provides a gradual and planned transition for the child from the home setting to the school environment and routine.

[5] UNESCO, *Mental Hygiene in the Nursery School* (Paris, UNESCO, 1953), pp. 9-10. (United States distribution through UNESCO Publications Center, U.S.A., 801 Third Avenue, New York 22, N.Y.)
[6] The term nursery school, as used in this report, includes both our nursery school and kindergarten age levels.

The UNESCO study continues:[7]

The nursery school period . . . is a time of capital importance in the moulding of the individual's personality, character, and behavior, and a period during which the effective environment is beginning to expand. During this period the transition is made from the family group of mixed ages—with its strongly affective values, revolving, so far as the small child is concerned, around the mother—to the non-family group of children of the same age, directed by a new adult who urges the acceptance of new authority and new values. It marks the first stage in the alternation of daily life—and very frequently in the alternation of behavior—between family life and life outside the family, between the home and the "work" atmosphere. It comes at the moment of the discovery of individuality, of partial weaning from emotional ties, and of the appearance of new interests and attachments.

The program offers young children an opportunity to become members of a peer social group and to develop social skills and values through continued and sequential guided learning experiences.

Programs for young children are planned to develop skills in social and group relationships. The children have an opportunity to work and play with other young children and to function as members of a group with varied social, economic, and cultural backgrounds. They learn to share and co-operate through play and work activities. They learn how to establish satisfactory relationships with adults other than their parents, and begin to develop an understanding of the restraints and privileges of socially acceptable behavior. Through such growth in co-operative group activities and skills the young child matures to a readiness for peer and group experiences in the primary program and for acceptance and use of socially acceptable behavior. If a youngster does not have the advantage of kindergarten (and/or nursery school) education, this growth must come at the primary level when he should be more concerned with moving ahead in other activities and learnings.

The program provides a foundation for wholesome personality development and mental health.

The early years are of key importance in building wholesome emotional attitudes and good health; the teacher, through guided group

[7] *Ibid.,* pp. 10-11.

learning situations and through individual direction, gives emphasis to this facet of development, and provides for the two basic emotional needs of young children, security and affection. The young child has an opportunity to grow in healthy self-confidence as an increasingly independent individual in an environment and learning situation scaled to his needs and abilities, and through doing those things that he is able to do successfully and well. Activities foster increasing independence from his family circle toward self-reliance and security in peer and social relations. In the organized program where he has freedom "to be, to do, and to explore," the child learns the beginnings of self-control. He learns to meet difficulties and to handle emotional problems. He adjusts to routine. He increasingly accepts the regulations and restrictions of group living. He experiences a widening world of new interests through firsthand, teacher-guided activities. He finds his problems of daily living easier in home and school because of the close relationship of the two through his mother and his teacher.

Important also to the child's personality development during this program is the attention given to individual abilities, needs, and problems. Each child has the advantage of guidance by a teacher who is not only qualified to understand and guide young children, but who has many school services and resources available to her for this phase of her work. Children with abilities are encouraged. Children with problems are noted and every effort is made to help them. Children with remediable defects in vision, speech, and hearing—all of which cause difficulty in primary level activities—are observed and the difficulty corrected, or at least helped.

The program provides space and equipment for health and safety experiences that supplement and reach beyond the home.

The school program is designed to satisfy the young child's need for much varied physical activity more adequately than the home; recommended equipment and planned play areas are provided. Knowledge and practice in habits of health and safety are encouraged. Fatigue and overactivity are guarded against. Full bodily and muscular growth are a primary concern.

Play, the child's natural way of learning and working, is the teacher's most effective method in furthering his development.

Too often adults evaluate children's play as purposeless activity rather than as the natural and very effective force it is in the learning process of young children. They think of play as recreation away from purposeful activity rather than an activity which in itself has purpose and gives pleasure.

All children play, and through their play grow, develop, and learn. The values of play are comprehensive and significant, so significant that play is accepted as the major form of learning of young children. Play is concerned in the child's total development and in every facet of his personality.

Play is directly related to the development of motor skills and physical growth. The child's natural and spontaneous activities, both quiet and vigorous, are play activities. Through them bodily growth, muscle co-ordination, and physical health are fostered.

Play is directly related to social skills and growth. Through play with other young children, the child learns to give and take as a member of a peer group, to share and co-operate, to plan and evaluate, to find his place as a member of a group or as a leader in that group, and to recognize the rights of others. True, group sizes for the young child are small, but here again he has situations and problems scaled to his maturity level.

Play is the child's means of understanding himself, other children, and adults, as well as his physical environment. Experiences that he has had in the home, school, and community can be happily repeated and relived in play. The work and activities of adults can be acted out in dramatic play through his identification of himself with their roles. Imitation of adult roles in children's activities in playing house, store, gas station attendant, harbor helper, postman, and so on, both in the classroom and on the playground, deepens and broadens the child's understanding and knowledge of family, adults, and community. Concomitent with the growth of social skills in these experiences are a widening knowledge of and interest in the environment, and an increase in the ability to form ideas and concepts, with the corresponding growth in language skills in communicating with others. This development, in turn, gives the child an excellent background of experience for a good beginning in the work of the primary level.

Play is directly related to emotional development and control.

109

Through play children give expression to feelings and emotions that are wholesome and satisfying. But they also give expression to unpleasant feelings and emotions, caused by their individual problems, through the acting out of such incidents and experiences. The alert teacher not only permits this play, with its therapeutic effect in the release of feelings, but uses her deepened knowledge and insight gained thereby to further her guidance of the child's development.

Through play young children develop beginning skills in the processes of thinking and problem solving at their level of maturity.

Play activities of young children are guided by the teacher toward constructive and functional learning. In this process the children begin to develop skills of thinking through questioning, planning individually and in groups, discussing, seeing relationships and effects, carrying out plans in play activities, and in evaluating the effectiveness of the plans as a guide to future thinking. The block play of the kindergarten illustrates this point. Children do not play aimlessly with blocks. Prior to block activity, they plan and discuss with the teacher what they will build and how they will go about it. The activity is guided in terms of the current learning interest in the social studies field. It may be building a harbor, an airport, or an entire community. They plan who will work together, what materials they will need, and how they will proceed. During the actual building play, problems that arise within any small group are worked out with the teacher. At the completion of the activity the entire group, with the teacher's help, evaluate what they have completed, their ways of working, what they have learned, and how they can use what they have learned in their next activities in block play. These skills of problem solving and the functional knowledge acquired through their use become the foundation for study and process skills in the primary level, and a part of the children's background and behavior readiness for further learning.

Summary

The nursery school and kindergarten programs are the natural and logical educational steps of a gradual transition into readiness for more mature developmental levels of learning. Such programs have important values for the child as an individual and as a member of groups, and for the parents and society in general.

Such programs help the child as an individual through: (1) supplementing his home experiences and opportunities; (2) providing a guided transition from home to school environment; (3) guiding development through the natural process of play; (4) widening interests and understandings through firsthand experiences; (5) influencing early experiences which are foundational in all personality development; (6) developing beginning skills in processes; (7) providing functional learning experiences and encouraging creative expression; (8) furthering readiness for formal learning; (9) extending language communication skills; (10) detecting and correcting remediable difficulties; and (11) providing for the development of the child as a unique person.

Such programs help the child as a member of the group through: (1) establishing peer relationships, group consciousness, and group skills; (2) developing readiness for group learning activities; (3) teaching socially acceptable behavior patterns; (4) increasing understanding of other children with varied and different social, economic, and cultural backgrounds; and (5) increasing knowledge and understanding of the physical environment.

Such programs help parents through: (1) providing professional guidance, environment, and opportunity for their children's development; and (2) making available the teacher's counsel and guidance.

Such programs help the school and society through: (1) children's achievement and development in later levels based on a good beginning; and (2) better citizenship because of early guidance in development, greater self-realization, increased co-operation with others, and the building of healthy attitudes and an appreciation of democratic values.

Interest

Many parents, lay persons, community groups, and professional educators *do* recognize the value to the child, his parents, and society in the downward extension of the elementary program to the four-year-old level. Groups working to extend these opportunities to all young children include UNESCO, The National Society for the Study of Education, The National Education Association, The American Association of School Administrators, The National Council of State Consultants of Elementary Education, The Educational Policies

Commission, The National Citizens Council for Better Schools, The Association for Childhood Education International, The National Association for Nursery Education, and The American Association of University Women. Some state departments of education exert leadership in encouraging educational programs for young children. Among outstanding publications of such departments are the California State Department of Education publications, *Teachers Guide to Early Childhood Education* (1956), and the Illinois State Department publication, *School Begins with Kindergarten* (1957).

The Association for Childhood Education International has worked consistently for the education of young children over a long period. Its most recent publication, aimed at further extending and improving the educational program of five-year-old children, is entitled, *How Good Are Our Kindergartens?* (1958).

Research

Many of the values inherent in nursery school and kindergarten programs are difficult to demonstrate or prove through controlled study because of their intrinsic nature. Others, such as growth in vocabulary, development of muscular skills and co-ordination, and improvement in vocal ability are more easily measured. Some of the available research and studies on the values and benefits of educational programs for four- and five-year-old children are:

ALMY, Millie C., *Children's Experiences Prior to First Grade and Success in Reading,* Contributions to Education, No. 954 (New York, Bureau of Publications, Teachers College, Columbia University, 1949).

DAWE, Helen C., "A Study of the Effect of an Educational Program Upon Language Development and Related Mental Functions in Young Children," *Journal of Experimental Education,* Vol. 11 (1942), pp. 200-209.

HATTWICK, B. W., "The Influence of Nursery School Attendance Upon the Behavior and Personality of the Preschool Child," *Journal of Experimental Education,* Vol. 5 (1936), pp. 180-190.

HILGARD, Josephine R., "Learning and Maturation in Preschool Children," *Journal of Genetic Psychology,* Vol. 41 (1932), pp. 40-53.

JERSILD, Arthur T., and FITE, Mary D., "Children's Social Adjustment in Nursery School," in Wayne Dennis, ed., *Readings in Child Psychology* (Englewood Cliffs, N.J., Prentice-Hall, Inc., 1951), pp. 567-576.

MORRISON, J. C., "Influence of Kindergarten on Age-Grade Progress of Children Entering School Under Six Years of Age," in Abstract: *The*

Role of Research in Educational Progress, Official Report (Washington, D.C., American Educational Research Association, 1937).

PRATT, Willie E., "A Study of the Difference in the Prediction of Reading Success of Kindergarten and Non-Kindergarten Children," *Journal of Educational Research,* Vol. 42 (March, 1949), pp. 525-533.

PROJECTS AND QUESTIONS

1. Develop an outline for a talk to "your own school faculty" on the values of the kindergarten program.
2. Adapt the outline developed in Project 1 for use with parents in:
   a. a low economic level community
   b. a predominantly professional level community
3. Assume that you have signed a contract for teaching kindergarten in a school system that expects some formal academic work in this program. What would you do?
4. Describe how you would handle the following:
   The Board of Education in your area is concerned because children in the community can have the advantage of kindergarten education only in private schools. They are considering establishing kindergartens as an integral part of all public elementary school education. You are invited to act as a consultant for them in their consideration of this undertaking. What values, research data, and other materials could you offer the Board to help them reach a decision?

GUIDE TO REFERENCES FOR FURTHER STUDY

ALMY, Millie C., "Are They Too Young for Problem Solving?" *Progressive Education,* Vol. 27 (March, 1950), pp. 143-148.

———, "Programs for Young Children," *Educational Leadership,* Vol. 8 (February, 1951), pp. 270-275.

BARNETT, Glenn E., "The Educational Setting of Early Childhood Education," *California Journal of Elementary Education,* Vol. 17 (February, 1949), pp. 134-138.

BERGAMINI, Yolanda, and SWANSON, Walter, "Does Kindergarten Make a Difference?" *School Executive,* Vol. 74 (December, 1954), pp. 54-55.

BOARDMAN, B. W., "Value Experiences with Children," *Educational Leadership,* Vol. 8 (May, 1951), pp. 485-487.

CHAMBERLAIN, Orlo R., and CHAMBERLAIN, Robert R., "Do Children Need Pre-School Experiences?" *Childhood Education,* Vol. 32, No. 8 (April, 1956), pp. 371-373.

COWIN, Shirley H., "Reading Readiness Through Kindergarten Experience," *Elementary School Journal,* Vol. 52 (October, 1951), pp. 96-99.

DRACOULIDES, N. M., "Preschool Education and Mental Health," *Understanding the Child,* Vol. 25 (June, 1956), pp. 84-85.

EAST, J. K., "Kindergarten Is a Good Investment," *School Executive,* Vol. 72 (May, 1953), pp. 52-53.

GANS, Roma, STENDLER, Celia Burns, and ALMY, Millie C., *Teaching Young Children* (Yonkers, N.Y., World Book Company, 1952).

GUTTERIDGE, Mary V., "Nursery School in the Public School," *School and Society,* Vol. 73 (May 19, 1951), pp. 309-312.

HARTLEY, R. E., FRANK, L. K., and GOLDENSON, R. M., *Understanding Children's Play* (New York, Columbia University Press, 1952).

HEADLEY, Neith E., "Kindergarten Comes of Age," *National Education Association Journal,* Vol. 43 (March, 1954), pp. 153-154.

————, "Good Education for Five-Year-Olds!," *Childhood Education,* Vol. 30 (March, 1954), pp. 314-316.

HEFFERNAN, Helen, "Teach Reading in Kindergarten?" *The Grade Teacher,* Vol. 75 (September, 1957), p. 16.

————, "Block Play in the Kindergarten," *The Grade Teacher,* Vol. 75 (January, 1958), p. 14.

Illinois State Department of Education, *School Begins with Kindergarten,* Illinois Curriculum Program Publication, Subject Field Series, Bulletin # C-1 (Springfield, The Department, September, 1957).

LAWS, Gertrude, "Early Childhood and Parent Education," *California Journal of Elementary Education,* Vol. 17 (February, 1949), pp. 190-194.

LLOYD, Elizabeth C., "Nursery Education, Our Responsibility," *Journal of Education,* Vol. 137 (May, 1955), pp. 2-4.

National Society for the Study of Education, *Mental Health in Modern Education,* 54th Yearbook, Part II (Chicago, The Society, 1955).

PRINDLE, Frances, "Education's Stake in the Nursery School," *Elementary Journal,* Vol. 56 (March, 1956), pp. 291-297.

SCHERER, Lorraine, and others, *How Good Is Our Kindergarten?* (Washington, D.C., Association for Childhood Education International, 1958).

TAYLOR, E. R., "Is the Kindergarten a Learning Situation?" *American Childhood,* Vol. 38 (April, 1953), pp. 23-25.

UNESCO, *Mental Hygiene in the Nursery School* (Paris, UNESCO, 1954).

CHAPTER 6

Theory of Teaching and Learning in Early Elementary Education

What an educator believes makes a great difference in how he teaches.[1]

INTRODUCTION

Theory concerns the basic principles and knowledge of the art of teaching; it is the foundation for practice. Our understanding of theory (centered in the philosophy and objectives of democratic education and in the science of the developmental and learning processes) is a sound guide for the translation of professional thought and research into practice in early elementary classrooms. Without such a basis, activities could become just activities, and not a means of effecting real individual and group academic and personality growth.

We have seen in our preceding discussions that all educational experiences are developed from within the basic framework of democratic ideology and its resulting objectives for the school's function in our individual living and in our society. We have also seen that how a child grows and develops in interests and needs and how he learns are starting points for educational planning within democratic goals.

Reflection on these considerations leads us to formulate the following basic principles and concepts as guides for classroom teaching,

[1] Freeman Glenn Macomber, *Principles of Teaching in the Elementary School* (New York, American Book Company, 1954), p. 4.

organized for our purposes under: (*1*) the child; (*2*) the learning experiences; and (*3*) the teacher.

THE CHILD

(1) *Each child must be given opportunity to develop to his maximum potential in all the facets of his personality.*

In planning all phases of classroom living we must give attention to the whole personality growth of each child. Mental achievement must not be attained at the expense of emotional, social, or physical development and adjustment. Should the development of one personality facet be forced or fostered at the expense of others, the interrelatedness of the various aspects of growth would limit the possible maximum development of even that one trait. Development of the whole individual furthers the growth of our society as a whole.

(2) *Simultaneously with his growth as an individual, the child must develop as a member of his several groups and of society as a whole.*

Our democratic society is designed for group living and interaction. Opportunities for group experiences which develop skills in social relationships involving the child's rapport and responsibility to others, his concern with socially acceptable behavior in making his best contribution to the group, and his wide interests in community and social activities must all be part of classroom living.

(3) *Each child must develop wholesomeness of personality through his realization of security, affection, and achievement.*

Classroom living must develop in each child a realization of the worth, value, and dignity of himself and other children and of all persons as individuals; this implies a program centered on and adjusted to individual child needs, interests, and abilities, rather than on subject content. Subject matter becomes the *tool or means* for achieving the development. Classroom living fosters self-realization for each individual. This type of program recognizes that early experiences largely determine later emotional patterns, and so provides encouragement rather than discouragement, and preventive rather than corrective processes when possible. It differentiates between causal behavior (which explains responses in terms of basic drives and problems) and surface behavior (which concerns itself with the response as it appears to an observer). It emphasizes the development of security and affection through relationships, achievement, and progress.

✓ (4.) *Each child must develop a sound sense of values.*

Functional learning experiences must give the child an understanding of and respect for democratic values. Co-operation, respect for others, and group thinking and acting are things the child can learn through direct and indirect or incidental teaching. The teacher of young children, through action and thought based on her own values, influences the values of the children.

Learning experiences must be concerned with intrinsic values more than with extrinsic, though the latter have some place in school experiences; it is the joy and sense of achievement in learning to read or in handling and using number concepts that is important, *not* the gold star, the check mark, or the 100 per cent mark.

(5.) *Each child must develop in self-reliance, resourcefulness, and independence.*

The learning experiences and the teacher's guidance must gradually but continuously help the child to develop in self-control, responsibility, and self-reliance through opportunities for choice, planning processes, self-evaluation, meeting and solving of problems and difficulties, and increased understanding of social behavior.

Principles based on policies and practices directed toward helping each child to develop self-control and self-direction include: (*1*) a permissive classroom atmosphere; (*2*) good teacher-pupil rapport; (*3*) emphasis on acceptance of the teacher as a guiding and working member of the class group; (*4*) a positive rather than a restrictive approach in group control and discipline; (*5*) gradual release of control to children as they mature to accept it; (*6*) attention to causal behavior and background experience; (*7*) attention to individual needs; (*8*) recognition of individual contributions; (*9*) emphasis on instrinsic values rather than on extrinsic rewards; and (*10*) emphasis and recognition placed on the effect of each individual's behavior on the group as a whole.[2]

[2] California State Department of Education, *Guidance in the Elementary School,* Bulletin Vol. 23, No. 4 (Sacramento, The Department, August, 1954), p. 46.

6. *Each individual child must develop in the use of the scientific method and approach.*

In our society, educational objectives are centered in democratic ideals and procedure. Each member of our society is highly valued as an individual. He must be educated to function as an intelligent person in a democratic culture, which means that he must see and recognize problems, think them through objectively and realistically, plan for their solution, and carry out and evaluate these plans. Such is the pattern of our daily living. To do this, the individual must have firsthand experiences, research and study skills, and training in the processes of thinking and problem solving. He must come into contact with community and social problems and interests, and learn to meet them in their changing setting as science and our culture advance. The *unit method* of instruction, the principal method used today, is built directly on this process; it is designed to help the child develop in these basic democratic procedures of seeing problems in their changing setting, and understanding their relationships, meeting these problems, and then evaluating the results in terms of future action. The beginning of education in these processes should be in the young child's program.

THE LEARNING EXPERIENCES

1. *Learning experiences have their goals and evaluation in the objectives of democratic education.*

Democratic living and ideals are the basic criteria in planning and evaluating the functional content of learning experiences for children. These objectives are realized through the teaching-learning process; in it the learning experiences are designed to meet the child at his various maturational levels and in his needs of daily living in our culture.

2. *Learning experiences are designed for continuity of growth and development toward maturity.*

Flexible, long range planning for the development of children is characterized by a continuing sequence of learning experiences, advancing the child through knowledge and development from early childhood through maturity. Planning for any one level is always considered as a part of the total educational program of development. Learning experiences use as their starting point the immediate and known in the child's family, community, and background of experience; they build extensively and deeply in a continuing pattern as the child matures, using the family, the community and its resources, and our culture as means of growth.

3. Learning experiences are the actual living experiences of the child under the guidance of the school.

Learning experiences are the immediate means through which the teacher realizes the basic goals with a particular group of children. The experiences planned for all children of a specific level will not be identical even though the basic goals are. Variations in planning will occur as the goals are realized through the means that makes them most meaningful to the particular group or class with which the teacher is working. The maturity level of classes of the same chronological age will vary, as will individual interests and abilities, and immediate backgrounds and knowledge. Without deviating from the basic goals of education, the teacher will develop learning experiences through an approach that is most effective with her immediate group.

4. Learning experiences are centered in functional learning and in the development of process skills rather than in rote memory work.

Learning experiences are planned to give the child a functional use of the knowledge and skills he has acquired rather than a rote memory collection of facts which are quickly lost. They are planned, too, to give him increased skill in the processes of thinking and problem solving; such skill will extend directly into his daily living in an increasing degree as he matures. To achieve such learning, experiences must involve the child both in the planning and in the doing, must challenge him through purposes that become his own, and must reach his individual needs and background. This type of experience-learning must be begun with the very young child, adapted to his maturity level, and continued throughout the whole educational program.

5. Learning experiences should occur in an environment which is physically and psychologically stimulating and challenging.

The emotional climate of the classroom must be relaxed and easy, the physical environment must be rich and stimulating through centers of interest in music, reading, and science, and in other materials and resources. The program must include regularly alternating active and quiet periods, which provide change to meet the attention span of the children. Timing or pacing must be emphasized in planning so that experiences occur at the time of the children's greatest readiness for them.

6. *Learning experiences are broad, varied, and flexible; they provide for a wide range of interests, needs, and abilities.*

Planning learning experiences for any group of children involves planning for individual differences and rates of learning; it necessitates planning through the various types of sensory learning, since some children are basically visually minded, some auditorially minded, and others kinesthetically inclined. Fundamentally it means an awareness and an acceptance of each child in the group and provision for him in the total planning.

THE TEACHER

1. *The teacher plays a role of central importance in the teaching-learning process.*

The teacher, as the mature guide, plays a key role in the teaching-learning process. Sensitive to individual child needs, to program timing and rhythm, and to knowledge content, it is her privilege to provide a creative, enriched environment which will motivate, stimulate, and challenge development in any child with whom she is working. It is she who gives the "spark" to the learning situation.

2. *The teacher understands and accepts all children.*

The teacher who understands the process of growth and development, who knows the "what," the "when," and the "how," who differentiates causal and surface behavior, who guides the child in terms of this understanding, and who often serves as a help to the parent is the teacher who accepts *all* children regardless of behavior, personality, and background. It is her function and privilege to serve all children.

3. *The teacher continues to grow professionally in interests, values, and achievement.*

The teacher must continue to grow in order to help children develop. This she does through constant professional study and evaluation, and by broadening her interests and meeting her professional and social problems intelligently in our changing society.

PROJECTS AND QUESTIONS

1. Describe fully an observation you have made in one of the early elementary levels. Analyze the observation by considering each of the principles given in this chapter and showing how each was or was not evident in the learning situation.

2. Summarize the ideas in this chapter as an introduction to your consideration of curriculum. (Chapter 9.)

GUIDE TO REFERENCES FOR FURTHER STUDY

Association for Supervision and Curriculum Development, NEA, *Toward Better Teaching,* 1949 Yearbook (Washington, D.C., The Association, 1949).

BOTTRELL, Harold R., ed., *Introduction to Education* (Harrisburg, Pa., The Stackpole Company, 1955).

BROGAN, Peggy, and FOX, Lorene K., *Helping Children Learn: A Concept of Elementary-School Method* (Yonkers, N.Y., The World Book Company, 1955).

BURTON, William H., *The Guidance of Learning Activities,* 2nd ed. (New York, Appleton-Century-Crofts, Inc., 1952).

CANTOR, Nathaniel, *The Teaching-Learning Process* (New York, Henry Holt & Company, Inc., 1953).

Department of Elementary School Principals, NEA, *Bases for Effective Learning,* 31st Yearbook, Vol. 32, No. 1 (Washington, D.C., The Department, September, 1952).

HAGGARD, Ernest A., "Learning: A Process of Change," *Educational Leadership,* Vol. 12 (December, 1955), pp. 149-156.

HOPKINS, L. Thomas, *Interaction: The Democratic Process* (Boston, D. C. Heath & Company, 1941).

HYMES, James L. Jr., *A Child Development Point of View* (Englewood Cliffs, N.J., Prentice-Hall, Inc., 1955).

IMHOFF, Myrtle M., "The Teacher Sets the Sights," *Childhood Education,* Vol. 33 (October, 1956), pp. 60-62.

LEE, J. Murray, and LEE, Dorris M., *The Child and His Curriculum,* Rev. ed. (New York, Appleton-Century-Crofts, Inc., 1957).

LINDBERG, Lucile, *The Democratic Classroom: A Guide for Teachers* (New York, Bureau of Publications, Teachers College, Columbia University, 1955).

MACOMBER, Freeman Glenn, *Principles of Teaching in the Elementary School* (New York, The American Book Company, 1954).

MCAULEY, J. D., "Qualities of a Good Teacher," *Peabody Journal of Education,* Vol. 32 (July, 1954), pp. 22-25.

MURSELL, James L., *Principles of Democratic Education* (New York, W. W. Norton & Company, Inc., 1955).

NESBITT, Marion, *A Public School for Tomorrow* (New York, Harper & Brothers, 1953).

OTTO, Henry J., *Principles of Elementary Education* (New York, Rinehart & Company, Inc., 1956).

SAUCIER, W. A., *Theory and Practice in the Elementary School* (New York, The Macmillan Company, 1951).

STEPHANS, Ada Dawson, *Providing Developmental Experiences for Young Children* (New York, Bureau of Publications, Teachers College, Columbia University, 1952).

TROW, William Clark, *The Learning Process*, What Research Says to the Teacher Series, No. 6 (Washington, D.C., National Education Association, 1954).

TYLER, Ralph, *Basic Principles of Curriculum and Instruction* (Chicago, University of Chicago Press, 1950).

Part III

TRANSITION INTO PRACTICE

CHAPTER 7

Administrative Organization

Schools exist to further the continuous growth of the child through realization of the objectives of the teaching-learning process as defined in our society. Organization has purpose and justification only as it serves and furthers these objectives.

INTRODUCTION

Within any structure or program as vast and comprehensive as the American educational system, there must exist some form of purposeful and orderly relationship. This relationship we term *organization*.

Organization of the present-day American educational program into three major divisions or levels is well known to you from your own experience of having attended first the elementary school, then the high school, and later the college or university. This three-fold division (graphically represented in Chapter 1, pp. 16-17) evolved as the educational program of our country developed and expanded.[1]

We have also seen that the major purpose of such division is to further the effective functioning of the school in its development of

[1] Dr. W. H. Burton points out in his discussion of the school system of our country that, though around 1900 our educational system was reorganized into a "single, sequential, democratic system open to all" and extending from kindergarten through higher education, it is to be remembered that each of the levels (that is elementary, secondary, and higher education) had developed independently and with different aims. Further, that the history of our education since that period has been concerned with "the struggle to co-ordinate the units into a unified school system." This effort to co-ordinate the levels still continues today even though they do constitute an organized system of American education. William H. Burton, *Introduction to Education* (New York, D. Appleton-Century Company, Inc., 1934), pp. 187-193.

the child as an individual and as a member of society. These smaller divisions, as part of the whole educational system, offer increased services and resources, better programs, and more efficient management and instruction.

The chart in Chapter 1 indicates variations in the over-all organization in that some elementary school programs extend through the eighth grade while others extend only through the sixth grade. Nursery schools and kindergartens are included as an integral part of the elementary school organization.

It is to be noted that each of the major divisions likewise has variations of organization within the schools of its level. The elementary division has, for example, individual schools organized on one of several plans such as the graded, the unit, or the multigrade plan. Again, we note that within the classrooms of any individual elementary school various plans of organization may exist. So long as such plans of organizational structure are based on one accepted curriculum philosophy within an individual school and contribute to the realization of the basic purposes of the educational program, organization will continue to be a definite and constructive factor in the education of children.

It is evident, then, that organization is not an end in itself. It is, rather, a means of increasing the effectiveness of the instructional program through smaller working units, increased attention to developmental and individual needs, improved opportunities for learning experiences, extended services, and more effective use of the facilities and equipment. Schools exist to further the continuous growth of the child through realization of the purposes of the teaching-learning process as defined in our society. Organization has purpose and justification only as it serves and furthers these objectives.

ORGANIZATION RELATED TO CURRICULUM

Organization is determined by and dependent on the program of curriculum in the school. As curriculum changes occur, corresponding changes must occur in the organization used to realize such purposes if it is to be effective. Hence, organization, while a necessary technique, is always secondary to and dependent on basic school purposes and philosophy.

Gradual but continuous change is characteristic of the curricula and programs of our schools. This is due to our advancing knowledge acquired through research in child development and in how a child learns and through action research in classroom situations, as well as through the increasing responsibility of the school in its community-centered role.

The basic objectives of our democratic education are centered in our democratic philosophy. Chapter 4 reviewed these objectives and showed their immediate relationship to the development of the individual as an individual and as a member of his social group. The means by which the school achieves these basic goals change and evolve as our continuing research indicates more effective ways of working.

Curriculum change has been most rapid in recent years. We have moved in most school systems from the strictly subject-centered program, in which the core of interest and concern was the subject content, toward a curriculum centered in development of the child and of social processes. Today, aware of our need to recognize and provide for developmental growth, individual differences, and skills in academic, intellectual, and social processes, we have increased our ability to plan and guide effectively the learning experiences of children. Attention is centered on:

1. continuity of experience based on continuity of growth
2. psychological readiness of the individual child for learning
3. broadened functional and social scope of learning
4. organization of knowledge into blocks more readily learned and used
5. increasing recognition of the central importance of the communication skills
6. the very real need in our democratic society for early beginnings in experiences in the process skills of problem solving, critical and creative thinking, and in research skills in studying, using, and evaluating knowledge
7. use of the scientific method
8. the essential value of subject matter as a tool for development and not as an end in itself
9. personality and mental health factors of security, affection, and achievement in the young child

10. involvement of the educational process with democratic and community daily living

The elementary school program today, offering continuous experiences planned on the developmental sequences natural to the child from the public nursery school or kindergarten age through the upper levels, recognizes differences in areas within this elementary scope; the early elementary program is such an area within the whole.

ORGANIZATION IN EARLY ELEMENTARY EDUCATION

Organization (or design) at the early elementary level varies in different schools and school systems. Three principal types of organization exist. These include *(1) the primary unit, (2) the graded organization,* and *(3) the multigrade grouping* (interage and intergrade) plan. Some programs are housed in an elementary school building where the total program extends through sixth or eighth grade, while others are carried on in a building designed especially for young children. The housing arrangement for the early elementary level is not a direct index to the type of curriculum program or organizational plan in effect.

THE PRIMARY UNIT[2]

Form

The *primary unit* is a flexible, ungraded plan of administrative organization at the early elementary level, designed to facilitate teaching in a curriculum which stresses child development. The term "primary unit" is the one most widely used for this type of organization which is demanding increasing interest and attention. Various other terms such as the "primary school," "ungraded primary," and "continuous progress program," are all used to indicate the same basic type of plan.

The structural organization of the primary unit is such that a child entering kindergarten or first grade can be placed in a group which continues as a class or unit through the completion of the first three or four years of the elementary program, often under the guid-

[2] Myrtle M. Imhoff, *The Primary Unit,* Selected References, No. 1, rev. ed. (Washington, D.C., United States Office of Education, May 1957).

ance of the same teacher. These plans are characterized by provision for: (1) continuous learning experiences for each child; (2) teacher assignment to a group for longer than a one year period; (3) flexible groupings which permit regrouping as needs are indicated; (4) increased attention to individual development; (5) removal or minimizing of grade lines, thereby placing emphasis on achievement and recognition rather than on failure; and (6) promotion based on an evaluation of all-round development and maturation, and on psychological readiness for further learning experiences, rather than on academic achievement alone.

Variations exist in the way the plan is carried out in various school systems. The Junior Primary Plan, as used by Richmond, Virginia and Tampa, Florida, combines only the kindergarten and first year programs, giving the child the first two years of school experience under the same teacher. Some school systems tried a form in which the first and second grades were combined into a unit while the third grade remained a regular graded classroom. Still another form is the two-year kindergarten plan covering the four-year-old nursery school and the kindergarten levels. Regardless of the form, the purpose is the provision of an improved learning program for young children.

Variations are also found in the emphasis within the program. In some primary units the emphasis is on growth and developmental stages; in others, the developmental growth is related directly to academic or reading levels as the core emphasis.

Such an organizational plan in any form is an effort to create a learning environment in which the young child can develop to his maximum academically at the same time that his social and emotional needs are met. To date it is one of the most promising and soundest plans we have developed for young children; continuing research substantiates it. In general, parents and teachers who have experience with it support it wholeheartedly.

Advantages

Advantages of the primary unit form of organization are many. They may be grouped as follows: (1) Attention is given to all-round and continuous development of the individual child. Studies show growth to be markedly uneven in the early years; in this plan learning experiences can be paced according to each child's growth rate. The very bright as well as the slow child finds the pace suitable to his gifts and needs. The value of such emphasis on the young child cannot be over-emphasized. (2) Provision is made for personality and mental health factors such as the need for security and affection, and for recognition of achievement. Through the teacher's increased attention to each individual, and through each child working at his own rate and on his own level without the frustration and emotional block produced by failure, the children develop positive and healthful attitudes. Adjustment and success follow when the academic and social challenges are geared to the child's ability and readiness. (3) Encouragement of greater academic growth is possible through firsthand experiences centered in needs, interests, and functional learning. (4) Development of more effective teacher guidance is possible through the longer and more intimate knowledge of each child gained in a two- or three- or even four-year period as compared to the one-year period. This permits also greater rapport and understanding with parents, and therefore more opportunity to help them.

Disadvantages

The disadvantages are few, it appears. (1) Parents are sometimes concerned over the placement of their child under one teacher for a long period of time *if* they consider the teacher weak or if she has not been able to establish good rapport with their child. (2) A more valid consideration is the broad background of experience the teacher must have in order to plan and carry on effectively such a program. This involves both firsthand and scientific knowledge and understanding of young children and of their developmental pattern over a long period, plus a thorough understanding of the particular educational program and learning experiences of the whole early elementary period. Though the range of maturity in any classroom requires both these factors, the breadth and depth of such knowledge should be greater in a program where the teacher's work covers three or four years instead of one. Like the teacher in the self-contained classroom, the primary unit teacher guides all experiences in all areas—but for a longer period than one year with a specific group.

Practice

Though it is possible to locate an increasing number of school systems throughout the country that are using some form of the primary unit organization, it is still considered an experimental form.

Milwaukee was among the first cities to try this plan. Many others followed with some form of it until now it is being used in certain locales in all areas of the country. Interesting charts giving the location and form of the primary unit have been developed by Slater and by Goodlad and Anderson (see general bibliography).

Among the systems of various sizes and geographic locations that have been or are now interested in experimentation with the primary unit are: Aliquippa, Pennsylvania; Athens, Georgia; Barstow, and Berkeley, California; Billings, Montana; Cleveland, Ohio; Corona, California; Cranston, Rhode Island; Dearborn, Michigan; East Orange, New Jersey; Glencoe, Illinois; Park Forest, Illinois; Phoenix, Arizona; Provo, and Randolph, Utah; Randolph County, West Virginia; Richmond, Indiana; Richmond, Virginia; Rochester, New York; Savannah, Georgia; Springfield, Vermont; Tampa, Florida; Torrance, California; Wayne, Michigan; and Wichita, Kansas.

The introduction of the primary unit into a school system requires careful and deliberate preparation. There must be staff study and understanding of (*1*) the philosophy and purpose of such an organizational plan, (*2*) the growth and learning patterns of young children, (*3*) the academic program of the first three years and the placement of such skills and knowledge in the primary unit, and (*4*) the basis and techniques of effective grouping. After thorough staff orientation, parents must be educated to the program for a period of time before it is begun, and such instruction must continue as a regular part of the school's responsibility.

Research

Reports of primary units being carried on in school systems, and research concerning such organizations, are becoming more readily available in professional journals and publications. Though no text on this topic has as yet appeared, there are several in preparation. The earlier materials which appeared concern, in general, the theory of the primary unit and first unit organization plans actually used in school systems; materials of a more recent date are concerned with the psychological and mental health aspects of the program, grouping, promotion practices, inter-age combinations, and evaluation of the program design and progress with in-service and parent groups.

References helpful for further study of this form of organization include:

ANDERSON, Robert H., "Ungraded Primary Classes: An Administrative Contribution to Mental Health," *Understanding the Child,* Vol. 24 (June, 1955), pp. 66-72.

Association for Childhood Education International, "Experiments in Re-organizing the Primary School, A Symposium," *Childhood Education,* Vol. 15 (February, 1939), pp. 262-271.

BUFORD, Florence, "We Looked at Our Schools," *National Elementary Principal,* Vol. 34 (December, 1954), pp. 20-22.

GLENNON, Vincent J., ed., "The Ungraded Primary School as a Contribution to Improved School Practices," *Frontier of Elementary Education II* (Syracuse, Syracuse University Press, 1955), pp. 28-29.

GOODLAD, John I., and ANDERSON, Robert H., "The Nongraded Elementary School," *NEA Journal,* Vol. 47 (December, 1958), pp. 642-643.

HILDRETH, Gertrude H., "Hazards of Straight Promotions," *Educational Administration and Supervision,* Vol. 32 (January, 1946), pp. 19-26.

KELLY, Florence C., "Ungraded Primary Schools Make the Grade in Milwaukee," *National Education Association Journal,* Vol. 40 (December, 1951), pp. 645-646.

LEBARON, Walter A., "Some Practical Techniques in Developing a Program of Continuous Progress in the Elementary School," *The Elementary School Journal,* Vol. 46 (October, 1954), pp. 89-96.

MERCILLE, Margaret C., "The Primary School Unit: Suggestions with Regard to Some Persistent Elementary School Problems," *Bulletin of the School of Education,* Indiana University, Vol. 25 (January, 1949), pp. 13-17.

MILLER, Edith, "Two Years with the Same Teacher," *Elementary School Journal,* Vol. 49 (May, 1949), pp. 531-535.

POLKINGHORNE, Ada R., "Parents and Teachers Appraise Primary Grade Grouping," *Elementary School Journal,* Vol. 51 (January, 1951), pp. 271-279.

POTTER, Gladys L., "Making Continuity Possible," *Childhood Education,* Vol. 25 (November, 1948), pp. 128-131.

SLATER, Eva May, *The Primary Unit,* Curriculum Bulletin No. 3 (Storrs, University of Connecticut, 1955).

SMITTER, Faith, "What Is a Primary School?" *California Journal of Elementary Education,* Vol. 17 (February, 1949), pp. 139-145.

THIMBLIN, L. M., "Adapting the School and Class Organization to the Varying Needs in Kindergarten through Grade III," in *Proceedings of the Annual Conference on Reading Held at the University of Chicago,* Vol. 16 (December, 1954), pp. 51-54.

THOMPSON, Ethel, "The Ungraded Plan," *National Education Association Journal,* Vol. 47 (January, 1958), pp. 16-17.

THE GRADED ORGANIZATION

The most widely accepted plan of organization today is the graded school[3] wherein each grade level represents a year of work and subject content; the pupils in each grade are approximately the same chronological age. This plan, begun in early times, has changed in focus from subject-centered to child-development-centered in many instances though some traditionally subject-centered classrooms do remain. It offers in its single-teacher-per-class plan many outstanding classroom programs.

Development of the Graded School

Historical beginnings and sources of the graded school as it exists in our educational system have been reported from two different viewpoints. One position states that our graded school was an adaptation of the Prussian school organization; the other maintains that the graded school developed as our educational system expanded.

Burton,[4] in discussing these opposing points of view cites the work of F. F. Bunker and C. H. Judd. In maintaining their position, these historians report various records and contacts of our early educators with the Prussian plan, our study of it, and instances of its recorded use as a plan for our schools (as in the 1852 Report of the Michigan State Superintendent of Schools).

Cubberly maintains that the graded school evolved through a gradual process as our educational system developed. He reports that the elementary school began in the ungraded room where children

[3] R. Preston and E. Reddin, "Status of the Curriculum," *Review of Educational Research,* Vol. 27 (June, 1957), p. 250.

[4] William H. Burton, *Introduction to Education* (New York, D. Appleton-Century Company, Inc., 1934), pp. 205-209.

of all ages were taught by one teacher. Increases in enrollment gradually required two rooms instead of one and division of the subjects to be taught between the two teachers. Further increases in enrollment necessitated the division of the school into two schools, a primary school and a grammar school; later the Infant School was added as a preparation for the Primary School, and assistant teachers were hired to help "hear lessons" in small side rooms called recitation rooms.

As growth continued and new buildings were required, individual classrooms (each under a regular teacher) were planned. The total instructional outline was divided into content material to be covered in each year and pupils were assigned to the various rooms according to their ages and academic advancement, thus beginning the modern graded school with grade-level rooms. Cubberly states that between 1850 and 1860 the graded school began because[5]

. . . Teaching had by this time become an organized and a psychological process; graded courses of study began to appear; professional school superintendents began to be given the direction and supervision of instruction; and the modern science of school organization and administration began to take place. . . .

Though disagreement as to the exact origin of the graded school does exist, nevertheless it is (and has been) an important part of the organization of the elementary school. Interesting variations within this organization have been made in the past years through introduction of such plans as the Dalton, the Platoon, the Winnetka, departmentalization, and ability grouping. Of lesser importance were such plans as division of the year into two semesters, or into four quarters.

The Self-Contained Classroom

The graded school today at the early elementary level is usually the single-teacher-per-room type in what Caswell[6] calls the "self-contained" classroom. The room teacher plans, develops, integrates, and evaluates all the learning experiences of the class group in all areas, using the help and guidance of principal, consultant, and specialist as needed. This plan fosters good teaching. Planning the curriculum

[5] Ellwood P. Cubberly, *The History of Education* (Boston, Houghton Mifflin Company, 1948), pp. 756-758.

[6] H. Caswell and A. W. Foshay, *Education in the Elementary School,* rev. ed. (New York, The American Book Company, 1957).

on basic objectives, the teacher is able to guide growth in all the varied learning experiences according to the differing ranges of ability, readiness, and maturity of the children in the group. Working constantly throughout the day and during the year with the same group gives the teacher a deeper insight into the children's special needs and problems, and thereby enables her to guide them and their parents more effectively. It further enables her to plan more effectively for the gifted child, to give more attention to the slow child, and to give specific help in problems of speech and emotional health, using help from specially trained personnel in these fields. Her overview of the learning experiences enables her to make learning more functional through social application and through broader, and more integrated and related wholes. The flexibility of such a plan encourages teacher-pupil planning and evaluation.

References helpful for further study of this form of organization include:

CASWELL, Hollis L., and FOSHAY, Arthur W., *Education in the Elementary School*, rev. ed. (New York, The American Book Company, 1957).

KOOPMAN, G. Robert, and SNYDER, Edith R., "Living Room for Learning —a Self-contained Unit," *National Education Association Journal,* Vol. 47 (January, 1958), pp. 18-20.

OTTO, Henry J., *Elementary School Organization and Administration* (New York, Appleton-Century-Crofts, Inc., 1954).

RICKARD, Garett E., "Establishment of the Graded Schools in American Cities," *Elementary School Journal*, Vol. 48. (February, 1948), pp. 326-335.

SHULKEY, S. C., "Fort Worth Has a Middle-of-the Road Organization," *Childhood Education*, Vol. 28 (December, 1952), pp. 175-178.

MULTIGRADE GROUPING

Another form of structural organization used experimentally in a few locations to date is the *multigrade* or interage and intergrade grouping plan. It, too, is attracting professional and public interest. In this organization classes are made up of pupils from three grades and cover a chronological age range of three years or more, in contrast to the usual classes in which there are children of one grade level.

In primary multigrade classes the group is made up of approximately an equal number of children from each of the first, second, and third grades, covering the academic and chronological span of three years, as opposed to the regular class group or the primary unit, both of which are made up of children of approximately the same age and grade levels.

The Torrance Unified School District of California has made an outstanding beginning in the use of this plan. Written summaries are available in the following sources:

Walter Rehwolt and Warren W. Hamilton, *An Analysis of Some of the Effects of Interage and Intergrade Grouping in an Elementary School,* thesis, (Los Angeles, University of Southern California, November, 1956).

Hamilton & Rehwolt, "By Their Differences They Learn," *The National Elementary School Principal,* Vol. 26 (December, 1957), pp. 27-29.

Warren W. Hamilton, "Why Group By Grade Level?," *The Grade Teacher,* Vol. 76 (September, 1958), pp. 18-19.

Because of the significance of the Torrance Multigrade program, a short review of it is worthwhile at this point.

The Torrance program in Multigrade Grouping was begun in order to determine whether greater learning and growth of pupils would occur in this organization than in that of the one-grade-level grouping. Dr. Warren W. Hamilton summarizes the program as follows:[7]

Four primary multigrade classes were established in 1955-56. Each class contained approximately 33 children, 11 first grade, 11 second grade, and 11 third-grade level. Parents had approved the children being in the classes; teachers were selected on the basis of chance rather than on the basis of set criteria.

The major objective of the study was to make a careful scientific study of the amount of learning that took place in the areas of reading, arithmetic, language, personal adjustment, social adjustment, behavior characteristics and attitudes toward school among these multigrade pupils as compared to the pupils in the regular classes. (This program contained a primary multigrade group and an intermediate multigrade group.)

Most of the data of the study was secured from standardized tests. Tests were administered in the fall and again in the spring. The gains that the multigrade pupils made in all the aforementioned areas were compared with the gains made by the regular grade pupils for the same grade levels.

Other parts of the study included such things as parental attitude towards

[7] Personal interview, Dr. Warren W. Hamilton, Assistant Superintendent, Torrance Unified School District, Torrance, California.

Primary multigrade class

Intermediate multigrade class

the multigrade classes, teacher and administrator opinions of the classes, pupil-pupil relationships within the multigrade classes, etc.

In summary, it was found that with but two exceptions in a total of 48 statistical comparisons, the multigrade pupils showed greater gains in personal and social adjustment, social maturity, and behavior characteristics. In addition, the multigrade pupils showed a better attitude toward school, their school work, their peers, etc. than did the regular grade pupils.

In the area of achievement (reading, arithmetic, and language), the multigrade pupils rather consistently made greater gains than did the regular grade pupils.

The major evidence gathered indicated that children in multigrade classes in which there were greater differences among children generally made greater gains, improvement, and progress than children in single grade classes where the differences were restricted.

The plan of grouping in multigrade classes has been expanded in number; parental support and request for such classes continues to increase.

Studies of this method of organization are still too few for final conclusions to be drawn concerning the effectiveness of such a plan in general practice. It is worth noting, however, that in the limited use of this plan to date, results have been positive, indicating further study is certainly justifiable.

CLASSROOM ORGANIZATION

As pointed out earlier in this chapter (page 126), variations in organization may exist not only within the schools of the elementary level, and the schools of a particular system, but also within the classrooms of any individual school.

Classroom programs are planned to include activities for the group as a whole, for smaller groupings within the class, and for individuals working alone. Class teaching, however, does not provide sufficient opportunity for teachers to reach the individual child with his special needs, problems, interests, and abilities, unless it is supplemented by small group and individual teaching-learning situations.

Grouping

Grouping, like organization, is related to curriculum. When the basic philosophy of education was centered on subject-content mastery, class and interclass grouping was on the basis of academic achievement in the subject skills. Today, with emphasis on social and emotional maturity as well as on academic achievement, the grouping of children for the purpose of working together is more often on the basis of any one of a number of purposes rather than on academic achievement alone. Class groups or grades within the school are usually formed of children of approximately the same chronological age. This basis allows for a wide range in abilities, interests, achievement, and maturity. Interclass grouping is a direct approach to meeting these individual needs.

The various groupings that exist within a classroom during the day's program for young children are each determined by specific purposes for the development and immediate needs of children. Such formal grouping is flexible; children work in a group, as in reading or numbers, for such time as it contributes to their growth, but are regrouped (individually or as a class) at such time as evaluation shows need for or advantages to be gained through change. These groups are not identical for all activities; a child works with one group in reading, another in numbers, and still others in other learning experiences. Informal grouping by the children into play and work groups is an equally important facet of classroom organization. Grouping is done solely to further the learning experiences of children; therefore the purposes parallel and have their basis in the developmental pattern.

Grouping on the basis of similarity in one facet of personality or ability is termed *homogeneous* grouping; likeness in one facet does *not* mean likeness in whole personality and needs. Grouping covering a range of abilities is termed *heterogeneous* grouping. We have shown that both types are used in early elementary education.

Grouping in the Nursery School

Grouping at the four-year-old level is informal and limited. The young child, coming from the home where he has experienced close and affectionate ties, is given an opportunity to discover himself as an individual in his own peer group and in a beginning independence away from his parents. In the beginning, the teacher to some degree becomes his security as his mother was in the home. Then, according to his individual ability, the child begins to find an answer to his social needs in very small groups with which he begins to associate in play and work activities, such as free play, and play with materials. Observation of four-year-olds reveals varied levels of maturational behavior. Some children will continue to play alone (solo play) as they did at home, some will use parallel play (wherein they will play near another child rather than with him) and some make small beginnings in social play in which two or three children share an activity. In some activities the teacher will work with the group as a whole, as in story telling. Yet, even here, a few children may be noted who are not yet ready to enter into any form of group activity. The basic characteristic of all grouping at this level is informality.

Grouping in the Kindergarten

The five-year-old child begins his first real activities in groups as such. Though he continues to use solo, parallel, and social or co-operative play, the teacher gradually builds his learning experiences around whole group and small group activities. Organization becomes more characteristic of the program though the time periods are still kept very short. Whole group activities, such as sharing of experiences and materials, rhythms, music, games, and so on, are balanced by smaller group activities in block building, free play, and playhouse dramatic play, and with individual activities in room responsibilities such as plant care, easel painting, clay work, the exploring of books, or a science corner activity. The five-year-old child finds security and fun in working and playing with peers; he shows an increasing ability to work in the total group and in small groups as he moves toward six.

Grouping at the Primary Level

Grouping at the primary level is an essential and necessary facet of room organization. It directly serves child development in both academic and personality growth. The class continues to work and develop as a whole group in some activities such as music, games, and rhythms, but smaller groupings are formed for many activities throughout the day. Grouping at this level continues to have as its basic purpose the meeting of child needs.

Grouping is both formal (but still flexible) and informal. It is informal when the children group themselves in play or in art or dramatic play experience, to watch the class pet, or to read for recreation or some functional learning interest. But at the primary level, formal grouping has an increased importance and place in the program. The teacher, aware of individual differences and needs, groups her class for specific purposes. These include grouping (1) on the basis of readiness, ability, and maturity for experiences in each of the subject areas with regrouping as need arises; (2) for enrichment of activities for the gifted; (3) for special help of a particular kind as in speech, reading skills, and number concepts; (4) for planning, research, and committee work in a class undertaking; (5) for ability grouping; (6) for furthering individual interests; or (7) for furthering and developing social and working relationships between certain children.

Such grouping achieves a twofold goal of attention to individual learning needs at the same time it teaches those children not working immediately with the teacher self-direction and independent activity along with social skills.

Independent Activities

Opportunity, space, and motivation for the child to work alone with materials and in meaningful activities related to the class learning experiences are important in the primary program. Through this method not only do we have a further means of meeting individual needs and interests, but we are able to develop in the child a sense of independent achievement and self-direction. Intelligent planning for such growth offers an avenue of child development not otherwise possible. Just giving busy work to children to be done independently is not implied, but rather teacher guidance toward worthwhile individual activities and the provision of a challenging environment offering such choices for children. Any creative primary teaching situation offers many such possibilities; too, many excellent sources of ideas for independent work are available for teacher planning.

PROMOTION

Organization and grouping policies are directly related to policy and practice in promotion procedures.

The graded school form of organization with its subject-centered curriculum gave rise to the problems of promotion and failure. With the arbitrary subject-content requirements for each grade came the establishment of definite minimum standards of achievement for determining the mastery of such content. Children were expected to achieve in accord with such standards. Success in meeting the standards meant "passing," and promotion to the next grade. Not to achieve the standards meant "failure," and consequent repetition of the year's work, sometimes more than once. Subject-content achievement was the principal concern; the effect of failure on the child was not considered negative. Children who achieved beyond their grade level were often double-promoted or skipped a grade.

Elsbree and McNally, in an excellent presentation on this problem of promotion and failure, state:[8]

If one believes that the graded type of school organization is desirable, it then seems logical to maintain that those who do not qualify for the next grade should "fail." Such failure has been justified on the grounds that it serves several "practical" purposes, chief of which are the following:

1. It maintains the standards of the graded school.

2. It reduces the variability in achievement levels within each grade, making instruction easier.

3. It serves as motivation to pupils to work harder and learn better the subject matter required for promotion.

4. It provides an opportunity for slow learners to bring their achievement levels up to standard.

5. Nonpromotion brings about better emotional adjustment by placing children in a grade most consistent with their achievement level.

If these assumptions are true, then it must be granted that there is considerable justification for the practice. Actually, there is convincing evidence that not one of the foregoing purposes is served by the graded school promotional policy.

With the school's increasing emphasis on the development of the child in all facets of growth as well as the academic, and with our present flexible organization and grouping, attention to individual needs, and the teaching of a range of levels within each class group, we have moved toward what is known as "social promotion" in our present-

[8] Willard S. Elsbree and Harold J. McNally, *Elementary School Administration and Supervision* (New York, The American Book Company, 1951), pp. 141-142.

day graded school. In this plan children are advanced through school with their peer group in most cases, and adjustment to their abilities and needs are made within such groups. This does *not* mean there is no retention. Where it seems best for the child to remain at a level this is done, but only after conference and consideration. Such retention, however, is not the year-end decision which is accompanied by all the emotional frustration of the older failing procedure. The child's problems are recognized throughout the year; teachers and parents work together as much as possible to help the child, and together arrive at the decision that he will benefit by not advancing. Often the older primary child is included in making the decision. This development of the decision over a period of time and through recognition of the difficulty by the teacher, the child, and his family does much to make it a better form of handling such problems than just—as a second grader put it—"flunking" him.

Many research studies have been made on the effects of the type of promotion policy used. Herrick and his associates,[9] and Elsbree and McNally[10] give excellent overviews of these studies and their conclusions.

The development of organizational and grouping plans in our schools which encourage each child to work at his level of ability in a consistent and continuing sequential pattern in a self-contained classroom, whether it be in a graded school, a primary unit, or a multigrade group, offers a sound and effective solution to the problems concerning promotion and failure.

PROJECTS AND QUESTIONS

1. Identify the administrative organizational plans at the early elementary level in your community.
2. Plan and hold a panel discussion on the effectiveness of the three plans discussed in this chapter: the primary unit, the graded school, and the multigrade. In your discussion consider:
    a. the relationship of organization to curriculum
    b. the relationship of organization to child development
    c. the relationship of organization to teacher preparation and personality.

[9] V. E. Herrick, J. Goodlad, F. Estvan, and P. W. Everman, *The Elementary School* (Englewood Cliffs, N.J., Prentice-Hall, Inc., 1956).
[10] *Op. cit.*

3. Identify the organizational plan in which you feel you could do your best teaching. Explain.

GUIDE TO REFERENCES FOR FURTHER STUDY

Association for Childhood Education International, *Grouping: Problems and Satisfactions,* Reprint Service Bulletin, No. 26 (Washington, D.C., The Association, 1954).

Association for Supervision and Curriculum Development, *Group Planning in Education,* 45th Yearbook (Washington, D.C., The Association, 1945).

CASWELL, Hollis L., and FOSHAY, Arthur W., *Education in the Elementary School,* Rev. ed. (New York, The American Book Company, 1957).

ELSBREE, Willard S., *Pupil Progress in the Elementary School* (New York, Bureau of Publications, Teachers College, Columbia University, 1943).

————, and McNALLY, Harold J., *Elementary School Administration and Supervision* (New York, The American Book Company, 1951).

GOODLAD, John I., "Some Effects of Promotion and Non-Promotion Upon Social and Personal Adjustments of Children," *Journal of Experimental Psychology,* Vol. 22 (June, 1954), pp. 301-328.

HEFFERNAN, Helen, "Grouping Pupils for Well-Rounded Growth and Development," *California Journal of Elementary Education,* Vol. 21 (August, 1952), pp. 129-153.

HERRICK, V. E., and others, *The Elementary School* (Englewood Cliffs, N.J., Prentice-Hall, Inc., 1956).

KELIHER, Alice V., *A Critical Study of Homogeneous Grouping in Elementary Schools,* Contribution to Education No. 452 (New York, Bureau of Publication, Teachers College, Columbia University, 1931).

POLKINGHORNE, Ada R., "Parents and Teachers Appraise Grade Grouping," *Elementary School Journal,* Vol. 51 (January, 1951), pp. 271-279.

————, "Grouping Children in Primary Grades," *Elementary School Journal,* Vol. 50 (May, 1950), pp. 502-508.

READ, Katherine H., *The Nursery School* (Philadelphia, W. B. Saunders Company, 1950).

RILEY, Fay C., "Grouping Gives Each Child a Chance," *Nation's Schools,* Vol. 56 (August, 1956), pp. 51-55.

SANDIN, Adolph, *Social and Emotional Adjustments of Regularly Promoted and Non-Promoted Pupils* (New York, Bureau of Publications, Teachers College, Columbia University, 1944).

THEMAN, Viola, "Continuous Progress in School," *Childhood Education,* Vol. 18 (September, 1941), pp. 21-23.

THOMAS, Edith M., "Grouping in the Classroom," *Childhood Education,* Vol. 30 (October, 1953), pp. 69-71.

WALDROP, M., and SPIEGEL, R., "Group Processes in a Community Nursery," *Understanding the Child,* Vol. 25 (January, 1956), pp. 14-15.

WALLIHAN, Robert S., *A Comparative Study of Retardation in the Primary Grades of San Diego, California,* thesis (Boulder, University of Colorado, 1951).

WILES, Kimball, *Teaching for Better Schools* (Englewood Cliffs, N.J., Prentice-Hall, Inc., 1952).

WILLIAMS, Margaret, "What Are Children Learning Through Independent Work Periods?" *Childhood Education,* Vol. 31 (December, 1954), pp. 183-190.

WRIGHTSTONE, J. Wayne, *Class Organization for Instruction,* What Research Says to the Teacher Series, Bulletin No. 13 (Washington, D.C., National Education Association, 1957).

———, "What Research Says About Class Organization: Advantages and Limitations," *National Education Association Journal,* Vol. 46 (April, 1957), pp. 254-255.

CHAPTER 8

Environment: An Aid to Learning

As our understanding of children and how they develop and learn widens and deepens, our emphasis on the learning environment itself becomes more definite.

INTRODUCTION

When young children are happy, eager, and enthusiastic about school —when they can't wait until it is time to go in the morning and return home in the afternoon filled with happy conversation about the events of the day—we can be sure that their learning situation is a good environment for living and working.

Contrasts in the kinds of schools provided for children today are very easy to locate, even within small areas. Extremes in types of physical plants range from the two- or more-storied brick structures, some of which were built as recently as the late nineteen-forties, to the new, colorful, and attractive one-story contemporary buildings located on beautifully landscaped park sites. Change is not limited to the style of building. It extends far beyond this into all aspects of architectural and equipmental design—all of which have a direct influence on the learning process. But more important than such changes in form are the changes in the human relationships within the class group, and between teacher and pupil. All these changes together help to create a psychologically healthful and stimulating learning environment.

146

LEARNING ENVIRONMENT DEFINED

The physical and psychological setting of the classroom and school in which the learning experiences take place is the *learning environment*. Within the classroom it is created and planned by the teacher for her class group in terms of subject content to be taught, basic purposes to be achieved, and the maturational levels, needs, and interests of the children. It can and should be made a most effective aid in the learning process through effective planning and use.

The physical aspects of the learning environment include: (*1*) the physical site, the building, and the playground; and (*2*) the materials and equipment. The first aspect covers such factors as the determination of site, kind of building, the location of rooms within the building, exposure, window space and location, indoor and outdoor play space, storage areas, lockers, bulletin boards, display areas, use of room dividers, and so on. It includes consideration of all the factors of safe and healthful living such as safety measures, ventilation, and heating. The second aspect, materials and equipment, covers furniture selection (size, kind, color, material, flexibility), playground equipment (standard and sculptured), and the other resources needed for the various age levels and planned experiences, including rest cots; play materials such as a playhouse, games, toys, and dolls; indoor and hollow outdoor building blocks; materials for exploration, experiment, and study in science, music, art, rhythms, and woodwork; books; and the necessary audio-visual equipment and supplies. The physical aspects should be characterized by attractiveness, availability and ease for child use, as in low shelves, and flexibility in arrangements for social development of the child.

The psychological environment is directly concerned with the emotional climate of the classroom and the school. It involves the establishment of good rapport between the teacher and her pupils, the interaction processes in effective group and peer work, and the stimulation and challenge to child development through the use of centers of interest and varied materials within the room. It involves the children in the planning of the room environment through exhibits and displays of their work, and through co-operative planning of centers of interest;

thus, it views the development of the learning environment as an educational process as well as an educational setting.

Such a wholesome emotional climate is a most important factor in the learning environment. As our understanding of children and how they develop and learn widens and deepens, our emphasis on the learning environment itself becomes more definite. It can be established in *any* school or classroom under a capable teacher, but it is helped greatly by such physical factors as are being planned and constructed in our newer schools. Research shows that the school site, the building, the equipment, the room materials, and resources are all of importance and influence. They must be justified in terms of children's needs and be centered in the basic goals of education, and the problems and psychology of teaching and learning at the various maturity levels.

EDUCATIONAL PROGRAM: THE GUIDE TO PLANNING RESOURCES

The educational program of the school is the core around which all planning of the physical and psychological environment centers. Programs planned on the basic objectives of democratic education and on the developmental research data require facilities and materials that differ considerably from those needed in the older type of program, wherein rote learning was the principal method used, and the building, furniture, and materials tended to be formal and inflexible. Today, buildings, facilities, and materials play an important role in learning; through planned design and increased attractiveness and flexibility they aid in the realization of individual and social growth, in broadened intellectual and academic knowledge and interests, and in the development of emotional maturity. By their form and use resources encourage free and creative exploration and experimentation; they further understanding; they stimulate the solving of problems; they encourage peer social interaction; they deepen meanings; they extend the functional use of ideas and concepts.

THE PLANNING OF ENVIRONMENTS IS CO-OPERATIVE

Along with increased sensitivity to the importance of environmental factors in the learning process has come recognition of the wisdom and need of using the abilities and insights of all concerned with the educational program in the planning of the site, building, materials, and equipment. Environmental planning today is done by many persons, all having immediate interest and experience in helping. Sites and buildings are planned by educators, architects, and consultants, but interested community persons and specialists are invited to be a part of such groups. Schools today are community centers used for evening classes and meetings, and so must include planning for them. The selection of materials and equipment involves in addition to administrators, teachers, and supervisors, the help of parents, community consultants, P.T.A. committees, publishers, and manufacturers. Each, in terms of his abilities and experience, has contributions to make, while the educators give professional leadership. Environmental planning by such groups is done in terms of basic criteria which have been soundly developed, and in terms of the immediate needs of the area or classroom under consideration.

Study and determination of basic criteria involves educators and specialized personnel working at all levels, city, state, regional, and national. Illustrative of the best efforts of educators and architects to develop basic criteria for good schools is the work of the National Council on Schoolhouse Construction. This Council, long in existence, has among its membership educational administrators and architects, and specialists in school construction from the United States Office of Education, from state departments of education, from city and county school systems, from college and university staffs, and from architectural groups. It works closely and co-operatively with liaison representatives from such groups as The American Institute of Architects, The American Standards Association, The Association of Public School Business Officials, The American Society of Heating and Ventillating Engineers, The National Fire Protective Association, and The National Safety Council. Materials and equipment are also evaluated and studied by groups, both national and local. Outstanding among such groups is the Association for Childhood Education International. Over a period of years this organization has had committees of educators and consultants who have evaluated materials and equipment for classroom use, and set sound criteria for their selection. Constant study and evaluation of the resources of the learning environment by such groups helps us determine and evaluate physical and psychological factors of inherent value for learning.

Within the immediate classroom, planning of the learning environment is also often co-operative; the teacher involves the children in the process and uses it as a means of their development and learning.

THE PHYSICAL LEARNING ENVIRONMENT

Physical Site, Building, and Playground

The approach to school planning should be in terms of the purposes and activities of the educational program.

The Indiana and Midwest School Planning Conference: Proceedings states:[1]

Three basic principles should be the basis of all school building planning.

1) The whole child goes to school. He goes to school socially, emotionally, physically, and mentally.

2) The environment must require the expenditure of a minimum of bodily energy for mere adaptation.

3) The educational spaces must be functional both in size and in relation one to another, yet be adaptable to change.

Implied in this kind of planning are provisions for group work, class work, dramatization, dramatic play, hand work and construction work, free play, creative activities in art, music, and rhythms, rest periods and snack periods for pre-primary children, gardening, and use of all types of audio-visual equipment and aids; space for the development of exhibits, displays, centers of interest, and indoor and outdoor activities; and space and equipment for storage and work rooms. Implied also are provisions for the necessary administrative, health, library, cafeteria, auditorium, and playground units for a well-rounded program.

An excellent help in school plant planning has recently been developed by Heffernan and Bursch. It states, regarding building design:[2]

[1] Paul W. Seagers, "Planning School Facilities," *Indiana and Midwest School Building Conference: Proceedings,* Bulletin of the School of Education, Vol. 30, Nos. 5, 6 (Bloomington, Indiana University Press, 1954), p. 85.

[2] Helen Heffernan and Charles Bursch, *Curriculum and the Elementary School Plant* (Washington, D.C., The Association for Supervision and Curriculum Development, 1958), pp. 18, 20.

Just as the curriculum worker uses the purposes of education accepted by the local school system as a springboard into curriculum design, so may the entire staff of a school use its statement of purposes as a springboard into the task of designing the kind of school building, classrooms, equipment, and play areas which provide the most effective setting for realizing these purposes for the particular children and the particular community the school serves.

All members of the staff will seek the best solution to common problems, while the members of the staff primarily engaged in school planning will be concerned with the technical problems of translating educational specifications into school facilities.

Among the major questions with which all members of the staff will be concerned are the following:

1. What provisions in the school plant will facilitate health services, health education, and sound habits of self-care?

2. What provisions in the school plant will facilitate learning about the physical and natural environment?

3. What provisions in the school plant will facilitate learning about people and their activities in the local community, state, nation, and world?

4. What provisions in the school plant will facilitate aesthetic experiences and creative activity?

5. What provisions in the school plant will facilitate understanding of quantitative relationships and the acquisition of mathematical skills, and the understanding and the acquisition of skills of communication commensurate with each child's ability?

6. What provisions in the school plant will facilitate effective guidance services?

7. What provisions in the school plant will facilitate effective physical education and recreation?

8. What provisions in the school plant will facilitate home-school-community cooperation?

9. What facilities in the school plant will contribute to the effective administration of the school?

10. What facilities in the school plant will assure the widest and most effective use of instructional materials and equipment?

11. What provisions may be made in the architecture so that children will enjoy their place to live and work?

The answer to these questions will involve every aspect of the school site, orientation of the school building(s), placement on the site, access to entrances, relation of indoor to outdoor facilities, grouping of facilities, planning of classrooms, health unit, administrative unit, instructional materials center, multipurpose rooms and many other considerations. Although each question merits separate and considered judgment, it is equally important to understand that no question can be answered satisfactorily without consideration of its relationship to the total school facility.

Examination of the various facets of the physical environment as they relate especially to early elementary education follows:

Site. Sites selected for school location vary according to the educational level of the school to be erected, that is, early elementary or elementary, and the enrollment potential. Criteria for site selection are given by the United States Office of Education as follows:[3]

School sites fail to render the service for which they are intended if they do not provide a suitable setting for the building, if they do not have an aesthetic appeal to the patrons and pupils, and if they do not provide the play and activity areas needed by the school and the community. Adaptation of existing sites to a more complete school use may involve such things as fencing to separate the site from hazardous lanes or areas. It may mean terracing for slopes too steep for play usage. It may call for filling and surfacing of parts of the site to make it usable.

The size of a school site is given as a recommendation rather than a set standard that must be followed. In its revised publication, the National Council on Schoolhouse Construction recommends criteria for site size as follows:[4]

Sites of an inadequate size have been one of the primary causes of early building obsolesence and curtailed school-community programs.

In the 1953 edition of the *Guide,* the Council proposed minimum elementary sites of five acres plus an additional acre for each 100 pupils of predicted ultimate maximum enrollment. . . . Experience has clearly indicated that school sites of such areas are inadequate. Many school districts are exceeding these site areas, and are finding that larger sites result in substantial improvements in educational programs, community services, and efficiency of operation. The necessity for larger sites is due to a number of trends such as: 1) space for outdoor teaching areas; 2) single story structures; 3) single-loaded corridors; 4) campus and cluster-type layouts; 5) the little-school, or the school-within-a-school concept of school organization; 6) consolidation of attendance areas resulting in larger schools, more buses, and regulations and practices requiring on-site bus loading and unloading; and 7) parking space. . . . Experience has indicated that *ultimate* site requirements should be met with the initial site acquisition. . . .

The size of any school site should be determined largely by the nature

[3] U. S. Office of Education, *School Buildings,* Bulletin No. 17 (Washington, D.C., Government Printing Office, 1950), p. 30.

[4] National Council on Schoolhouse Construction, *Guide for Planning School Plants* (Nashville, George Peabody College for Teachers, The Council, 1958), Ch. 2.

and scope of the contemplated educational program. . . . While it is rec ognized that for many schools much larger areas are preferred, the acceptance of the following suggestions will be an improvement for a majority of the schools throughout the country:

1. For elementary schools, it is suggested that there be provided a minimum site of five acres plus an additional acre for each 100 pupils or predicted ultimate maximum enrollment. Thus, an elementary school of 200 pupils would have a site of seven acres.

. . . It must be recognized that each type of situation has its own specific variations which must be studied before sites are chosen.

The Playground. Recommendations for play areas for young children usually advise that such areas are best located immediate to the classroom. Many early elementary classrooms today are planned to open directly onto a play space. If possible, the area provided for younger children should be separate from that used by other levels. It should provide for various kinds of activity including free play, sand box or sand pile play, gardening, and apparatus play. The recommended size is an average of 75 to 100 square feet per child.

The Building. The newer school buildings are attractive and functional. Characteristic of such plants are the following:

1. Contemporary or modern simple style, rambler rather than multistoried. Such a type is usually less costly than the older and more ornate buildings.

2. Classrooms are built in sections joined to each other by covered arcades and immediately available to a centrally located administrative unit. Each section usually houses a level; this has the advantage of providing a separate section for young children. Such sections can be easily expanded to meet growing enrollment needs.

3. Classrooms open on one side to a long, connecting corridor which is often glass walled. On the other side they open to play areas immediate to the classroom; in some cases a sliding glass door in this wall makes it possible for the classroom to have an indoor and outdoor activity space.
   (The White Point School of San Pedro, Los Angeles Public School System, is an excellent illustration of this type of school. Each room has its own outdoor classroom or activity space separated from the indoor class space by a sliding glass door.)

4. Landscaping around the school is planned in many cases for use in nature study as well as for beauty.

153

5. Arrangements are flexible so that the building can be easily used as a community center at night as well as for children's learning experiences during the day. Room dividers, space partitioners, and multi-purpose rooms facilitate multiple use of the building.

6. Classrooms are designed for good and healthful living. They are airy, well lighted, spacious, attractive, and colorful. Permanent equipment such as shelves, storage lockers, etc., are scaled to the height and size of the child level for which the room is designed. Radiant heating is often provided. Facilities such as lavatory, drinking fountain, and toilet are included in each room. The atmosphere created by such design is homelike, warm, and friendly; it encourages a feeling of security in the young child.

Illustrations of newer Southern California schools are shown on page 155. Other reproductions are available in Lawrence B. Perkins' *Workplace for Learning* (New York, Reinhold Publishing Corp. 1957).

The usual pattern is for the early elementary level to be housed in the elementary building, or at least on the elementary campus. In some cases a primary school, housing only the young children through the primary level, is built; it is ideally located near the center of the area of the children's homes and is often termed a "neighborhood school." Its general characteristics are the same as those of the elementary school cited above.

The floor space recommendations, in general, suggest 50 square feet per child in the nursery school, 40 square feet per child in the kindergarten, and 30-40 square feet per child in the primary level. No set requirement is made, however.

By no means do all schools or even the majority reach the standards and ideals listed above. Many older school buildings are being used to advantage; many have been modified to approach what we now know as best for children in housing.

Through a nationwide school facilities survey, the United States Office of Education defined the characteristics of a good school plant as including:[5]

1. Construction and educational adequacy sound enough to last twenty years or longer.

[5] U. S. Office of Education, *Good and Bad School Plants,* Special Bulletin, No. 2 (Washington, D.C., Government Printing Office, n.d.), pp. 2-3.

Torrance Unified School District, Torrance, California

Long Beach Unified School District, Long Beach, California

2. Fire-resistive corridors, walls, and ceiling or roof in multi-storied buildings.
3. Space large enough for activities as recommended in modern school programs.
4. Space sufficient to encourage program changes when needed.
5. Sites that are good and reasonably free from traffic hazards.
6. Well developed school grounds with space for outdoor activities.
7. Adequate provision for lighting and ventilation.
8. Light, heat, water, and toilet systems that will meet reasonable standards for twenty years or more.
9. Furniture and equipment satisfactory for the program.

Materials and Equipment

Resources of materials and equipment include furniture (tables, chairs, lockers, storage bins, shelving, and rugs); playground equipment (standard and sculptured); play materials (playhouse, games, toys, and dolls); blocks (indoor, building, and hollow outdoor); materials for exploring, experimenting, and studying science, music, art, rhythms, woodwork, etc.; books; and audio-visual equipment.

The objectives of education give direction to the learning process. The resources of materials and equipment are the tools that help the teacher in the realization of these objectives and as such are an important facet in the learning process. Such resources *must* be carefully selected and continually re-evaluated through criteria such as the following:[6]

1. Does it contribute to the educational purposes?
2. Is it pupil oriented? Does it meet growth and developmental needs?
3. Does it meet high technical standards?
4. Is it practical and helpful in the immediate situation?
5. Is its learning content valid?
6. Does it teach the child the use of property?

Resources for the school and for the classroom are usually selected, as indicated above, by the classroom teacher, the supervisor or consultant, and the administrator in accord with the policies and philosophy of the school system. Often commercial specialists, parents, and community committees make sound contributions on school resources committees.

Basic lists of approved and recommended equipment and supplies

[6] Teacher Workshop, Tallahassee, Florida, 1956.

Teacher education students prepare classroom materials in Industrial Arts class

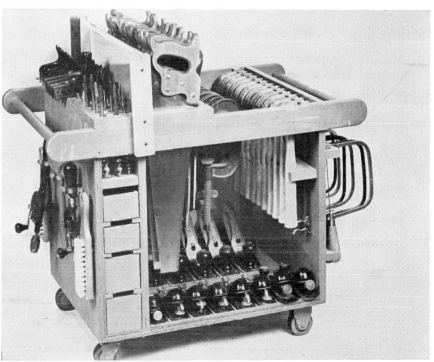

Portable tool cart for classroom use, made by
teacher education students in Industrial Arts class

are available to teachers in their school district publications. Other sources of lists include publications of professional organizations, state departments of education, and commercial companies. It is well worth the student's time to become acquainted with such basic lists. Good sources of basic equipment and supply lists include:

1. Publications and curricula of the various school systems.
2. American Association of School Administrators, *Choosing Free Materials for the Classroom.*
3. Association for Childhood Education International, *Supplies and Equipment.* A very complete guide giving lists for the nursery school, the kindergarten, and the primary level; criteria; evaluation; and recommended sources.
4. California State Supervisor's Association, *Guiding Young Children.* Kindergarten and Grades one, two, three.
5. California State Department of Education, *A Teachers Guide to Early Childhood Education.*
6. Creative Playthings, Inc., *Equipment and Materials for Early Childhood.*
7. National Council of State Consultants of Elementary Education, *Education for Children Below Six.* List compiled by consultants from all the states.

Illustrative of such lists is the following developed by consultants in early elementary education and published by the School Interiors Company and Creative Playthings, Inc. (5 University Place, New York 3, N.Y.).

EQUIPMENT CHECKLIST

Materials and equipment for class of 15 in Nursery, Day Care, or Kindergarten centers

FURNITURE

TABLES Stacking for space saving
For 2 and 3 yr. olds—16" & 18" high
For 4 and 5 yr. olds—20" & 22" high
5 Tables 18"—22" high, seating 4 to 6
4 Tables 18"—22" high, seating 2
Vari-shaped for multiple use.

CHAIRS One for each child—stacking for space saving
For 2 & 3 yr. olds, seats 8" & 10" from floor. For 4 & 5 yr. olds, seat 12" & 14" from floor
3 Chairs, rocking, small
16 COTS approx. 25"x54"x12" high
15 CLOTHING LOCKERS approx. 48" x54"Hx12"D with built-in seats. Use as room dividers.

SHELVING low, open for blocks, puzzles, books and records. 38"x42"x12"

SHELVING open for books and records

1 BLOCK STORAGE BIN approx. 24¼"x22"x18", on casters for picking up and moving blocks and other materials and used as play truck

SCREENS 32"x48" on base to separate quiet and active play as well as separating cots at rest time

STEPS nursery school type

Indoor and Outdoor Play Equipment and Materials

FOR CARPENTRY WORK (where supervision permits)

4 Hammers, 6-10 oz. weight
Nails, large heads, assorted sizes
1 Saw, crosscut, 12", good steel
Plane, small but sharp
Sandpaper
Brace and bits
Paint brushes, ¾" and 1"
Wooden wheels, assorted sizes
Lumber, soft pine, assorted sizes, large enough for sawing, small enough for nailing
Workbench with 2 vises—24" high, professional quality
Tool storage cabinet (peg board back and doors for greater flexibility)

Creative Art Equipment

10 Brushes, paint, japanese hair, 2" with 10"-12" handle
10 Brushes, paint, bristle, 1" with long handle

10 Paste Brushes
3 lbs. Plasteline—for occasional use only
25 lbs. Clay, modeling, keep moist and soft for easy manipulation
Clay Boards, 10"x12"
8 doz. Crayons, 1 doz. ea., red, orange, yellow, green, blue, violet, black, brown, ½"-¾"
1 Easel, double, 24"x24" wood or alum. adjustable to 4 heights, removable tray for easy cleaning
Paints, variety of strong, clear colors, always including red, yellow, blue, black and white. Either powder, cold water, or mixed depending on facility
6 Jars Paint, finger, ½ pt. ea.—red, yellow, blue, green, black and brown
Finger Paint Paper, 5 ply or glazed shelf paper
2 pkg. Paper, construction, 12"x18"
2 pkg. Paper, manila, 9"x12" or 12"x18"
500 sheets Newsprint, unruled
1 pt. Paste, library
1 doz. Scissors, blunt, high quality blades

Audio Visual Equipment and Supplies

Pictures, colored, black and white, animals, birds, nature, nursery, rhymes, etc.
Kindermobiles
Access to projectors
Reproduction of famous paintings
Picture books

159

Multi-purpose tables are designed in many shapes and made of light-weight, sturdy materials. They lend themselves to regrouping and arrangement according to the needs of the classroom, and permit easy stacking. Designs from School Interior Company, New York

SCIENCE EQUIPMENT
- Aquarium
- Vari-shaped magnets
- Magnifying glass
- Prism glass
- Terrarium
- Hamster and Cage
- Thermometer
- Flower Boxes
- Bird Feeding Station
- Cage for visiting pets

FOR MUSIC
- Piano or Autoharp
- Triangles
- Tambourines
- Snare Drum
- Gold Coast Marimba
- Wood Hoops
- Cymbals
- Tom-Tom, 10"x14"
  (skin heads)
- Sleigh Bells

Play sculptures, a new type of playground equipment consisting of animal, nature, and free forms is appearing in the schoolyards of today. Such forms stimulate active physical and creative play. Designs from Play Sculptures, Inc., New York

Jingle Clogs
Rhythm Sticks
Xylophone, chromatic
3 Speed Phonograph
Records, carefully selected
Music books
Tympany Drum
Barrel type Drums

FOR ACTIVE PLAY
 1 Cargo Net or Commando Gym
 1 Three-Way Ladder

1 10′ Bouncing Board
  Rocking Boat
2 Ladders, portable, 4′ & 5′, wood
  or steel
1 Climbing Gym with Firemen's
  pole—3 to 4 yr. olds
1 Climbing Gym—4 to 5 yr. olds
2-3 Kegs, painted often, bright
  colors
3 Packing Crates, 39″x26″x25″,
  or 30″x18″x15″
6-8′ Teeter Boards, rigid, bouncing

boards with cleats at end and center

1 Sand Box, 4'x6' or 6'x6', shelf or seat on two sides or sand table for indoor use

6 ea. Sand Pails (non rusting) spoons, shovels, cars, strainers, funnels, wooden spoons, etc.

4 Saw Horses or Rail Fences—18" or 24" high

1 Arcade Climber

1 TeePee Tent Climber

1 Turtle Tent

1 set Steel Climbing Bridges

6 Snow Shovels

Several assorted large rubber balls

4 Swings, hemp rope or doorway gym (for indoor use)

1 Water Play Enamel Tray

1 Climbing Rope

1 Ladder Box

1 Climbing Ladder

Metal and Wood Ladder House

Steel Gang Plank

Nesting 3 and 5" Metal Climbers

Heavy Rubber Balls 5", 10", 13"

Safety Signal

Derrick Hoist

Fiberglas Play Puddle

BUILDING BLOCKS

1 set Blocks, 500, hardwood, smooth finish, accurately cut, mostly straight cuts

Caroline Pratt type (Creative Playthings Unit Blocks)

26 Hollow Blocks—11"x11"x5½"

12 Hollow Blocks—22"x11"x5½"

12 Hollow Blocks—
5½"x11"x5½"

12 Hollow Blocks—Triangle

6 Playboards, 5½"x44"x¾"

1 set Giant Sta-Put Blocks for large project building (kindergarten or first grade only)

Steering Wheel Hollow Block

FOR LESS ACTIVE BUILDING AND MANIPULATIVE PLAY

1 Diesel Train, solid wood

1 Boat set, sculptured solid wood

1 Interlocking Train

1 Interlocking Boat

Bendable Rubber Figures—community and family, rubber wild animals

1 set Wedgie or Sculptured Dolls —community figures

1 set Wedgie or Sculptured Wooden Dolls—family figures

1 set ea. Wedgie or Sculptured Wooden Animals—farm and zoo

1 Transportation set—auto, truck, bus, airplane—wooden

1 set Rubber Farm Animals, large size

1 Barn, large wooden, open floor type

1" Wooden Beads

Assorted sizes wooden spools, colored

1 set large Nuts and Bolts

1 Color Cone

1 Pounding Peg Board

1 Three Form Block Cart

1 Lock Box, filled

See Inside Puzzles—junior 4-5 yr., senior 6-7 yr.

Assorted Puzzles—varying degrees of difficulty, simple wood inlays

2 Puzzle Racks

Examples of materials and equipment uniquely designed for the special needs of early elementary education. Designs from Creative Playthings, Inc., New York

Nested Blocks
1 Design Color Cubes—wooden box
1 Postal Station
1 Nok-Out Bench
1 Wooden Train Track and Blocks
1 Giant Jumbo Floor Train with flat cars
1 Giant Jumbo Floor Truck
1 Giant Jumbo Floor Boat
1 Giant Jumbo Tug Boat and Barge

Jumbo Toys—without wheels for young group, with wheels for 4 yr. and up
3 Lotto Games—single picture matching
Family Hand Puppets
Indoor Sand & Water Play equipment
Masonite Sewing Cards
Rubber Peg Boards
Jumbo Bolt'n Build and Lumber Logs

163

Snap Blocks, Blockcraft
Lock-Up Garage
Playforms Transportation Toys

WHEEL TOYS
2 Wheelbarrows—large and sturdy enough to hold child, wooden, 2 wheels for easy balance and to prevent tipping
1 Porters Hand Truck
1 Engine or Steam Roller—large enough to ride
2 Velocipedes or Tricycles, different sizes, full ball bearing, 16" for pre-school, 20" for Kindergarten
1 Wagon, small
1 Wagon, large
1 Platform Truck, wooden, large casters
  Wood or Steel Platform Truck (2" casters)
  Child Size Doll Carriage
  Push 'Em Box Truck
  Wood Doll Carriage
  Wood Doll Stroller
1 Live Doll Carriage

FOR DOLL PLAY AND HOUSEKEEPING PROJECTS
1 Doll, 10", rubber, baby, painted eyes
2 Dolls, 18", washable cloth, boy & girl
1 Doll, 24" or 36", girl, soft body, life size
1 set Doll Clothing, loose fitting, durable material, washable, large button holes, zippers, etc.
1 Chest for doll clothes, 3 drawers

1 Doll Bed, sturdy, large enough to sit in
1 Doll Bed Mattress, Blanket, Pillow and Sheets
  Clothes Line, Clothes Pins and Pulley
1 Housekeeping set—wet mop, dry mop, broom, dust pan, dust broom, push broom (must be good quality)
1 Wash Pail and Washboard, very large
  Kitchen pots and pans, aluminum, child size (not toys)
1 Stove, wooden, child size
1 Cupboard, wooden, child size
1 Refrigerator, wooden, child size
1 Sink, wooden, removable tray for water play, child size
1 set Doll Dishes, sturdy aluminum tea set
2 Telephones, sturdy, wooden
1 Rocker, child size
1 Round Table and 2 chairs for doll corner
1 Doll Carriage, wooden, school type construction
1 Floor Plan Doll House, folding
1 set Doll House Dolls
  Sturdy wooden doll house, furniture scaled
2 Irons, wooden
1 Stationary Ironing Board
  Clothing Cupboard for doll clothes
  Doll Bath (Aluminum and Polyethylene)
  Aluminum Bake Set (actually bake with them)
  Doll High Chair
  Bissel Carpet Sweeper
  Heavy Gauge Cutlery (4")

Because basic equipment used in the early elementary program is undergoing a change in its structure, kind of material, and form as pronounced as that in building architecture, it will be worthwhile to give it consideration at this point. Your observations will give you opportunity to note in a very general way the furnishings used in the various school systems; you will find that many classrooms are using the older types of wooden furniture with which you are already familiar. Hence, a few generalizations about and illustrations of some of the newer types may be of help.

The furnishings of today are light weight, durable, flexible, attractive, colorful, and functional. The materials used include molded plywood, cast aluminum, and others which give the definite advantage of light weight at the same time the quality of sturdiness is retained. This makes it possible for even young children to move, stack, or store such furnishings as tables, chairs, and cots. Too, the equipment is designed in such a way that it is flexible and usable according to the classroom needs. The tables, for example, have several basic forms which can be arranged in a number of helpful ways as well as used as separate units. (See page 160.) In conformity with the theory that attractive and colorful surroundings add to the desirability and effectiveness of a learning environment, the furnishings are made to fit into the comfortable and homey type of room recommended for young children. The functional and multi-use quality of these forms, designed in accordance with sound educational theory, highly recommends them for extensive use.

The equipment and materials illustrated on pages 160, 161, and 163 are copies of those available through Creative Interior Company, New York.

Community Resources

Extensive and rich resources are available to all teachers in their immediate communities. In the community-centered school of today (see Chapter 1) the curriculum draws heavily upon the community for firsthand, enriching experiences for children. Facilities and businesses such as those concerned with the harbors, health of the community, dairies, forestry, manufacturing, services including police, fire, stores, and post office should be part of the resources available to the children. In addition, each community has many persons of varied backgrounds who are happy to serve as resource persons. (See Chapter 10.)

One first-grade teacher intensified the interest of the children in their study of the harbor when one of the youngster's fathers, who was a harbor worker, visited with them; his suggestions on the breakwater and on the setting of piers in the classroom harbor the children were building added much in meaning and knowledge to their activity. In another instance, the father of a first-grade child visited the school in order to help with a health unit. Being a doctor, he had much to contribute regarding ventilation, room temperature, body temperature, and so on. His visit set off an extensive health unit study.

Participation of the teacher and her class group in community projects designed for children and their parents is another help teachers sometimes overlook. Illustrative of such a project is the excellent Book Fair held annually in Washington, D.C. Sponsored by the Children's Book Guild and co-sponsored by many groups, including a local newspaper, library associations, service clubs, and other groups, this project is unlimited in values and in motivation for books and reading. Conservation activities offer many opportunities for school community co-operation. An excellent bulletin recently published by Drs. Bathhurst and Hill,[7] of the United States Office of Education, illustrates such activities carried on in schools throughout the country.

The beginning teacher, or a teacher going into a new community, should become thoroughly acquainted with the area and its activities before school opens. A survey of the community for nature study and excursion possibilities, and an acquaintance with resources and resource persons are valuable preparations for the teaching in the academic year that follows.

Free and Inexpensive Materials

An acquaintance with free and inexpensive materials is useful to the teacher candidate in building her beginning teaching file and material resources preparatory to entrance into the profession, as well

[7] Effie G. Bathurst and Wilhelmina Hill, *Conservation Experiences for Children,* Bulletin No. 16 (Washington, D.C., Government Printing Office, 1957).

as to all in-service teachers. Such materials are widely accepted and used in our schools, though at their introduction some objections were voiced because of the advertising script which appears on them. A recent two-year study[8] showed that the majority of schools now set no restrictions on the use of such materials, and that where such restrictions are set it is on the theory that the materials are of more value to the sponsor than to children. In most areas where control

Early elementary education major explaining to her class some room environments she has planned

of free materials does exist it appears to be a policy within the local school system. However, selection of such materials for use should always be made on the basis of evaluative criteria.

PROJECTS AND QUESTIONS

1. Develop three basic floor plans for one early elementary level classroom; show permanent and movable furniture and equipment. One is to be planned as an ideal room, one as an average but acceptable plan, and one as a room you consider unacceptable. List the equipment in

[8] Marcella R. Lawler and others, "Free and Inexpensive Materials," *Review of Educational Research*, Vol. 26, No. 2 (April, 1956), pp. 175-176.

each plan. Evaluate each plan, giving the points supporting it and against it.

2. Use as your starting point a classroom with which you are familiar. Sketch it as it exists, and again as you would improve it as a learning environment without changing equipment or facilities.

3. Participation of the children in the setting of room environment is part of the educational process. Justify and illustrate.

4. A first-grade teacher and her class set up an excellent bulletin board comparing the local weather and climate with that of colder areas. Newspaper was effectively used to represent snow. What effective room environment ideas have you found in your observations or developed yourself?

5. Using the references on community resources listed in this chapter make up a list of such resources for early elementary classroom use.

6. Assume you begin teaching next semester in the immediate community where you are attending school. Survey the possible community resources for use in your teaching; report on this survey.

7. Choose five pictures from your teaching file. Evaluate your choices in terms of value to young children.

GUIDE TO REFERENCES FOR FURTHER STUDY

SITES, BUILDING, AND PLAYGROUND

Helpful Journals:

The American School Board Journal
The Architectural Forum
The Architectural Record
Childhood Education
Educational Leadership
National Education Association Journal
The Nations Schools
The School Executive

ALSCHULER, Rose H., ed., *Children's Centers,* National Commission for Young Children (New York, William Morrow & Company, 1942).

American Association of School Administrators, NEA, *American School Buildings,* 27th Yearbook (Washington, D.C., The Association, 1949).

American Educational Research Association, NEA, *School Plant and Equipment* (Washington, D.C., The Association, 1951).

Association for Childhood Education International, *Portfolio for Kinder-garten Teachers* (Leaflet No. 2); *Portfolio on More and Better Schools for Children Under Six* (Leaflet No. 3) (Washington, D.C., The Association, n.d.).

California Elementary School Administrators Association, *The Characteristics of the Good Elementary School* (Berkeley, University of California Press, 1955), Ch. 9.

Connecticut State Board of Education, *How Is Our School Growing?* (Hartford, State Board of Education, 1955), Ch. 2.

ENGLEHARDT, N. L., ENGLEHARDT, N. L., Jr., and LEGGETT, Stanton, *Planning for Elementary School Buildings* (New York, F. W. Dodge Corporation, 1953).

ENGLEHARDT, N. L. Jr., "The Home-School Unit," *The School Executive,* Vol. 68 (January, 1949), pp. 42-43.

GLENNON, V. S., and VANDEREOF, T., "Essential Characteristics of a Modern Classroom," *Educational Leadership,* Vol. 9 (December, 1951), pp. 200-201.

HASKELL, Douglas, "The Modern Nursery School," *Architectural Record,* Vol. 83 (March, 1938), pp. 84-100.

HEFFERNAN, Helen, "Freedom for Development of Individuality," *National Education Association,* Vol. 44 (May, 1955), pp. 282-284.

―――, "Space for Living," *National Education Association Journal,* Vol. 44 (March, 1955), pp. 142-145.

―――, "Stimulation for Learning," *National Education Association Journal,* Vol. 44 (April, 1955), pp. 218-221.

―――, and BURSCH, Charles, *Curriculum and the Elementary School Plant* (Washington, D.C., Association for Supervision and Curriculum Development, 1958).

HOLDEN, McLaughlin, and others, "Model Center for Child Care," *Architectural Record* (May, 1946), pp. 108-109.

National Society for the Study of Education, *Early Childhood Education,* 46th Yearbook, Part II (Chicago, University of Chicago Press, 1947), Ch. 9.

Research Report No. 1, "The Development of the Teaching Space Divider," *American School and University Journal,* Vol. 26 (1954-55) p. 435.

STEVER, Dorothy V., "The Kindergarten Environment," *California Journal of Elementary Education,* Vol. 17 (February, 1949), p. 3.

United States Office of Education, *Designing Elementary Classrooms,* Special Publication, No. 1; *Good and Bad School Plants,* Special Publication No. 2; *Planning and Designing the Multipurpose Room in Elementary Schools,* Special Publication, No. 3; *Basic Body Measurements of School Age Children: Handbook for Planning School Buildings, Furniture, and Equipment,* Special Publication, No. 4; and *Lighting*

Schoolrooms, Pamphlet No. 104 (Washington, D.C., Government Printing Office, n.d.).

WAECHTER, H., and WAECHTER, E., *Schools for the Very Young* (New York, F. W. Dodge Corporation, 1951).

WILSON, R. E., *Flexible Classrooms* (Detroit, The Carter Company, 51 W. Hancock, March, 1953).

EQUIPMENT AND MATERIALS

Good Sources of Magazine Pictures:

Arizona Highways
Holiday
Ideals
UNESCO Courier

Film and Filmstrip Sources:

California Association for Childhood Education, Helen Heffernan, ed., *Good Day Series, Kindergarten through Grade 8,* 9 sets (Mrs. Sadye Lewis, 1755 Belair Ave., San Jose, California).

Coronet Films (65 East South Water Street, Chicago, Illinois).

Encyclopedia Britannica Films (1150 Wilmette Avenue, Wilmette, Illinois).

United States Office of Education, *A Directory of 3,300 16mm. Film Libraries,* Seerley Reid, ed. (Washington, D.C., Government Printing Office, 1956).

AINSWORTH, Irene, "Today's Library Becomes a Materials Center," *Library Journal,* Vol. 80 (February 15, 1955), pp. 473-475.

Association for Childhood Education International, *Equipment and Supplies* (1955); *Creating with Materials for Work and Play* (1957); *Primary School Portfolio* (1956, Washington, D.C., The Association).

BOTTRELL, Helen K., "Textbooks Can Be Creative Sources," *Educational Leadership,* Vol. 12, No. 7 (April, 1955), pp. 418-422.

BRODERICK, Catherine M., "Research in the Use and Purposes of Instructional Materials," *Educational Leadership,* Vol. 13 (April, 1956), pp. 418-422.

California Elementary School Administrators' Association, *Instructional Supplies and Equipment for the Four and Five-Year-Olds of the Good Elementary School* (San Francisco, 693 Sutter Street, The Association, 1956).

————, *Instructional Supplies and Equipment for the Five- and Six-Year-Olds of the Good Elementary School* (San Francisco, The Association, 1956).

CASWELL, Hollis, "A Curriculum Viewpoint on Educational Television," *Educational Leadership,* Vol. 14 (November, 1957), p. 107.

COREY, Stephen M., *Audio-Visual Materials of Instruction* (New York, Bureau of Publications, Teachers College, Columbia University, 1949).

Creative Playthings, Inc., *Equipment and Materials for Early Childhood* (New York, 5 University Place, n.d.). Catalogue.

CURTIS, Dwight K., "The Contribution of the Excursion to Understanding," *Journal of Educational Research,* Vol. 38 (November, 1944), pp. 201-212.

Department of Elementary School Principals, NEA, *Basis for Effective Learning,* 31st Yearbook (Washington, D.C., The Association, 1952).

EAST, Marjorie, *Display for Learning: Making and Using Visual Materials* (New York, Henry Holt & Company, Inc., 1952).

GARRY, Ralph, "Psychological Tools Assist the Teacher," *Educational Leadership,* Vol. 12, No. 7 (April, 1955), pp. 402-406.

HAWKINS, Reginald R., *Easy-to-Make Outdoor Play Equipment* (New York, The Macmillan Company, 1957).

JACKSON, Margaret M., "Understanding is Better with Felt Boards," *Instructor,* Vol. 64 (June, 1955), pp. 18, 20.

JOHNSON, June, *Home Play for the Preschool Child* (New York, Harper & Brothers, 1957).

KAWIN, Ethel, *Wise Choice of Toys* (Chicago, University of Chicago Press, 1938).

KINNEY, L., and DRESDEN, K., *Better Learning Through Current Materials* (Palo Alto, Stanford University Press, 1949).

KOSKEY, Thomas A., *Baited Bulletin Boards: Handbook for Teachers* (San Francisco, Fearon Publishing Company, 1954).

LANGDON, Grace, *Children Need Toys* (New York, American Toy Institute, 200 Fifth Avenue, n.d.).

MILLER, Bruce, *So You Want to Start a Picture File* (Riverside, California, Bruce Miller, Box 369, 1954).

REDDING, Frank, "T is for Textbooks," *National Education Association Journal,* Vol. 46 (March, 1957), pp. 156-159.

School Library Association of California, "Recommended Standards: Elementary School Library," *Bulletin* (March, 1955).

WILLIAMS, Catherine, "Pictures with a Purpose," *National Education Association Journal,* Vol. 46 (March, 1957), pp. 197-198.

COMMUNITY RESOURCES

Association for Supervision and Curriculum Development, *Large Was Our Bounty,* 1948 Yearbook (Washington, D.C., The Association, 1948).

BLACKWELL, Gordon W., *Toward Community Understanding* (Washington, D.C., American Council on Education, 1943).

BROWNELL, Baker, *The Human Community* (New York, Harper & Brothers, 1950).

CLAPP, Elsie R., *The Use of Resources in Education* (New York, Harper & Brothers, 1950).

GRINNELL, J. E., and YOUNG, Raymond J., *The School and the Community* (New York, The Ronald Press Company, 1955).

HILLIS, Charity, *Preparation and Evaluation of Instructional Materials on Community Agencies,* Bulletin of the Bureau of School Service, Vol. 21, (Lexington, University of Kentucky Press, 1948).

MILLER, Bruce, *Sources of Free and Inexpensive Pictures* (Riverside, California, Box 369, 1952).

National Society for the Study of Education, *Citizen Co-operation for Better Public Schools,* 53rd Yearbook, Part I (Chicago, University of Chicago Press, 1954).

————, *The Community School,* 52nd Yearbook, Part II (Chicago, University of Chicago Press, 1953).

OLSEN, Edward G., ed., *The Modern Community School* (New York, *view of Educational Research,* Vol. 26 (April, 1956), Ch. 3.

OLSON, Clara M., and BHARNURATNA, Sai, "Community Resources," *Re-* Appleton-Century-Crofts, Inc., 1953).

FREE AND INEXPENSIVE MATERIALS

American Association of School Administrators, NEA, *Choosing Free Materials for Use in the Schools* (Washington, D.C., The Association, 1955).

Association for Supervision and Curriculum Development, *Using Free Materials in the Classroom* (Washington, D.C., The Association, 1953).

Field Enterprises, Educational Division, *Sources of Free and Inexpensive Educational Materials* (Chicago, Field Enterprises, 1955).

George Peabody College for Teachers, *Free and Inexpensive Learning Materials* (Nashville, The College, Division of Surveys and Field Services, 1952).

HARAP, Henry, "Use of Free and Inexpensive Learning Materials in the Classroom," *School Review,* Vol. 63 (October, 1955), pp. 378-383.

SINCLAIR, Thomas J., *An Analysis of Certain Factors Relating to Business-Sponsored Teaching Aids,* thesis (Evanston, Illinois, Northwestern University, 1948).

WILLIAMS, Catherine M., "Sources of Teaching Materials," *Educational Research Bulletin,* Vol. 34 (May, 1955), pp. 113-140. (Also available from: Columbus, Ohio State University, Bureau of Educational Research, Teaching Aids Laboratory, 1952.)

THE EMOTIONAL CLIMATE

The emotional and social climate of the young child's classroom is one of the most important factors in the learning situation. Young children need a free, spacious, and wholesome environment where they can find personal security and satisfaction in achievement at the same time that they are liked and respected as individuals. This implies:

1. Guidance of a friendly, understanding teacher who has a deep, personal interest in each child.
2. Programs encouraging controlled freedom "to do" and "to be" and "to learn" in activities paced to child needs in spacious areas.
3. Peer relationships fostering appreciation for each child's individuality and encouraging socially acceptable behavior.
4. Opportunity for the child to be his natural, growing self rather than conforming to a rigid pattern of "good"; this implies teacher understanding of surface and causal behavior and guidance in how to handle feelings and relationships.

The teacher is the key to creating such a climate in the classroom.

A good classroom climate, while helped greatly by good physical factors, is possible in any environment. You can find it in beautiful, ultra-modern schools which are ideally located, in well built and well equipped schools in any area, in meagerly furnished and neglected schools in underpriviledged localities, and even in drab and colorless, poorly equipped schools. It is the teacher's understanding and values that determine it—resources alone *can't* produce it.

In visiting schools across the country it is possible to visit many classrooms where the teacher is especially able in helping children grow and develop. It is encouraging to note, on entering these classrooms, the way the social climate and the rapport between the group and their teacher seem to foster learning. A second grade visited was located in an old college building that had been remodeled for use as an elementary school. These youngsters were talking about the zoo. They named and recognized the kinds of animals they expected to see on their coming field trip; they identified those animals that are tame and those that must be kept in strong cages; and they described the habits of the various animals. Their discussion led directly into interest in a poem about the zoo which the teacher developed with them, and then into a two-part response song which they sang with enthusiasm.

To watch the interest and eagerness in the faces of these responsive youngsters; to feel the freedom in this classroom's rapport and the oneness of the group with its acceptance of each child as an individual within it; to observe the sparkle of this excellent teacher and her careful attention to the needs of each child as she developed knowledge and skills made one aware that real learning and growth were taking place. This teacher's program showed understanding of goals, long range and immediate, and made one sense keenly that behind the present situation lay careful planning, a knowledge of child development processes, an awareness of the importance of meeting social and emotional needs of young children, the personal integrity of the teacher, and real love and joy in working with young children. The teacher's manner was quiet but enthusiastic, the material simple, but she had created an environment for the maximum learning and growth of these children. It was evident that broad goals, which weighed developmental patterns and needs of children as a group and as individuals for wholesome personality development, were the source of classroom activity.

Another classroom was housed in a portable building, with few environmental helps such as modern equipment and bulletin board space. It could have been a very inadequate learning situation. Instead, it was a room rich in academic and social experiences for children. The youngsters, through study of their immediate environment and community, were engaged in building their own classroom post office. Orange crates, unprinted newssheet, construction paper—all free or inexpensive materials—had been used by an effective teacher to create a real and meaningful situation to deepen understanding and enrich play. Among other things, the children were learning how to find answers to their questions, how to write and mail a letter, how to plan and work together, and how to function as citizens in our democratic society— under the best of classroom environments. Yes, this teacher had provided opportunities for experiences in harmony with the needs and maturity level of the group in a wholesome learning climate.

Through such an emotional climate in the classroom, through the teacher's goals and understandings, children have the kind of experi-

174

ences that foster *greater academic achievement, maximum development,* and *wholesome living. Such teaching is creative!*

GUIDE TO REFERENCES FOR FURTHER STUDY

Association for Supervision and Development, NEA, "A Good Environment for Learning," *Educational Leadership,* Vol. 5 (March, 1948), entire issue.

————, *Creating a Good Environment for Learning,* 1954 Yearbook (Washington, D.C., The Association, 1954).

DILLON, Ina K., "Firmer Boundaries for Greater Freedom," *Reprint,* Association for Nursery Education, Southern California (Los Angeles, Office of Consulting Service, 1955).

HILL, W., and others, *How Children Can Be Creative,* Bulletin 1954, No. 12 (Washington, D.C., Government Printing Office, 1957).

LIPPITT, Ronald, "An Experimental Study of Authoritarian and Democratic Group Atmosphere, Studies in Topological and Vector Psychology I," *University of Iowa Studies in Child Welfare,* Vol. 16 (1940), pp. 44-195.

MIEL, Alice, "When Resources Are for Children," *National Education Association Journal,* Vol. 45 (October, 1956), pp. 401-403.

STENDLER, Celia Burns, and YOUNG, Norman, "The Impact of Beginning First Grade Upon Socialization as Reported by Mothers," *Child Development,* Vol. 21 (December, 1950), pp. 241-260.

THOMAS, M. J., and others, *Climate for Learning* (Pittsburgh, University of Pittsburgh Press, 1953).

CHAPTER 9

Curriculum: Learning Experiences

What we try to accomplish through education at any growth level should be in keeping with the individual's capacities and potentialities at that level.[1]

INTRODUCTION

What are the learning experiences of young children like today? Let us look again at classroom groups, first a primary and then a kindergarten.

As we enter the primary room we find ourselves responding immediately to the warmth and freedom of the social climate and stimulating environment in which learning is taking place. Chairs and tables (rather than screwed down desk-and-seat furniture) have been arranged in small groups which offer inviting work places for four to six children; a plant or flower has been placed in the center of each table, helping to make it a friendly, pleasant place to talk and work with others. Equipment such as blocks, paints, paper, paste, beads, puzzles, peg boards, and records are stored on open shelves at a level where they are immediately accessible to the children.

Centers of interest for reading, numbers, science, music, and "quiet work" activities have been arranged within the room. Children are busy exploring, observing, manipulating, discovering, and reading with deep interest. In the science corner we see the classroom pet, a rabbit (though at other times we would have seen a turtle, a hen, a hamster,

[1] Arthur T. Jersild, *Child Development and the Curriculum* (New York, Bureau of Publications, Teachers College, Columbia University, 1950), p. 8.

176

or one of the many other kinds of pets children love). The children are lovingly caring for the pet, cleaning his pen, changing the drinking water, and rearranging the straw. As they finish their tasks they watch —their eyes big with wonder—while the small bunny holds and nibbles the carrot they have given him. Observing, learning, giving attention to detail, sharing, and working together in responsibilities and pleasures, these children are developing. At the aquarium a small group are watching as Tom enjoys his turn at feeding fish; Peggy, close by, is watering the plants and taking care of the rock and shell collection.

At the reading center the teacher is encouraging a small group in their success and achievement in reading stories they have written about their recent trip to the harbor. This reading area contains picture books and magazines of varying levels of difficulty about the people and pets and things that young children know and love—these further stimulate their interest in reading and learning. In this wholesome environment, planned around their interests and needs, the children are secure in achievement and affection within their group.

Other children are hard at work in another center at the far end of the room; they are expressing themselves creatively through the various mediums of art. Some are telling a story or expressing a mood through finger paint; their hands, moving in fast, broad strokes across the paper, show freedom of movement and the flow of ideas. Others have preferred the tempera or water paints and brush to express what they want to communicate to others through painting. Chalk, paints, charcoal, crayons, clay, and other materials for this developmental level are available for children to choose in their creative expression work. Evident in the behavior of these children is the satisfaction of self-expression, achievement, creativity, and the feeling of belonging.

Seated at one of the table groups are children intent on so-called quiet or independent activities, which we learn are games and other materials designed to give the child individually or in very small groups opportunity to develop skills in reading and numbers. In the center of the room a "committee" is busily engaged in beginning the building of a harbor patterned on the one they visited recently with their class and teacher. Earnest thought and research are evident in their concern with the problem of setting up the breakwater and the docks in the places where they will best serve the harbor and vessels.

On the bulletin boards and display areas of the room are pictures, stories, and paintings made by the children, either individually or in groups. These materials are meaningful and real because they were developed as the children observed, read, discussed, and studied their environment. Firsthand experiences such as using materials in the classroom and making trips into the community to visit locations and talk with workers are an important part of the learning, just as is the use of secondary sources such as reading materials, films, maps, records, and stories told by the teacher. Knowledge is not acquired through rote learning or a mere mastery of facts and skills isolated from the children's background and experience in daily living. Rather, knowledge and skills are learned functionally in an environment planned to challenge wholesome interests and self-expression; the children are learning and developing in many facets of personality in a class group where they feel secure and loved.

No matter which of the activities in this classroom we consider, we find that they have been provided in the learning environment *not* just as activity, but rather as a means to stimulate and further the children's development and functional learning, as a way of meeting individual needs, as a way to foster individual and group growth through continuous learning, and as a step toward the realization of basic educational goals.

Viewing the curriculum as it develops we see that the experiences of young children are sometimes organized around individual subject content, but more often are planned around a central area of experience or core problem. The study of the place and work of the harbor in the community, which the group mentioned above were beginning, is an example of a core problem in which many related learnings in social studies, language arts, numbers, art, and music are involved. Such a problem is planned for development by the teacher and then developed through further planning with the children so that it becomes their problem, for only so far as it becomes a problem to them is it a challenge to learning. Such problem-centered experiences further the child's development through increased understanding, knowledge, skills, appreciation, and participation in his environment. It gives him widened functional knowledge as it gives him opportunity for developing his skills in the basic processes of thinking and problem solving.

Or we may visit the four- or five-year-old child in his environment for learning. The basic approach to learning would be the same as at the primary level but the learning experiences would be changed to accord with his maturity. In the kindergarten, which is spacious and allows for much more freedom and informality, children are busily engaged in block play. Some are working co-operatively in small groups, some are engaged in parallel play, and some are working or playing alone. Whether the child is playing alone, close to another child carrying on a comparable activity, or whether he plays with a group, the activity gives him an opportunity to participate in terms of his individual needs, social growth, and maturity. Materials and resources of many kinds are available to these children; many of them have been obtained without cost or have been made by the teacher or parents. Security and achievement are reflected here, too, in the satisfaction seen in the children's faces and in their behavior. The learning situation meets the developmental needs for social and emotional maturation, as well as for knowledge and skills. It reflects the teacher's goals based on her educational philosophy. These goals, in turn, determine the approach, use of resources, and interpretation of the community and the class needs.

Thus we see curriculum in the classroom. What is the theory of curriculum which underlies it?

CURRICULUM DEFINED

Good learning experiences for children are organized and based on democratic values. (See Chapter 4.) The determination of the kinds and content of learning experiences in terms of the immediate living needs of children, and in terms of the values and insight of adults in our culture, is called curriculum organization and planning. *The actual living experience of the child and group in the classroom under teacher and school guidance is the curriculum.* So defined, curriculum includes all experiences and activities, informal as well as the more formal; it includes field trips, indoor and outdoor play activities, all types of programs for parents and other groups, as well as academic learning experiences. Curriculum, as it is used currently in educational thinking, is to be differentiated from the "course of study" (which is usually termed *guide*). The course of study is a study guide of suggested outlines of academic content to be taught at the various levels, including methods, resources, teacher aids, and other helps in curriculum planning; such helps are related to child growth patterns, needs, and interests for the teacher. Though in an earlier period we used the terms *curriculum* and *course of study* interchangeably, today there is this clear differentiation in the concepts implied: On the basis of the guide, the teacher plans in terms of child growth, background, the way children learn, individual and group needs and interests, and the community setting, as well as content to be taught. The *actual* experiences developed in the classroom as a result of the planning are the curriculum.

CURRICULUM CHANGE

Curriculum is planned around problems of living in our society; children learn to meet the "here and now" problems, and through this process are prepared to meet future situations and problems as they occur. They study primitive life in order to contrast our culture with non-technical societies. They study other ways of life for contrast, comparison, and appreciation of man's ingenuity in meeting his basic needs. We know today that we help children in their later living only through having them learn functionally and live effectively in the present. We cannot foretell what problems will exist in the society of 1980 or 2000, but we do know that the basic skills of processes will enable an individual continually to meet and adjust to changing and advancing society and culture. Knowledge and skills must be learned *not* for themselves, but for their *use* in solving problems. They are means, not ends! They are functional, not static! Effective learning situations are centered in problems of daily living; they are characterized by normal social relationships and situations, co-operative planning, doing, and evaluating, use of supplementary and enriching materials, pleasant and challenging environments for working, flexibility to meet individual needs and evaluation of development rather than grading.

Though our basic guidelines of education have always been democratic, the form of our curriculum has not always been that described above. Form has changed in proportion to our growth in knowledge and understanding of children, the educative process, and our dynamic society.

The A.S.C.D., through committees, has reported a study of such change in curriculum for the hundred year period between 1857 to 1957.[2] During this time

both theory and practice have changed as result of the development of the new sciences of psychology, psychiatry, cultural anthropology, and sociology. The century of Pierce, James, and Dewey has given new meaning to the philosophy of democracy and to the relationship between experiences and learning. New insights have been gained into the relationship between the growing individual and the society of which he is a part. . . .

Throughout the discussions in the preceding chapters we have implied many changes in curriculum and in educational thought. Statement of these significant changes during the hundred year period follows:[3]

Change from the faculty psychology of learning with emphasis upon memorization and mental discipline to an organismic, dynamic psychology with emphasis upon the powerful forces of purpose, meaning, goal seeking, differentiation and integration in the learning process.

Change from reliance on tradition and subjective judgment as a basis for educational procedures to concern for scientific research and the application of scientific method and scientific findings.

Changes in methods and materials that have grown out of the idea that how we learn is as important as what we learn.

Changes in patterns of participation in curriculum building.[4]

Change in curriculum has been accompanied by change in curriculum guides (courses of study) as we would expect. Harap and Merritt,[5] in a comprehensive study of the curriculum guides published between 1951 and 1953, report these changes. Included in their summary of trends of change are the following:

[2] P. Bostwick, J. C. Parker, and G. L. Potter, *One Hundred Years of Curriculum Improvement, 1857-1957* (Washington, D.C., Association for Supervision and Curriculum Development, 1957), pp. 2-3.

[3] *Ibid.,* pp. 3-6.

[4] The change in patterns of participation in curriculum building has been from subject content, prescribed by specialists in the content fields, to teacher and even parent participation in curriculum planning, and teacher-pupil co-operation in classroom planning.

[5] E. Merritt and Henry Harap, *Trends in the Production of Curriculum Guides,* Division of Surveys and Field Services (Nashville, George Peabody College for Teachers, 1955), pp. 40-43.

1. Increased use of the term guide rather than course of study, implying that the manual's function is suggestive rather than prescriptive.
2. Increased number of guides covering the whole school program, giving emphasis to the continuity of growth and the continuous curriculum.
3. Continued emphasis on the cooperative development of guides through committee processes with teachers taking an important part in leadership as well as in development of the publication.
4. Increased acceptance of the community-school role through suggested use of community resources and study of community.
5. Organization of social studies content into teaching units.
6. Interest in long range curriculum development.

The following guides are illustrative of the many excellent ones being developed by school systems at the present time. They are suggested for examination and study in the light of this chapter.

Baltimore Public Schools, Maryland, *Living and Learning in the Kindergarten*

California State Department of Education, *A Teacher's Guide to Education in Early Childhood*

Cincinnati Public Schools, Ohio, *New Primary Manual: A Teacher's Guide to Kindergarten and Grades One, Two, and Three*

Connecticut State Board of Education, Hartford, *How Is Our School Growing?* (nursery school and kindergarten)

Long Beach Public Schools, California, *A Teacher's Guide for Kindergarten Education*

Los Angeles County Board of Education, California, *Educating the Children of Los Angeles County*

New York State Department of Education, Albany, *Child Development Guide for Teachers of Three-, Four-, and Five-Year-Old Children*

Richmond Public Schools, Virginia, *Handbook for Junior Primary Teachers*

BASIC CURRICULUM PATTERNS

Curriculum design (or structural organization) in the elementary school is currently classified into four major types, but it is recognized that many variations exist within the four divisions. These include the subject-matter curriculum, the broad fields or areas curriculum, the emerging needs curriculum, and the problems-of-living curriculum.[6]

[6] See Virgil E. Herrick, "Design of the Curriculum," *Review of Educational Research,* Vol. 27, No. 3 (June, 1957), p. 270.

We noted in Chapter 7 that the historic development of the graded school included the development of subject content and its subdivision into amounts of content to be covered in each grade level. This division of knowledge into subject fields, to be taught independent of each other and within set time allotments, is the older concept of the *subject-matter curriculum*. Today, in view of the factors already considered, that is, the sciences of growth and of how children learn, the improved ways of planning for and with children, and the impact of social change on education and daily living, the subject-matter curriculum has been modified. It gives attention to the psychology of learning within the content organization and places some emphasis on the social usage aspect, but it is still essentially subject-content- or knowledge-centered. As a curriculum pattern it does not meet the need for daily, functional living and developing in our society.

The *broad areas curriculum* is a variation of the subject-centered form of curriculum organization; however, it combines several related subject fields into whole areas instead of teaching each content as an isolated subject. The subjects of history, geography, and civics or citizenship are combined into a broad area termed social studies. Language arts as a broad field covers study of the communication skills, and includes such subjects as reading, spelling, oral and written language, literature, speech, poetry, and dramatics. Not all subject fields are combined into broad areas; some, like arithmetic, remain isolated or nearly isolated subjects.

The third type, the *emerging needs curriculum,* goes to the opposite point of view from the subject-centered curriculum; it has been called the child-centered curriculum. Its emphasis is entirely on the needs and interests of the child. Contrary to the planning of a logical sequence of materials to be taught, it calls for planning in terms of the immediate and developing needs of the group of children concerned. Continuity of learning experiences is dependent on continuing staff planning in terms of the children's needs and teacher-pupil planning in class groups. While such curriculum organization considers at length child needs and functional living, it appears to many to by-pass the guidance and insight of mature educators in giving direction and basic planning to classroom living, and to assume superior professional guidance by outstanding teachers in every classroom.

The last of the classifications listed, the *problems-of-living curriculum,* is the most widely accepted. It is neither completely subject-centered nor child-centered. In it the learning experiences are organized around broad areas concerned with group and individual living in the family and social setting; it is centered in the development of knowledge and acceptable behavior in terms of our democratic values. Emphasis is placed on:

1. Development of child interests, needs, and potentialities.
2. Skills of group living and interaction.
3. Basic functional knowledge, understanding, and appreciation.
4. The thinking processes of problem solving, and critical and creative thinking.
5. Purposeful functional living in everyday situations in our immediate communities and changing world.

This curriculum pattern considers the child in terms of maturity, individual differences, and background experiences and opportunities. It sets long range and immediate objectives of democratic values and wholesome personality development. Within this framework it creates learning experiences which are real and meaningful to children, which challenge development, and which build through functional learning in a continuous and sequential pattern toward fuller maturity.

Basic to such a curriculum is organization that brings to planning and to actual learning experiences: (*1*) the best of the past in our democratic heritage, culture, and educational processes; (*2*) present scientific knowledge and research; and (*3*) professional insight and evaluation for future needs and activities as far as possible.

The scope and purpose of such education for young children covers *whole growth.* It involves firsthand and other learning experiences that help the child develop and mature in:

1. Physical growth, skill, and co-ordination
2. Skill in communication, which involves increased understandings and concepts, enriched vocabulary, facility in oral and written expression, and the reading skills of the maturity level
3. Foundations of personality and mental health in behavior and attitudes
4. Knowledge and understanding of a widening natural and cultural environment
5. Appreciation, understanding, and skill in human relationships

6. Growing self-direction, self-reliance, and independence
7. Skills in the thinking processes as a basis for behavior
8. Creativity

Also, such curriculum planning is co-operatively developed. The teacher, as the professional person guiding the immediate learning experiences of the children, plays a most important role in this process. Principles and supervisors provide leadership and guidance for the teacher. Parents and community members also have a role in the planning. Within the careful planning done by the teacher is ample opportunity for child planning and the emergence of group and individual needs. Teachers who plan in advance are in a better position to make adjustments in sequence of experiences.

The immediate goals of the teacher, developed through such curriculum planning, deeply influence the value of the curriculum experiences. They are the guide for her over-all planning of units and daily work with the children. They are the immediate source of the kind of experiences that develop in the classroom. The teacher's purposes are the direct approach to the realization of basic values of good education, irrespective of the type and amount of materials used, the environmental setting, the course of study or guide books, and community resources, even though all such helps are of great value. The method usually used to realize purposes in classroom procedures is problem solving.

EARLY ELEMENTARY CLASSROOM PLANNING

Curriculum planning for the individual classroom must be a *broad* process. It *should not be limited* to planning for a specific subject, level, unit, or day *only*. It should begin at the beginning of *each* school year with a reconsideration of the basic goals and values of the *total* educational program, and *within them* of the basic goals and values for a specific teaching program such as a nursery school, kindergarten, or primary class. On this foundation the teacher should consider the maturity level, needs, and readiness of the particular group she is to teach. This involves determination of the individual differences in potentiality and experience. Then, using the basic content to be taught as her tool, the teacher plans for sequential child growth in present experiences and toward next developmental levels on the basis of her knowledge of the growth and learning processes of children. It is suggested that the student restudy at this point the materials and chart presented on pages 50-60.

The organization of curricular activities is termed the program. Planning for the whole early elementary program gives attention to certain basic considerations, while planning for specific levels within the whole involves greater differentiation. After consideration of the total early elementary program, we will examine more closely each of the programs of specific levels within its scope.

Program Guidelines

Basic in the planning of programs for young children is the determination of: (*1*) What are good learning experiences? and (*2*) At what point in the children's development and program should they be placed? Briefly, good experiences are those determined on the basis of the objectives of education; where they are placed in the program is determined by the developmental pattern and readiness of children; and how they are taught is determined by the psychology of the learning process.

Guidelines for broad planning of young children's programs must consider the following:

Total growth of the children. We have discussed at length that the focus of all planning is centered in the child's total individual and social development; and that all experiences are designed for realization of this objective.

Continuity and sequence of experiences. Learning experiences are planned in an ever-widening scope of meaning, functional knowledge, skills, and processes. The "when" of the placement of such experiences is determined by the developmental task and growth patterns of children, following the sequence of the child's natural development. Hanna, Potter, and Hagaman set the criteria for determining sequence in unit learning experience as follows:[7]

[7] L. A. Hanna, G. L. Potter, and N. Hagaman, *Unit Teaching in the Elementary School,* 3rd ed., (New York, Rinehart & Company, Inc., 1956), p. 84.

Is it suited to the maturation of pupils and to their physical and psychological needs?

Is it one which pupils at that grade level are likely to find interesting?

Does it provide for articulation between grades and between segments of the school system so that there is continuity and co-ordination of learning experiences?

Is adequate and suitable material available?

Does it provide for comprehensiveness and balance in the program?

Does it provide for flexibility so that teacher-pupil planning can be used?

Emphasis on individual differences. The child must be guided to set purposes for learning experiences if they are to have meaning for him. To give this guidance the teacher must have insight into the individual motivation, interests, and abilities of the children. Then, on the basis of such individual differences, the teacher provides for a range of learning levels, and opportunities for individual contributions to the group. She helps the child to understand himself and the purposes for his activities, and to plan for his growth. She organizes her class into groups on the basis of special or common needs. She helps the child successfully find his place and way of contributing in the group at the same time that he learns to appreciate differences and values in others. Individual differences are the key to helping each child develop to his maximum. Every individual achieves in terms of his strengths, not his limitations.

Provision for varied experiences. Experiences must cover a wide range of interests and needs; each experience must build from the known and immediate to wider horizons. Experiences must offer opportunity for the child to "explore" and "experiment." They must be meaningful, and so far as possible, firsthand experiences. They must provide for flexibility in doing and for creativity in expression.

Every kind of learning experience that will contribute to the child's development should be offered. For the young child especially, many experiences will be firsthand contacts with concrete objects and with actual situations. Books, auditory and visual aids, and other secondary sources become increasingly important as the child matures.

Types of experiences vary widely. They include planning, doing, and evaluating, as well as understanding, appreciating, listening, and creating. They involve participation, responsibility, enjoyment, knowledge, and understanding.

Development of skills in the processes. The "how?" is best answered in the *unit* method of teaching, since it most effectively develops the process skills of thinking and problem solving. The basis for this method is found in everyday living in democratic society. Democracy presumes intelligent self-direction on the part of all individuals within the scope of group good. Each individual must recognize and formulate his own problems and needs, plan for them, carry out the plans, and then evaluate the process as a whole for future action and behavior. This same procedure is the foundation of the unit method of teaching. Children learn through living in the classroom. They are guided within the scope of a need to consider a problem in terms of the purpose, the knowledge needed, the plan for solving, the activities necessary to carry out the plan and to solve the problem, and to evaluate the whole process for the next activity. This democratic living is functional in classroom learning and living, rather than in theory studied.

The unit method has been defined as:

. . . a purposeful learning experience focused upon some socially significant understanding which will modify the behavior of the learner and enable him to adjust to a life situation more effectively.[8]

Further:[9]

A unit of work is a series of learning experiences focused upon the achievement of a common goal which pupils have accepted as their own. A unit must possess cohesiveness and wholeness, be based upon the personal-social needs of children, cut across subject lines, be based upon the modern concept of how learning takes place, require a large block of time, be life-centered, utilize the normal drives of children, take into account the maturational level of pupils, emphasize problem solving, provide opportunity for the social development of the child, and be planned cooperatively by teacher and pupils. . . .

. . . The fact that it (unit) cuts across subject matter lines makes subject matter more meaningful and the interrelationships between subject disciplines at once apparent. The unit is rich in opportunities for children to satisfy their innate drives to be active, to manipulate and construct, to satisfy curiosity, to create, to communicate, to dramatize, and to satisfy the ego-integrative urge. It is replete with opportunities for children to use functionally skills of reading, writing and arithmetic, to live democratically with

[8] L. Hanna, and others, *op. cit.,* p. 101.
[9] *Ibid.,* p. 124.

their peers, to satisfy their individual needs, and to progress at their own rate. . . .

PROGRAM FOR THE FOUR- AND FIVE-YEAR-OLD CHILD

In most cases, the young child at his entrance into nursery school or kindergarten is experiencing his first living outside the home and family. This is an important experience for him and one that must be made pleasant, for it will do much to form his attitudes toward school life. The learning activities during this early period are focused on guiding the child in a growing independence of the home and of adults, in learning social skills in relationships with adults as well as with others of his own age, in using socially acceptable behavior, in physical activity to build sound health and good muscle co-ordination, in emotional control in meeting situations, and in beginning the individual and group use of problem-solving skills.

The program designs at these levels vary widely. In general, the program builds from an informal and free schedule into a balanced day of free activity and routines, with more organized activity becoming increasingly prominent. By the time the child reaches six he is usually oriented to the more formal organization of the primary program. The individual class program is built directly on the needs of the children in the immediate group and in terms of the variations of maturity levels. Many school systems group children of kindergarten age into morning or afternoon classes according to their background and maturational development, so that programs can be more directly planned in terms of immediate needs.

To help the child make as smooth and comfortable a transition from the home as possible, the learning experiences are concerned basically with those persons and things which the child knows in his immediate environment. It is important that interest in the physical and social environment and an eagerness and curiosity to learn be developed during this period of growth. The home, the family, pets, the work of community helpers, and interest in plants, birds, and trees, as well as in weather and the four seasons, are all explored. As the child grows to be part of the school group his interests and experiences widen.

The interest span of the young child must be considered in planning. Two methods are used to meet this need. First, a challenging environment is planned which offers the young child an opportunity to move on to something different when he has exhausted the possibilities of his present activity. Secondly, for the most part activities are planned for short periods and are changed frequently. The rotation of quiet and active periods in the program is termed the "rhythm of activities."

Learning is most effective if it occurs at a time when there is need for and strong interest in it. The placing of learning activities at a time when the children will most quickly and effectively benefit from them is important; this placement is termed "timing."

The program at the beginning of the year allows much time and freedom for play in self-chosen activities, especially for the four-year-old children. Much time must be provided for physical activity, both indoors and out. At the same time a beginning is made in the establishment of routine. The child learns how to care for and use materials; he learns to assume responsibility for his clothing and for his personal habits; he learns that time is provided for rest periods, snack periods, and for health care. Gradually for the four-year-old child, and more quickly for the five, the balance between free activity and guided activity and routine is established, and then the guided activity is increased until by the end of the kindergarten year the child is usually well adjusted to the school routine and is prepared for the primary program.

Social skills are of key importance in the program. The child begins by learning the name of his teacher and classmates, and later the names of the nurse, principal, and other adults in the school. Courtesy through consideration, morning greeting, and like practices throughout the day is made a part of all relationships. Ease and growth in social skills comes from relating to and communicating with others. Activities such as free conversation in all play periods, telling time, story and library periods, puppet play, dramatic play, discussion of happenings and study trips, and talking about pictures and picture books all help the child to communicate and mature in needed skills of group living. Teachers use interesting little devices to help this growth. One teacher made a bulletin board display of black paper silhouettes of her class with the name of each child beneath a cutout. The children had great fun identifying themselves (and at the same

190

At school with four- and five-year-olds

At school with four- and five-year-olds

At school with four- and five-year-olds

time they were learning to observe characteristics and to differentiate shapes and forms). Another teacher made a big paper book entitled, "Our Class"; inside, each child had made a picture of himself, and in some cases of his family. Thus a child grows from being an egocentric individual to being an outgoing individual and a member of the group —a necessary step to later learning experiences.

Creativity and self-expression are encouraged. Music activities such as rhythms, singing, listening, and playing rhythm instruments encourage self-expression and release of feelings, and at the same time give children pleasure. Art activities are used to encourage expression and creativity through work with brush and paints at the easel, finger paint (perhaps to music such as "The Nutcracker Suite"), clay, scissors, paper cutting and tearing, drawing, and beginnings in construction work.

Number or quantitative concepts are introduced to young children through the counting of concrete objects and the incidental teaching of number concepts as a part of the other learning activities.

Much attention and individual guidance is given the young child as he works and plays. As a basis for her guidance, the teacher observes such factors as individual interests, emotional needs, attention span, health, ability to finish a job that is begun, special abilities, creativeness, use and care of materials, adjustment to routine, reaction to suggestion and authority, independence and initiative or the tendency to lean on or follow another child, and relationships with the group.

Problem solving is begun as a process with young children. The teacher, with the class group, discusses the problem, plans the method of meeting it, the activities involved, and later evaluates with the class the process used. For example, block play lends itself to the development in process skills. The unit interest may be the harbor or the airport. Teacher and children together plan the doing; during the block activity the teacher gives help and guidance to individual children or to small groups; at the end of the activity teacher and children come together to evaluate the plan and the work, and then decide on next steps for the next block play period. Planning, doing, evaluating— all are process skills which operate in these basic beginnings.

Toward the end of the kindergarten year, the teacher begins to plan more in detail for the children's transition to the primary level.

The whole kindergarten year, with its emphasis on emotional maturity, physical development and co-ordination, social growth, and functional learning has been a foundation for primary learning experiences. Now the teacher acquaints the children with first grade through a visit to the classroom. She does *not,* however, start the children in readiness books and formal academic work; such practices are definitely not in accord with what we know as "best" for young children.

THE PRIMARY PROGRAM

Just as the kindergarten teacher ended the school year with activities that were transitional to the primary program, so the primary teacher begins her year using some of the kindergarten interests and activities in order to give the children a feeling of "at homeness" in first grade.

Classroom living at the primary age is an extension and enrichment of that in the nursery school and kindergarten in that it is adapted to the maturing children and their basic needs of much physical activity, social relations with others, growing independence and self-reliance, and skills in processes. But the scope and kinds of learning experiences and the program organization are adapted to the more mature growth and developmental patterns of children six through eight years of age. Individual differences, too, are greater among the children than they were at a younger age.

As a general rule, the primary program has all areas of study and group living organized within each "self-contained" classroom. The teacher directs and interrelates as far as possible all learning experiences, continuing in sequence on the basic experiences the children have already had.

A pictorial overview of these activities has been prepared by the Teachers Club of the Huntington Beach Elementary School in a filmstrip, *Let's Take a Look.* (See pages 196-199.)

Learning experiences at this level are designed to continue the widening of the children's social horizon. The nursery school and kindergarten were concerned with the home, family, and immediate community; the primary continues these interests but gradually broadens and deepens them to include a more comprehensive study of the physical and social environment, and some acquaintance with other cultures.

*At school
in the
primary*

*At school
in the
primary*

At school in the primary

At school in the primary

It continues the building of functional knowledge and understanding of citizenship, the roles of people in our society, interdependence, and communication.

Broad area learnings in the curriculum are organized into major units related to group and individual social living such as the school, the community (and helpers in the community), the farm, the harbor, and the city. Each unit, building on past and immediate experiences, is planned to develop functional learning of interrelated knowledge. Social studies, science, reading and the language arts, numbers or quantitative concepts, music, art, and all related learnings are taught so far as is practical in relation to the general unit, problem, or area of living being studied. For example, a unit on the harbor would give children a functional knowledge of the physical environment, the function of the harbor, the role of workers involved, and effect on the community, that is, information and knowledge in the social studies and science fields. It would involve number concepts in construction and problems concerning harbor work. It would involve art activities such as painting, illustrating, drawing, clay modeling, and reproducing scenes and activities in murals. It would involve language arts in discussion activities, reading, chart work, research activities, and dramatic play. The room environment, the firsthand experiences in field trips, and the audio-visual aids all supplement and enrich the knowledge of subject content. So far as possible, learning in the various content and skill fields would all be related to the scope and purpose of the unit.

Thus subject fields at the primary level are planned in relation to the total needs of young children; this avoids the danger of meaningless rote learning, or such narrow considerations as skill outcomes *only,* for:

The social studies give knowledge and understanding of the physical and social environment in which we live.

The language arts develop the skills of communication: reading for meaning and understanding (in developmental reading for skills through systematic instruction, in recreational reading for fun, and in functional reading for information to use in problem solving); writing and spelling for written communication; and oral speech for spoken communication. The language arts involve activities of reading, telling and sharing, puppet dramatic play, following directions, story telling, choral speaking, listening, writing, and spelling. It involves reading class-dictated stories, individual stories, and books. The language arts field is a skill development field; it uses as its materials the content of the social studies and science fields.

Numbers develop the social usage of computational skills in problem solving.

Physical education builds good health, and knowledge, habits, and attitudes for wholesome living.

Creative activities and art encourage self-expression through painting, modeling, murals, papier-mâché, and three-dimensional posters.

Creative activities and music further aesthetic development through rhythms and songs, and in developing creative music.

The unit program continues to follow the basic guidelines of good programs for young children; it is varied, flexible, based on firsthand experience, free and creative, timed to children's readiness, and characterized by a rhythm of active and quiet periods. It offers continued opportunity for individual and group growth in functional knowledge, group rapport, and process skills. It fosters total personality growth.

It is to be noted that not all materials of the primary program can be taught in interrelated broad areas of units. Some content must be taught independently. However, this learning, too, is often organized with the problem-solving approach.

PROJECTS AND QUESTIONS

1. Compare, in column form, the strengths, then the weaknesses of the two differing forms of curriculum pattern, that is, the subject-content-centered versus the problems-of-living pattern. Use research data and democratic philosophy of education as guidelines.

   Content-Centered Curriculum—Problems-of-Living Curriculum

Strengths:

Weaknesses:

2. Justify for kindergarten parents the lack of formal instruction in the program for four- and five-year-old children.

3. Evaluate the use of the unit as a method of teaching young children.

4. Trace the sequence of development of broad experiences in the social

studies program in early elementary education; do the same for the language arts. (Use curriculum guides as basis.)

5. In the light of the programs discussed, plan (in a general way) for the first few days of a kindergarten program; a primary class.

GUIDE TO REFERENCES FOR FURTHER STUDY

ADAMS, Fay, *Educating America's Children* (New York, The Ronald Press, 1954).

ALMY, Millie C., "Are They Too Young for Problem Solving?" *Progressive Education,* Vol. 27 (March, 1950), pp. 143-148.

Association for Childhood Education International, *Pictures of Children Living and Learning* (Washington, D.C., The Association, 1951).

Association for Supervision and Curriculum Development, NEA, *Continuity in the School Program,* 1958 Yearbook (Washington, D.C., The Association, 1958).

————, *Toward Better Teaching,* 1949 Yearbook (Washington, D.C., The Association, 1949).

————, *Group Planning in Education,* 1945 Yearbook (Washington, D.C., The Association, 1945).

————, "Creativity and the School," *Educational Leadership,* Vol. 14, No. 1 (October, 1956), entire issue.

BALDWIN, Louise, and others, "Reducing the Gap Between the Kindergarten and First Grade," *The Nations Schools,* Vol. 54 (August, 1954), pp. 38-41.

BATHURST, Effie, *Where Children Live Affects Curriculum,* Bulletin 1950, No. 7 (Washington, D.C., Government Printing Office, 1950).

BURTON, William H., *The Guidance of Learning Activities,* 2d ed. (New York, Appleton-Century-Crofts, Inc., 1952).

California State Department of Education, *Teachers Guide to Education in Early Childhood* (Sacramento, State Department of Education, 1956).

Cincinnati Board of Education, *Primary Manual* (Cincinnati, Board of Education, 1948).

Department of Elementary School Principals, *Contemporary Society-Background for the Instructional Program* (Washington, D.C., The Department, 1957).

FRANK, Lawrence K., "Play in Personality Development," *American Journal of Orthopsychiatry,* Vol. 25 (1955), pp. 576-590.

HANNA, L. A., POTTER, G. L., and HAGAMAN, N. C., *Unit Teaching in the Elementary School* (New York, Rinehart & Company, Inc., 1956).

HAVIGHURST, Robert J., *Developmental Tasks and Education,* rev. ed. (New York, Longmans, Green & Company, 1953).

————, *Human Development and Education* (New York, Longmans, Green & Company, 1953).

HILDRETH, Gertrude H., *Readiness for School Beginners* (Yonkers, N.Y., The World Book Company, 1950).

————, *Child Growth Through Education* (New York, The Ronald Press Company, 1948).

HILLIARD, Pauline, *Improving Social Learning in the Elementary School* (New York, Bureau of Publications, Teachers College, Columbia University, 1954).

JERSILD, Arthur T., *Child Development and the Curriculum* (New York, Bureau of Publications, Teachers College, Columbia University, 1956).

————, and TASCH, R., *Children's Interests and What They Suggest for Education* (New York, Bureau of Publications, Teachers College, Columbia University, 1951).

LEE, J. Murray, and LEE, Dorris May, *The Child and His Curriculum,* rev. ed. (New York, Appleton-Century-Crofts, Inc., 1957).

Long Beach Public Schools, *Kindergarten Guide* (Long Beach, Board of Education, 1954).

MACOMBER, Freeman Glenn, *Guiding Child Development in the Elementary School* (New York, The American Book Company, 1948).

MIEL, Alice, "Planning for Continuity in the Curriculum," *Teachers College Record,* Vol. 54 (December, 1952), pp. 131-138.

————, and BROGAN, Peggy, *More Than Social Studies* (Englewood Cliffs, New Jersey, Prentice-Hall, Inc., 1957).

MURSELL, James L., *Successful Teaching: Its Psychological Principles* (New York, McGraw-Hill Book Company, 1954).

PRESCOTT, Daniel A., *The Child in the Educative Process* (New York, McGraw-Hill Book Company, 1957).

RUDOLPH, Marguerita, *Living and Learning in the Nursery School* (New York, Harper & Brothers, 1954).

SHEEHY, Emma D., *The Fives and Sixes Go to School* (New York, Henry Holt & Company, 1954).

SMITH, B. O., STANLEY, W. O., and SHORES, J. H., *Fundamentals of Curriculum Development* (Yonkers, N.Y., The World Book Company, 1957).

STEPHANS, Ada R., *Providing Developmental Experiences for Young Children* (New York, Bureau of Publications, Teachers College, Columbia University, 1952).

STRATEMEYER, F., and others, *Developing a Curriculum for Modern Living,* rev. ed. (New York, Bureau of Publications, Teachers College, Columbia University, 1957).

THEMAN, Viola, *A Good School Day* (New York, Bureau of Publications, Teachers College, Columbia University, 1950).

WILLCOCKSON, Mary, ed., *Social Education for Young Children* (Washington, D.C., National Council for Social Studies, 1956).

CHAPTER 10

Role of the Early Elementary Teacher

The teacher of pre-school children has the challenging task of helping the child to direct his energies away from self absorption to a concern about the world around him, and this she does effectively by what she herself is, rather than by what she says or does.[1]

INTRODUCTION

What is the role of the teacher in early elementary education? Today the teacher is the most effective and direct answer to America's educational needs and problems. Within her lies the key to an immediately effective learning situation in the classroom where she is at one time both guide and co-worker as well as the direct link between school and community. Research data, well planned functional buildings, excellent equipment, enriching resources, and other helps are more effective today in the learning experiences of children than ever before, *but* all are secondary in importance to the teacher.

The role of the teacher has been different at different times in our educational history, determined by the immediate thinking of the time in terms of what was good education for children. The transition from the earliest role of authoritarian keeping rigid control of pupils and charged with the transmission of information to them, to her present role of "guide," has been a long series of step-by-step progressions based on every possible source of study, theoretical and practical.

The teacher's role, of its very nature, demands excellent and broad personal and professional qualities of dedication and ability. Now,

[1] Florence Clothier Wislocki, "Teachers as Human Beings," *Vassar Alumnae Magazine* (December, 1956), p. 21.

popularly characterized by the term "guide," it implies one who gives direction and leadership in the classroom to individual child development, and to group living, and who builds understanding and friendly relations in the community with parents and lay persons. It involves creative planning, doing, and evaluating. It demands continued personal and professional growth. It *assumes* sound knowledge and skills in academic and scholastic areas. Such a role, in its far-reaching and intensive demands, requires thought as well as knowledge. Within this exacting role for all teachers, the teacher of young children plays a most important part, for it is she who lays the foundation in attitudes, in skills of academic work, in personality development, and in home relations.

THE EARLY ELEMENTARY EDUCATION TEACHER

Though teaching is a satisfying and challenging profession at any of the various levels, the teaching of young children offers many teachers the greatest challenge. When education was strictly subject-centered some held that the importance of the teaching position varied in direct relation to the age taught. Hence, high school teachers were held in higher esteem than elementary, and, in turn, the teacher of the upper grades in the elementary school rated greater respect and often more salary than those who worked with younger children. Less subject content was required at the lower level, it was argued! Contrary to this point of view, we know today that in some ways the teaching of younger children makes greater demands on the teacher than teaching at other levels. This is evidenced in the continuing and far-reaching influence of school beginnings on *all* later growth and development, in the flexibility and psychological implications in planning and guiding learning experiences for young children, and in the close parent relationships which the teacher of early elementary levels must maintain.

Evaluation of the profession of teaching young children and interest in this work involves reading and practical experiences, as was pointed out in Chapter 1. For theoretical considerations, we will look first at the teacher in the early elementary field, and then at her role in its various relationships to: (*1*) the profession; (*2*) the children; and (*3*) the parents and community.

Teachers of young children share in common with all teachers the basic qualifications for professional excellence, but *must* have in addition that special interest, creativeness, and insight for the problems and needs of young children. Careful consideration of the following questions will help to determine interest in this teaching level.

1. *Do you have a genuine love, knowledge, and understanding of young children?*

This implies interest from a realistic and mature point of view, not from a sentimental belief that young children are "cute," and that teaching them would be "easy."

This connotes a respect for and understanding of children that you show in your relations with them. It involves seeing "through their eyes," understanding their developmental problems and tasks, and enjoying helping the child and his parents at difficult as well as at delightful times. It involves *much* listening. It means accepting *all* children regardless of race, creed, color, or personality.

2. *What are your personality qualifications?*

This implies good health, sparkle, attractive posture and manner, and reserves of physical energy. It presumes a neat, well-groomed, poised appearance, and pleasing voice qualities. It connotes emotional balance, a sense of humor, outgoingness, flexibility, adaptability, and self-confidence. *It requires scholastic ability and achievement, a sense of responsibility, and an open and scientific mind.*

3. *What are your skills in human relations?*

This asks: Do you act on values, philosophy, and convictions? Are you vitally interested in family, school, community, and world happenings, and their effects on our daily living? Do you objectively evaluate yourself and others? Do you give leadership and co-operation? Have you wide interests? Have you respect for others as individuals at all times? Do you have an understanding of surface versus causal behavior?

4. *How effective are your skills of communication?*

Do you speak well? with emphasis on thought? Do you write well? Do you use a scientific approach to problems? Do you increase your understanding of others through contact and study?

5. *What do you believe is the place of psychological insight and creativity in the teaching-learning process?*

This implies that you believe in "guiding," not telling. It assumes that you want to work for children and others, and that their problems are a challenge to you; that you have insight, creativity, resourcefulness, and ability to plan, organize, and do. It requires professional activities based on an understanding of basic values and goals translated into classroom activities and professional self-evaluation.

A most helpful description of the teacher of young children is written by Florence Clothier Wislocki,[2] a Vassar graduate and a practicing psychiatrist. Excerpts from it follow:

. . . The teacher, especially the teacher of young children, whether he knows it or not, is helping the child to extend his horizons of conscious control over himself and his environment by developing his means of self expression. The more freely and accurately the child can observe and integrate and express, the greater is his capacity for reality, for testing, and the wider are the areas over which he has conscious control. A goal of the educator is to give to each individual the capacity freely to use skills and techniques for dealing with the natural world, with society and with the self—and this last is the particular prerogative of the parent and teacher of young children.

. . . The kindergarten and nursery school teacher performs a function quite different from the teacher of older pupils or students. Preschool plays a unique and important role in character and personality formation as well as preparing the child for his future school adjustment. It is in the nursery school that the child first meets new authority figures outside of his own family and household. His nursery school teacher is interested in him, but unlike his parents, she is not exclusively focused on him and she is not emotionally tied up with him. His nursery school teacher is just as interested in his peers as she is in him, and adult attention must be shared with ten or more equally self-centered creatures of his own dimensions. It is in nursery school that the child begins to learn how to deal with his peers and how to work and play cooperatively with them. He discovers that frustration is the lot of all mankind but that it need not undermine security. He moves slowly from demanding instant gratification towards postponement of his own pleasure for the sake of the group. His chances to test reality are expanded in this, his first relatively independent group experience.

The teacher plays a role more analogous to that of a parent than to that of an instructor, because the young child learns by acquiring behavior patterns and reactions and attitudes without conscious awareness that they are

[2] *Ibid.,* pp. 19-21.

being acquired. The young child identifies himself with persons who have, emotional significance for him. He acquires large blocks of reaction patterns and behavior traits from another person by a process of incorporating that person's personality into his own personality. The acquisition of personality traits by identification is the most primitive and all-pervasive form of learning. It occurs normally right into adolescence, but is most conspicuous in the early years of childhood. Parents who are permanently fixed objects in the child's life are, of course, the most important objects of identification, but as I have stressed before, rich personality development requires a variety of suitable models from whom to borrow traits and reaction patterns which will be woven into the personality. The teacher of pre-school children has the challenging task of helping the child to direct his energies away from self absorption to a concern about the world around him, and this she does effectively by what she herself is, rather than by what she does or says.

So we see that the selection of teachers for very young children is a peculiarly difficult and important responsibility. It is very easy to flunk a student who D's and E's in academic work, but very hard to weed out prospective nursery school teachers who get A's and B's in all their courses, but who nevertheless would not be good teachers for pre-school children because of personal insecurity, immaturity, or subtle neurotic problems. The profession needs mature, out-going women (and perhaps some men, too) whose personal and emotional life are satisfying and who go into pre-school teaching as a challenging, creative job.

The attributes that make a good teacher of very young children are more subtle and difficult to evaluate than are the attributes that make a good teacher of older students. However, education is a field as broad as life itself. There is room in the profession for many kinds of personalities, and the differing needs of these many types of personality can be met in the most challenging field.

PROFESSIONAL RELATIONSHIPS

The teacher as a dedicated member of a profession has four major responsibilities. These concern: (1) philosophy of education; (2) scientific approach to the teaching-learning process; (3) ethical attitudes and relationships; and (4) professional organizations.

A Functional Philosophy of Education

It is the privilege and responsibility of each teacher in our democratic educational structure to work from a well defined philosophy of education which is deeply and personally meaningful to her. This enables her to give a sound direction to all her work and therefore to be a more effective teacher.

The teacher's philosophy, gradually developed through understanding of basic democratic concepts and professional knowledge, will cover the ideals, responsibilities, and opportunities for service within its scope. It will not be a mere verbal adoption or memorization of some formulated statement of philosophy of education, though such may be the beginning of the individual's own meaningful statement.

A Scientific Approach to the Teaching-Learning Process

The teacher, functioning with a democratic philosophy and through democratic group processes, works through a scientific method of teaching. This involves: (1) approach; (2) method; and (3) evaluation.

Approach. The teacher has a responsibility to develop and increase her skills in creating learning environments and in planning and organing experiences. Her approach is through creative and critical thinking involving seven facets: (1) Determination of the specific problems presented by the children within the framework of the particular classroom situation in which she is working; (2) Recognition of the group and individual developmental stages and variations; (3) Attention to the individual as such; (4) Understanding of the learning process; (5) Understanding and appreciation of cultural forces; (6) Mastery of the knowledge and skills involved; (7) Continuous adaptation to the immediate group of children.

Method. The teacher uses the problem-solving approach in her teaching, in analysis of the bases of problems arising in the teaching situation, and in the effective handling of such problems.

Evaluation. Continuous evaluation of classroom activities and learning experiences in the light of the needs of the particular group situation and of the research and readings in the field gives opportunity for continued improvement and effectiveness in teaching.

Ethical Attitudes and Relationships

The National Education Association, the largest and most comprehensive professional teachers' organization, has been the instrument most effective in moving teaching forward to the status of profession. In

CODE OF ETHICS[3]

WE, THE MEMBERS of the National Education Association of the United States, hold these truths to be self-evident—

—that the primary purpose of education in the United States is to develop citizens who will safeguard, strengthen, and improve the democracy obtained thru a representative government;

—that the achievement of effective democracy in all aspects of American life and the maintenance of our national ideals depend upon making acceptable educational opportunities available to all;

—that the quality of education reflects the ideals, motives, preparation, and conduct of the members of the teaching profession;

—that whoever chooses teaching as a career assumes the obligation to conduct himself in accordance with the ideals of the profession.

As a guide for the teaching profession, the members of the National Education Association have adopted this code of professional ethics. Since all teachers should be members of a united profession, the basic principles herein enumerated apply to all persons engaged in the professional aspects of education—elementary, secondary, and collegiate.

[3] National Education Association, *Code of Ethics* (Washington, D.C., The Association, 1952).

FIRST PRINCIPLE: *The primary obligation of the teaching profession is to guide children, youth, and adults in the pursuit of knowledge and skills, to prepare them in the ways of democracy, and to help them to become happy, useful, self-supporting citizens. The ultimate strength of the nation lies in the social responsibility, economic competence, and moral strength of the individual American.*

In fulfilling the obligations of this first principle the teacher will—

1. Deal justly and impartially with students regardless of their physical, mental, emotional, political, economic, social, racial, or religious characteristics.

2. Recognize the differences among students and seek to meet their individual needs.

3. Encourage students to formulate and work for high individual goals in the development of their physical, intellectual, creative, and spiritual endowments.

4. Aid students to develop an understanding and appreciation not only of the opportunities and benefits of American democracy but also of their obligations to it.

5. Respect the right of every student to have confidential information about himself withheld except when its release is to authorized agencies or is required by law.

6. Accept no remuneration for tutoring except in accordance with approved policies of the governing board.

SECOND PRINCIPLE: *The members of the teaching profession share with parents the task of shaping each student's purposes and acts toward socially acceptable ends. The effectiveness of many methods of teaching is dependent upon cooperative relationships with the home.*

In fulfilling the obligations of this second principle the teacher will—

1. Respect the basic responsibility of parents for their children.

2. Seek to establish friendly and cooperative relationships with the home.

3. Help to increase the student's confidence in his own home and avoid disparaging remarks which might undermine that confidence.

4. Provide parents with information that will serve the best interests of their children, and be discreet with information received from parents.

5. Keep parents informed about the progress of their children as interpreted in terms of the purposes of the school.

THIRD PRINCIPLE: *The teaching profession occupies a position of public trust involving not only the individual teacher's personal conduct, but also the interaction of the school and the community. Education is most effective when these many relationships operate in a friendly, cooperative, and constructive manner.*

In fulfilling the obligations of this third principle the teacher will—

1. Adhere to any reasonable pattern of behavior accepted by the community for professional persons.

2. Perform the duties of citizenship, and participate in community activities with due consideration for his obligations to his students, his family, and himself.

3. Discuss controversial issues from an objective point of view, thereby keeping his class free from partisan opinions.

4. Recognize that the public schools belong to the people of the community, encourage lay participation in shaping the purposes of the school, and strive to keep the public informed of the educational program which is being provided.

5. Respect the community in which he is employed and be loyal to the school system, community, state, and nation.

6. Work to improve education in the community and to strengthen the community's moral, spiritual, and intellectual life.

FOURTH PRINCIPLE: *The members of the teaching profession have inescapable obligations with respect to employment. These obligations are nearly always shared employer-employee responsibilities based upon mutual respect and good faith.*

In fulfilling the obligations of this fourth principle the teacher will—

1. Conduct professional business thru the proper channels.

2. Refrain from discussing confidential and official information with unauthorized persons.

3. Apply for employment on the basis of competence only, and avoid asking for a specific position known to be filled by another teacher.

4. Seek employment in a professional manner, avoiding such practices as the indiscriminate distribution of applications.

5. Refuse to accept a position when the vacancy has been created through unprofessional activity or pending controversy over professional policy or the application of unjust personnel practices and procedures.

6. Adhere to the conditions of a contract until service thereunder has been performed, the contract has been terminated by mutual consent, or the contract has otherwise been legally terminated.

7. Give and expect due notice before a change of position is to be made.

8. Be fair in all recommendations that are given concerning the work of other teachers.

9. Accept no compensation from producers of instructional supplies when one's recommendations affect the local purchase or use of such teaching aids.

10. Engage in no gainful employment, outside of his contract, where the employment affects adversely his

professional status or impairs his standing with students, associates, and the community.

11. Cooperate in the development of school policies and assume one's professional obligations thereby incurred.

12. Accept one's obligation to the employing board for maintaining a professional level of service.

FIFTH PRINCIPLE: *The teaching profession is distinguished from many other occupations by the uniqueness and quality of the professional relationships among all teachers. Community support and respect are influenced by the standards of teachers and their attitudes toward teaching and other teachers.*

In fulfilling the obligations of this fifth principle the teacher will—

1. Deal with other members of the profession in the same manner as he himself wishes to be treated.

2. Stand by other teachers who have acted on his behalf and at his request.

3. Speak constructively of other teachers, but report honestly to responsible persons in matters involving the welfare of students, the school system, and the profession.

4. Maintain active membership in professional organizations and, thru participation, strive to attain the objectives that jusify such organized groups.

5. Seek to make professional growth continuous by such procedures as study, research, travel, conferences, and attendance at professional meetings.

6. Make the teaching profession so attractive in ideals and practices that sincere and able young people will want to enter it.

1924 a committee was appointed to prepare a professional code of ethics; the first code was presented and adopted by the profession in 1929. Amendments were approved in 1941, 1944, and 1948. In 1952 the latest revision was adopted.

The Code of Ethics states the basis for professional relationships in five basic principles. Because of its importance for every member of the profession it is reproduced here in full.

Each of these principles is of extreme importance in its own right. It is important to note also that teacher-in-school relationships of co-operation and rapport should extend to all members of the school team working for children. The often overlooked member of this team is the school custodian. His work, while differing in kind, is important for the welfare of all. He contributes directly to many health and safety factors of the school environment and can be a definite help at times in planning school environment and projects such as gardening and construction activities. Then, too, let us not forget that he is another human being in the total educational picture.

Professional Organizations

Professional organizations, non-existent in early times, came into being as a result of need. Teachers, as they became aware of common professional problems, developed an interest in organizing. It is a professional responsibility to know in general what organizations exist, their purposes, services, and publications; and further, which would be of especial help in our individual professional work and personal growth.

Professional organizations exist on the national, state, county, regional, and local levels for both in-service and pre-service personnel.

The National Education Association is the largest and most important of all organizations in the teaching profession. Founded as the National Teachers Association on May 15, 1857, by 43 representative teachers, it has now passed its hundredth year.[4] It has now nearly 700,000 members, over a million affiliated members, 66 state and 6000 local affiliated associations, 30 departments, 13 headquarter divisions, 24 commissions and committees, and one council. Each of

[4] See Edgar B. Wesley, *NEA: The First Hundred Years* (New York, Harper & Brothers, 1957), pp. 374-380.

the units works independently on its own program at the same time it reinforces and supplements the work of the other units.

Murra states:[5]

Despite changes in nature and changes in name to National Educational Association (1870) and to National Education Association (1907), the officially stated purpose of the association has remained unchanged. The NEA of 1957 operates under the authority of a charter from the Congress of the United States, in the preamble of which are the same words that were adopted on August 26, 1857, as part of the original constitution of the NTA: "to elevate the character and advance the interests of the profession of teaching, and to promote the cause of popular education in the United States."

This historic statement of purpose identified the two main foci of attention for NTA-NEA activity during the past century, namely, teacher welfare and educational movement. At all times the NEA has been concerned actively with both categories. . . .

In NEA usage a department is typically an autonomous national organization of individuals concerned with a particular professional specialty in education, such organization being more or less loosely connected with the NEA. But some departments are not autonomous, being dependent on the "parent" association for both financial support and a measure of control. Some departments are organized on the basis of subjects taught, some on the basis of educational level. In two departments membership is for women only; in one, it is for institutions only.

The teacher of young children will find many groups and publications within the NEA organization of immediate help. Among these are:

N.E.A.	National Education Association	*N.E.A. Journal* *N.E.A. Handbook*
A.A.S.A.	American Association of School Administrators	Yearbooks
A.S.C.D.	Association for Supervision and Curriculum Development	*Educational Leadership* Yearbooks Bulletins
D.E.S.P.	Department of Elementary School Principals	*National Elementary Principal*
E.P.C.	Educational Policies Commission	Yearbooks Bulletins
K.P.	Department of Kindergarten-Primary	Publications

[5] Wilbur F. Murra, "The First Century of the National Education Association," *School and Society* (May 11, 1957), pp. 157-158.

The NEA forms a joint committee with The National Congress of Parents and Teachers.

Other national groups and organizations and their publications of especial interest to early elementary education teachers are:

A.C.E.I.	Association for Childhood Education International	*Childhood Education* Bulletins
N.S.S.E.	National Society for the Study of Education	Yearbooks
N.A.N.E.	National Association for Nursery Education	Publications
	Children's Bureau, Department of Health, Education and Welfare	*Children*
	Office of Education, Department of Health, Education, and Welfare	Briefs Selected References Bulletins

State and local professional organizations began before the national, state groups beginning in 1845 and local groups existing as early as 1794. Students, and teachers in service, should become familiar with the publications of the organizations of the state in which they plan to teach or are teaching.

Participation in professional organizations is stressed for beginning and prospective teachers. We find that:[6]

Early membership in professional organizations at local, state, and national levels is almost universally recommended by those who have written extensively on the orientation of the beginning teacher. In such organizations, the first-year teacher gets to know his fellow workers, becomes informed with regard to trends and developments in the teaching profession, and learns about the current public issues with which educators at all levels must deal.

Too, emphasis on student membership in professional organizations as a phase of pre-service professional education has become widely accepted. Bent says of the NEA for students:[7]

[6] "First-Year Teachers in 1954-55," *NEA Research Journal,* Vol. 24, No. 1 (February, 1956), p. 14.

[7] Rudyard K. Bent, "Contributions of Student Organizations to the Professional Growth of Teachers, *Journal of Teacher Education,* Volume 8 (September, 1957), p. 276-277.

The purposes of membership in the Student NEA are that of orienting students to their professional responsibilities, aiding them to learn to participate effectively in educational organizations, and developing professional atttudes. Those who have developed professional attitudes have an interest in teaching and in its possibilities and an interest in the problems of education, and a wish to aid in their solution. They participate in professional activities and organizations, attend professional meetings, and read professonal literature. Teachers who possess these characteristics will make efforts to improve themselves and to remain educationally vital. The process of developing them is low and cannot be postponed until after they start teaching.

Many of these characteristics are developed in professional classes; but the Student NEA develops them further and also gives the student a chance to put them into practice by engaging in a series of activities designed to promote professional attitudes. The types of activities in which they engage depend upon the school, the students, and the sponsors.

The NEA is a professional organization covering the activities for all levels, elementary, secondary, higher, and administrative. Other organizations are available to students in pre-service education. Many of these are designed to meet the needs of particular groups. The ACEI is the organization of especial value to students entering elementary and early elementary fields. Students should also have a special interest in the state organization of the area where they will teach; state association journals are of much help and value.

In addition to the professional organizations discussed above, the teacher candidate should be familiar with W.O.T.P., the World Organization of the Teaching Profession. This group, begun by 38 national organizations and 9 professional inter-governmental organizations, is concerned with world unity and co-operation in our profession.

GUIDE TO REFERENCES FOR FURTHER STUDY

Ashby, Lyle W., "The Teacher Shapes Tomorrow," *National Parent-Teacher*, Vol. 50 (February, 1956), p. 8.

Biber, Barbara, and Lewis, Claudia, "An Experimental Study of What Young Children Expect from Their Teachers," *Genetic Psychology Monographs*, Vol. 60, No. 1 (1948), pp. 3-97.

Bottrell, Harold R., ed., *Introduction to Education*, Division IV (Harrisburg, Pa., The Stackpole Company, 1955), pp. 303-409.

Brown, James, "First a Person, Then a Teacher," *Educational Leadership*, Vol. 13 (February, 1956), pp. 299-302.

COREY, Stephen M., "Interpersonal Relations and the Work of the School," *Baltimore Bulletin of Education* (March-June, 1952), pp. 16-22.

JERSILD, Arthur T., *When Teachers Face Themselves* (New York, Bureau of Publications, Teachers College, Columbia University, 1955).

LEONARD, George B., Jr., "What Is a Teacher?" *Look,* Vol. 20, No. 4 (February 21, 1956), pp. 29-39.

MCAULEY, J. D., "Qualities of a Good Teacher," *Peabody Journal of Education,* Vol. 32 (July, 1954), pp. 22-25.

MASSEI, Renato, "Desirable Traits of Successful Teachers," *Journal of Teacher Education,* Vol. 2 (December, 1951), pp. 291-294.

MITCHELL, Morris R., "The Whole Teacher in a Divided World," *Childhood Education,* Vol. 30 (February, 1954), pp. 267-269.

MOUSTAKES, Clark E., *The Teacher and the Child* (New York, McGraw-Hill Book Company, Inc., 1956).

National Commission on Teacher Education and Professional Standards, *The Teacher and Professional Organizations* (Washington, D.C., The Commission, 1956).

SHARPE, D. Louise, ed., *Why Teach?* (New York, Henry Holt & Company, 1957).

WILES, Kimball, "When Is a Teacher Mature?" *Educational Leadership,* Vol. 8 (May, 1951), pp. 493-496.

ZIRBES, Laura, "Teachers for Today's Schools: A Symposium," *Educational Leadership,* Vol. 10 (December, 1952), pp. 152-156.

RELATIONSHIPS WITH THE CHILD

Every child is unique! Not a new concept but often one more verbalized than understood! Only through a study of children can a teacher really know children and learn to plan effectively for their development.

Child study today is becoming a specialized field touching on many other fields and using many approaches and methods. Its immediate importance to the professional teacher lies in the information and understanding it gives her for the guidance of individual children and of groups.

Many helps in child study are available to the teacher. Organized programs called the Child Study Programs are offered in all areas of the country under the direction of the University of Maryland specialist, Dr. Daniel Prescott, and his staff. Much research and publication is carried on in this field of child study. A helpful reference to students, teachers, and school staffs is that developed by the Commission on

Teacher Education.[8] Supervisors, principles, and child specialists in the school systems assist teachers in this activity. In addition to these many avenues of help, the teacher has two major approaches to use in getting to know her class group well. These are: (*1*) observation, and (*2*) records.

Observation

The classroom teacher of young children has many different relations with the children assigned to her group. She has an excellent opportunity to observe and study the child in his whole personality pattern. Such observation, interpreted in terms of her scientific training in child development, gives her the guides she needs in planning for the children's learning experiences and for their further growth.

The observations of a child or group may be formal (scheduled) or informal. Many opportunities for the latter offer themselves during the course of a normal school day. The child may be observed in the classroom in individual activity, small group activity, or in relation to peers in a class project. He may be studied as he plays on the playground. Relationships to siblings and parents in the home or during parent visits to school offer other possiblities for observation. Getting to know the child in both the home and school situation is important; sometimes his reactions at home and school differ greatly.

It is important for valid observation that the teacher has created a wholesome learning environment in which the child feels secure and free; it is further absolutely necessary that the teacher appreciate and accept all children as worthy of respect and capable of making a contribution to group living. Assuming this, the teacher can observe each child and come to know his intricate and unique pattern of personality, his needs, and his abilities. Then such knowledge is supplemented by information regarding the child in his family, home, and community.

An excellent outline for the study of children is available in the Teacher Education Commission publication cited above.[9] It covers:

1. Organic factors that influence growth, development, and behavior
   a. Health: disease, history, corrected and uncorrected defects, nutrition, health habits

---

[8] Commission on Teacher Education, *Helping Teachers Understand Children* (Washington, D.C., American Council on Education, 1945).
[9] *Ibid.,* pp. 431-432.

      b. Characteristic rate of energy output: quality of physical endurance and recovery from fatigue

      c. Growth history: present maturity level and rate of growth

      d. Skill in managing body: physical attractiveness

2. Relationships to others, social roles, and family status

      a. Social roles of family members in the community

      b. Interpersonal relations within the family, past and present

      c. Child's interaction and relations with peers

      d. Child's interaction and relations with adults outside the family

3. The child as a developing self

      a. Conceptions about physical and social processes; his attitudes toward them

      b. Conceptions of aesthetic and ethical principles; his attitudes toward them

      c. Skill in using symbols in thinking and communication

      d. Patterns of emotional behavior; situations that evoke them

      e. Common dense mechanisms

      f. Present adjustment patterns

      g. Developmental history and present developmental tasks

      h. Basic evaluation of self as a physical being, an object of love, a social being, and a "self"

      i. Values and aspirations

4. Summary: the child's major assets and needs

      a. As a physical being

      b. As to personal relations with others

      c. As to social roles

      d. As to experience, knowledge, and skills

      e. As to attitudes, values, and aspirations

      f. As to his evaluation of himself

      g. In relation to his adjustment problems and developmental tasks

Records

Records are an important help to the teacher in getting to know the children for the purpose of guidance. The form and content of records differ somewhat in the various school systems but in general cover the same basic material and data.

Kawin lists the general characteristics of a good record system. She states:[10]

Although the criteria for satisfactory records may vary in different kinds of situations and for different objectives, there are general characteristics which apply to most good record systems. These are:

[10] National Society for the Study of Education, *Early Childhood Education,* 46th Yearbook, Part II (Chicago, University of Chicago Press, 1947), pp. 283-284.

1. That an individual cumulative record (preferably a record folder) be started for every child upon his entrance to a school or child care group.
2. That such records be simple, accurate, and not too difficult to maintain.
3. That most of them be readily available to teachers but that certain types of information be kept in special, confidential files available only to special personnel.
4. That the record be cumulative, extending from preschool through high school or college, transferred (at least in summary form) from school to school when the child transfers.
5. That records should present as complete a picture as possible of the child and his environment.
6. That records should show a broad picture of the child in relation to his own capacity and growth, in relation to the group of which he is a member, and in relation to children of his age in general.
7. That *facts* and *opinions* should be distinguished from each other in the record.
8. That the records should be, on the whole, uniform through a school system, so that a comparable picture of the child is shown from year to year.
9. That data gathered in individual records should *constantly function* in the guidance of the individual child.
10. That records should be used to help parents as well as teachers and others who have the responsibility for the care and guidance of a child to understand the child. (That does not imply that records should actually be shown to parents.)

The Cumulative Record. The cumulative record is one form of record that is nationally accepted and is kept by most school systems. It is a comprehensive recording of information begun at the nursery school or kindergarten preschool roundup or at least at the time of the child's school entry. Its purpose is a continuous and growing summary of data concerning the individual child; such data is immediately useful to the teacher and the staff in planning for the child's personal and academic growth. It is a confidential file used only for professional purposes by those directly concerned with the child involved. In some school systems such files are kept by the teacher; in others, they are filed in the principal's office and checked out by personnel as needed.

The kinds of information contained in the cumulative record vary a little from system to system. Los Angeles, California, and Webster

Groves, Missouri, have developed excellent record forms. In general, the information on such records concerns:

Personal and family data: child's name, birth date, birth place, proof of birth date and location (as through birth certificate registration), sex, and race; name, birth date, birth place, race, religion, occupation and education of each parent; marital status of parents, languages spoken, residence, names of siblings, and like information. Community backgrounds are also noted.

Medical record: a complete health record of the child giving physical examinations, dates, results, illnesses, follow-up action if any, and the like. The medical history of the family is also noted.

School record and progress: levels attended, record of attendance, progress, and problems.

Test data: records on mental ability, achievement, personality rating, and social growth.

Other: some forms include personality and social record in detail; curriculum experiences and units at each school level; data on social experiences and opportunities outside the school; photographs of the child at each age level and of class groups.

In addition to individual city cumulative record forms, various state cumulative forms are widely used. An excellent illustration of such a form is the California Cumulative Record (Kg. through Grade 14) which is used throughout most of the State. Information data is comparable to that illustrated above. Manuals of use in keeping such records accompany the forms.

Anecdotal Records. Anecdotal records are also included in the cumulative folders. These are objective descriptions of the child's behavior written by teachers as a further index to the understanding of the child and his behavior patterns, and as a guide to planning for further growth. Only to the extent that such a record is *objective* is it of value.

Prescott, of the Child Study Movement, describes the characteristics of a good anecdote as follows:[11]

Observing behavior with the idea of writing an anecdote about it changes the teacher's mental set, alters the way he views the behavior of a child, and thereby alters his perceptions. Discriminating the essential components of the anecdote he will write, enables the teacher to be objective, and to forget his feelings of being helped or hindered by the child.

[11] Daniel Prescott, *The Child in the Educative Process* (New York, McGraw-Hill Book Company, 1957), pp. 113-114.

The characteristics of a good anecdote are:

1. It gives the date, the place, and the situation in which the action occurred. We call this the setting.
2. It describes the actions of the child, the reactions of the other people involved, and the response of the child to these reactions.
3. It quotes what is said to the child and by the child during the action.
4. It supplies "mood cues"—postures, gestures, voice qualities, and facial expressions that give cues to how the child felt. It does not provide interpretations of his feelings, but only the cues by which a reader may judge what they were.
5. The description is extensive enough to cover the episode. The action or conversation is not left incomplete and unfinished but is followed through to a point where a little vignette of a behaviorial moment in the life of a child is supplied.

Anecdotes may concern any one of a number of incidents such as peer relationships, emotional problems, family status, changes of problems in the home, and the like.

Study of Social Growth. Social growth is studied through *sociometric techniques* which are devices designed to give insight into the social structure of the class or group, the interaction within the peer group, and the place of the individual in the group.

Sociometric techniques prove more useful with older children than with younger, though they may be beneficially used toward the end of the early elementary program. One of the commonly used techniques is the sociogram. Through determining individual preferences for other members of the group as learning, play, or social partners, the teacher secures data which enables her to chart or picture graphically the small groups, friendship preferences, the much-liked children, and the isolates, and thus to understand more clearly the relationships and rapport between class or group members. This affords still another method for study of children—but it is only one means and must be supplemented by others. The booklet published by the Horace Mann-Lincoln Institute of School Experimentation entitled, *How to Construct a Sociogram*,[12] gives a clear and detailed description of this process. Again, we note that because of the flexibility of the young child's preferences, this technique is not recommended for use below second grade.

---

[12] Horace Mann-Lincoln Institute of School Experimentation, *How to Construct a Sociogram* (New York, Bureau of Publications, Teachers College, Columbia University, 1951).

Observation of the child in many situations and in interaction with his peer group seems to be the more satisfactory and effective way of recognizing social interrelatedness among the children four to seven years of age. However, some measures, such as the *Vineland Social Maturity Scale*,[13] are a help to the teacher working with children of nursery school and kindergarten age.

GUIDE TO REFERENCES FOR FURTHER STUDY

BARUCH, Dorothy, *Understanding Young Children* (New York, Bureau of Publications, Teachers College, Columbia University, 1953).

California State Department of Education, *California Cumulative Record Kindergarten through Grade 14,* and *Manual* (Sacramento, The Department).

Commission on Teacher Education, *Helping Teachers Understand Children* (Washington, D.C., American Council on Education, 1945).

CUNNINGHAM, Ruth, and others, *Understanding Group Behavior of Boys and Girls* (New York, Bureau of Publications, Teachers College, Columbia University, 1951).

DRISCOLL, Gertrude, *How to Study the Behavior of Children,* rev. ed. (New York, Bureau of Publications, Teachers College, Columbia University, 1954).

MILLARD, Cecil V., and ROTHNEY, John, *The Elementary School Child: A Book of Cases* (New York, Henry Holt & Company, Inc., 1957).

National Committee on Cumulative Records, *Handbook of Cumulative Records* (Washington, D.C., Government Printing Office, 1945).

PRESCOTT, Daniel, *The Child in the Educative Process* (New York, McGraw-Hill Book Company, 1957).

REDL, Fritz, *Teachers Study Their Children* (Washington, D.C., American Council on Education, 1940).

TABA, Hilda, and others, *Diagnosing Human Relation Needs* (Washington, D.C., American Council on Education, 1955).

TORGERSON, Theodore L., *Studying Children* (New York, The Dryden Press, Inc., 1947).

RELATIONSHIPS WITH PARENTS AND COMMUNITY

The teacher of young children plays a key role in the establishment and furtherance of home-school relations. The parents of the young

[13] Edgar A. Doll, *The Vineland Social Maturity Scale* (Minneapolis, Educational Test Bureau, 1947).

child are often experiencing their first school contacts as adults at the time of the child's entry and their interest is keener and more intense at this time than it will be at a later date. The early elementary teacher, in her responsibility for beginning the parents' orientation to the school and for laying groundwork for parent-child-school-community relationships, recognizes that the school is only one of the many forces and agencies working for the development of the child and that the school program begins by supplementing home education. Hence, she knows that it is extremely important for her effective guidance of the child that she understand his parents, home, and community. The young child brings to school in his personality and growth pattern his home background and experiences. Understanding of the school and its objectives by the parents is equally important.

The teacher makes every effort to help the parents through friendliness and understanding; through sound information on the need for public education, its provision for learning experiences for young children, and the kinds of programs provided; through guidance on specific and individual problems; and often in parent education work. Her co-operation and guidance increase the parents' confidence in their own guidance of the child. She uses every opportunity to reach parents through preschool roundups (see Chapter 1), parent handbooks, home visits, mothers' clubs, parent organizations, workshops, conferences, and use of community. All become avenues of meeting the needs of parents in her immediate group. In these relationships the teacher needs the ability to meet parents well and to see problems from their point of view as well as in the educational perspective. She must be able to communicate with them in a common, lay terminology and to suggest well-written parent educational materials for their use. An illustration of such materials are those by Jenkins and Baruch (see general bibliography). She keeps in mind that her function is to guide and help, not to "tell" or "give solutions" to problems.

In all these contacts and through her pupils, who "love" school, the teacher becomes an effective public relations agent for education; she wins the understanding, support, and co-operation of the parents for the school program.

The teacher's role in relations with parent and community is two-fold: (1) as a teacher, and (2) as a citizen. The two roles are interrelated since both are concerned with the improvement of individuals in their environment. Consideration of this dual role follows.

The Role as Teacher

The teacher in her professional role contributes through parent education, and through interaction with the community as a staff member of a community-centered school.

Parent Education. Parent education work for teachers of young children usually involves the teaching and guiding of parent groups in child growth and related problems of family living. Programs are based on the immediate needs and interests of the groups involved; objectives, plans and methods used, resources involved, and evaluation for future planning all depend on such needs.

Various types of programs exist. Parent education programs are organized under the sponsorship of the Parent Teacher Association. Teachers may be called upon to serve as consultants or speakers; in other cases they assist with the planning and guiding of such programs. Mothers' Clubs are another parent education activity. In many schools the kindergarten mothers meet once or twice a month for study under the guidance of the kindergarten teacher. Common problems concerning the growth and behavior patterns of five-year-olds are studied and discussed. This offers the kindergarten teacher an excellent opportunity and method of informing parents on many basic aspects of growth and on common problems. It leaves the follow-up discussion of individual problems for parent conferences.

Child Development Center Programs offer still another excellent form of parent education. Parents in these programs combine theory work, discussion, and actual participation in the nursery school program. Examples of superior programs of this type are those in California at Long Beach and at Santa Monica. In these programs mothers enroll in Preschool Parent Education and in any other college course of their election; they attend college classes one or more mornings per week. They also spend one morning per week in participation in the nursery school program in which their children are enrolled. They help with the care of play equipment, snack and rest periods, story hour, and supervise play periods under the guidance of the regular nursery school teacher. Additional discussions each week under pro-

228

fessionally trained leaders help the parents to understand ways of working with and guiding young children. In addition, both the fathers and mothers attend a night class twice a month.

One of the highlights in the Long Beach Preschool Parent Program is the toy workshop in which the parents study and make the toys and equipment best suited to young children. This workshop terminates in a yearly "Toy Fair." Placing emphasis on creative toys and materials, the Fair displays samples made at the workshop and on the commercial market. Included are woodworking and construction equipment; manipulation and construction toys; blocks and block accessories; equipment for active play including those for sand and water play, and those for playing house and store; puppetry materials; large and small toys; and children's books and records. Publications distributed to parents concern a child's need for toys at various age levels; the choosing of toys and the kinds and makes developed in accord with educational standards and values; ideas for parent construction of equipment and toys; safety; play therapy; lists of records and books for youngsters and for parents; and information regarding further course and lecture helps for parents. The enthusiastic response to such Fairs and to the Center's Program, and the further interest motivated in parent education are evidence of their need and value.

Interaction with Community as a Staff Member of a Community-Centered School. The teacher as a member of the staff actively shows her interest in children and in all activities related to them; and she participates in all school activities designed to further school-community relations. She encourages parent participation in the school program; parents and teacher grow through planning and doing together.

For teachers of young children this usually covers activities related to: (*1*) interpretation of the program and planned learning experiences to the class parents as a whole group, in small or so-called "cottage groups," and as individuals; (*2*) evaluation of the child in individual parent conferences and reports; (*3*) encouragement of parent participation in the school program through workshops, curriculum planning, committees, commissions, and councils; and (*4*) use of the community and its resources in the learning experiences of the children. In all activities the teacher keeps in mind the readiness, needs, and interests of the immediate group or person.

229

1. Interpretation of the program. Meetings of the class parents as a group, a small group, and as individuals with the teacher have key importance in the teacher's professional work. These meetings serve four essential purposes: (*1*) opportunity for interpretation of the educational learning experiences of children to parents and community members; (*2*) a means of securing information by the teacher for use in guiding child development; (*3*) a way of involving parent interest and co-operation in the school; and (*4*) an opportunity for showing parents practical ways in which they can help.

The teacher's preparation for any of these three types of meetings should be well planned. Helps are immediately available to the teacher in staff meetings, district bulletins, school handbooks, and in the immediate guidance of her principal or supervisor. When possible, parent representatives should be included in the planning of group meetings.

In many school systems throughout the country it has become the practice for each teacher to meet with the parents of her class group during the early fall. At this time she explains the objectives of the year's program in her grade level in terms of academic and child development, displays the materials to be used, and answers questions of the parents. Handbooks, helpful in such planning, have been prepared by most school systems. An illustration of such a help is the handbook, *The Group Conference*,[14] developed by the Torrance Public Schools.

Teachers show resourcefulness in their planning for group conferences. One teacher, using an idea from the Cincinnati *Primary Manual,* made a wall chart showing the activities of the children throughout the day in order to capture parent interest and attention; another began with an actual class demonstration of an activity by the youngsters. Illustrative of talks given parents at group meetings is the following developed by Jacqueline Mulholland[15] for her kindergarten parent group.

THE WHY OF KINDERGARTEN

All over our nation the five-year-olds walk, run, and skip home from kindergarten with that happy, satisfied feeling. What happens at school that

[14] William B. Forrest, Marion G. Steele, and Lester I. Foster, *The Group Conference* (Torrance, California, Torrance Unified School District, 1957).

[15] Paper presented in the Master's Program, Long Beach State College, California (Fall, 1957).

gives them that feeling of belonging and acceptance in their world at school and at home? Is kindergarten part of the answer? Is it really necessary? To answer these questions we need to take the hand of a five-year-old child and enter with him into his world at school.

As you enter his class, take a good look at the kindergarten children. They come in varied sizes and shapes, quick to laugh and sometimes quick to cry, with imagination that can have them soaring across the skies piloting their planes, or an attention span that can plunge them into deep intent on a story. Curiosity that never lessens plus energy that can run circles around you—this is a five-year-old. How do you cope with these amazing children? How do you guide them? Look at the needs of kindergarten children . . . herein lies the answer.

Intellectually, the five-year-old is brimming over with interest in investigation. He wants to know about the things that he sees in pictures, books, and in his everyday environment; and he wants an answer that will satisfy him. To feel, to touch, to explore, and to experiment along with an opportunity to do things for himself are necessary for him to develop a feeling of self-confidence and satisfaction. His intellectual needs demand opportunities to participate in a variety of activities, and a chance to change from one interest to another as the attention span is short. Above all, he needs a meaningful background of experience which gives him an understanding of the world in which he lives.

Socially the five-year-old needs children his own age to work and play with him. He needs a chance to learn to be a part of the peer group, to meet children with different personalities and different backgrounds, and to give as well as to take. His social nature demands that he be not only a member of the group but one accepted by the group as having something to offer. As much as he needs this chance to be with other children, he also needs time to do things for and by himself.

Physically the young child needs a daily routine of both work and relaxation. He needs many opportunities to be active indoors as well as outdoors. Playground apparatus, large balls, outdoor blocks, and rhythms help him to develop his large muscles and coordination; woodworking tools, small blocks of different sizes and shapes, scissors for cutting, and art materials help him develop small muscles and coordination.

Emotionally the kindergarten child needs to find in his school environment affection and a feeling of belonging. Routine adds to his security, while consistency from adults helps him progress in socially acceptable behavior. Above all, he needs praise and encouragement. When he has a happy outlook, then he can turn his attention to learning.

Parents certainly supply many of these needs as they have been teachers of their children in the important days and months since birth; however, there are some needs that can only be supplied by a group situation such as is found in the kindergarten. By looking at one activity in the kindergarten program such as indoor block play, we can see an illustration of how the educational experiences are designed to meet needs and help the child grow.

As the children sit and plan what they will build with the blocks on a particular day they are learning to work in a group. They have an opportunity to express themselves before others and to listen carefully when another child shares his experiences. During this time the teacher has an opportunity to stimulate their thinking and to make concepts more meaningful by showing pictures and discussing the particular social studies unit they are studying. As the children build with blocks they can carry out the plans that they have made, noticing the likenesses and differences in the block shapes, experimenting in building, and meeting small difficulties and problems that arise. During the evaluation period when the group meets together again to talk about what they have done, the children share their activities and bring up problems that occurred, and review the standards set by the group for this type of work at the beginning of the year. During clean-up time, the children remember to put the toys away first, then the blocks. They help make the room neat and orderly before they return to the rug for a short discussion of their work that day.

One of the major values of block play is the experience which grows out of studying a particular unit. When the need arises the children have an opportunity to take various trips to their local grocery store, drug store, bakery, fire station, and post office. If these experiences are meaningful the child loves to talk about what he saw, what he did, how things looked, and how he felt. The child's own experience is the basis for his learning for these experiences give him a background of concepts and a fund of information essential for the interpretation of reading in the first grade.

In summary, we could say that indoor block play meets the needs of children intellectually, socially, physically, and emotionally. Intellectually the activity increases vocabulary, gives a background of meaningful experiences, gives opportunity for experimentation with blocks, clarifies concepts in his here-and-now world, offers opportunity for expression of ideas and growth in poise, and develops good work habits involving completion of work, willingness to work to capacity, ability to follow directions, and opportunity to do problematic thinking. Socially the activity gives the child an opportunity to learn to work and play and share with others, and to listen while others speak.

Physically the activity provides a routine with a balance of activity and quiet time, and it helps in the development of coordination of muscles through manipulation. Finally, emotionally the child is provided an atmosphere that has routine and security, an acceptance of him, and offers him a chance to feel wanted and a part of the group.

Indoor play is just one part of the kindergarten curriculum. As shown, this activity is based on the need of five-year-old children; so are all other facets of the program: the science, numbers, literature, music, language, physical education, outdoor play, and art work. Every five-year-old should be given the advantage of attending kindergarten not only because his growth phase demands it, but also because with the background of a successful year, he can move easily and with security and anticipation into the first grade for another year that is exciting and satisfying.

Meetings with small numbers of parents from time to time to supplement the general group sessions and give more opportunity for teachers and parents to become better acquainted and to work on a more individual basis. Torrance Unified School District uses this technique in so-called "cottage meetings"; five or six mothers and the kindergarten teacher meet at one of the homes for discussion, film or filmstrip viewing, use of materials, and study concerning the learning experiences of the children. The social and relaxed setting is an excellent background for working together.

Interpretation of the program to parents is done through individual parent-teacher conferences (see next section), and through parent visits to the child's classroom. It is the teacher's responsibility to see that the parent be made to feel wanted and welcome; too, the teacher should, if possible, be available to answer questions after the children are dismissed. One system has prepared a mimeographed four-page folder for parents; it serves to stimulate interest in visitation and to give information regarding visits which makes the parent feel more at ease. (See pp. 236-239.)

2. Evaluation. Evaluation is an important and continuing part of the teaching-learning process. It is[16]

the process of gathering and weighing evidence which will reveal changes in the behavior of pupils as they progress through school. It is an integral part of education and is important because it focuses on the goals of education. Changes in behavior include all phases in the life of the learner. Evaluation is concerned not only with growth in the basic skills, the traditional "three R's," but also with growth in the attitudes and knowledge needed for effective living in our American society.

Evaluation, then, is much broader in connotation than grading or reporting. It involves a total picture of the child's behavior from many

[16] California State Department of Education, *Evaluating Pupil Progress,* Vol. 21, No. 6 (Sacramento, The Department, April, 1952).

sources such as records, child study, and study of the child's reactions to classroom and outside situations. Reporting, which at one time implied only academic grading, is directly concerned with indicating to a parent the child's progress in academic and personality growth. At the present time reporting is done both through personal conferences and in written reports.

How do you evalute? Rothney, in his research report, states:[17]

. . . you will decide what important changes you are trying to produce in pupils. You will state how those changes may be expected to be shown in pupil's behavior and you will measure the changes that take place. You will then study and interpret the observed changes so that your reports will be meaningful to the pupil himself, to his parents, and to anyone who wants to know what progress a particular pupil is making.

When do you evaluate? This, too, is best answered through Rothney's report. He states:[18]

. . . evaluation is a continuous process and an integral part of instruction. . . . Evidence of accomplishment, growth, and development are needed throughout the whole school year so that the classroom teachers may see that progress is being made toward the objectives. . . . We must be alert to recognize readiness when it appears lest we lose the golden opportunities when pupils are eager to learn. As classroom teachers, we must recognize lack of readiness, too, lest we require the pupil to study something too soon and actually set him back so that he does not learn it at the usual time. With a plan for continuous evaluation we are more likely to identify readiness (or lack of it) than we are when we depend upon chance.

. . . Progress must be observed and recorded when it occurs. . . . New patterns of behavior or retrogressions to past patterns need to be evaluated so that action may be taken upon them at the right time. . . . Evaluation should provide a moving picture rather than a snapshot of pupil development.

Who should evaluate? Rothney continues:[19]

Ultimately the responsibility for evaluation falls upon those who teach. Parents may assist and pupils may contribute to the process. . . . Evaluation may be the cooperative product of several teachers, pupils, parents, counselors, . . . visiting teachers, physicians, school nurses, . . . in fact,

[17] John W. M. Rothney, *Evaluating and Reporting Pupil Progress,* What Research Says to the Teacher Series, No. 7 (Washington, D.C., The National Education Association, 1955), p. 6.

[18] *Ibid.,* pp. 25-26.

[19] *Ibid.,* pp. 26-27.

any persons who have had sufficient opportunity to observe the pupil. . . . Pooled data have generally (but not without exception) been found to be more valid than information from single sources. . . . All these findings suggest, then, that evaluating and reporting a pupil's development will be more effective if all those who have had sufficient opportunity to observe him have the responsibility of reporting their observations.

Reporting to parents is done through parent conferences and written report cards.

The teacher-parent conference is being used increasingly in most school systems; it has many advantages over the written form. Through personal contact the teacher is able to learn much about the child and his background; hence, the conference is a source of child study. It further offers the teacher a direct means of helping and guiding the parent, and through him the child. It deepens the home-school rapport, which in turn has a favorable effect on the child; it deepens the parent's understanding of the child; it wins parent co-operation in setting plans and expectations for their child; and it improves school-parent relations.

The preparation of the teacher for any parent conference requires intelligent planning. All information she has on the child and on the parents and home situation should be reviewed. Samples of the child's work should be made ready for the parent to see in folder or similar form. Anticipated questions regarding program and school policy should be considered; possible avenues of guiding the parent should be thought out; and usable materials and references provided in case they are needed. The child should know of the conference and be helped to look forward to the parent's visit. In turn, the parent should be made to feel that the conference is a friendly, helpful meeting with someone deeply interested in his child. The beginning teacher has to be certain that during her first experiences in conference work she uses specific illustrations rather than generalities in her evaluations, and that she avoids "professional lingo."

Conferences during the year or longer that a teacher works with an individual parent should be progressive; the first might be a get-acquainted session, the others building and planning sessions, and the last an evaluation, and a looking forward to continuing work with the child's next teacher.

Planning A Visit to Your Child's Classroom

Torrance Unified School District
Torrance, California

INTRODUCTION

Have you ever thought, "I'd like to visit my child's room, but I never know when to go or what to do when I get there."? If so, you are not the only one - other parents feel the same as you do.

We encourage you to visit your child's classroom and we encourage you to confer with the teacher and principal.

This brochure may answer some of your questions and encourage you to look in on a Torrance classroom in action.

GETTING READY FOR A VISIT

As a matter of interest - but not required - why not drop the teacher a note asking about a good time to visit - or ask to observe a specific lesson such as reading, arithmetic, social studies, etc.?

Time your visits for twenty minutes to a maximum of forty minutes, at any one time. Two such visits will be more informative than one prolonged visit.

Pre-school children should be brought to school on special invitation only. Normally we do not have personnel to handle them.

The object of your visit might be to observe your own child as he works in the group or just to see a modern classroom at work.

THE VISIT ITSELF

Stop in the principal's office so the school is aware of your presence. Upon entering the classroom introduce yourself to the teacher and find a chair.

Avoid unnecessary conversation.

In general, a good time to terminate your visit is at the end of a particular lesson or at recess time.

AFTER THE VISIT

Do you have questions about your child's school
  work?

Do you have questions about how your child is
  getting along with other children?

Do you have questions about the school program
  in general?

Why not arrange a conference with the teacher?

Naturally, it is not possible for the teacher to
  confer with you during the time she is responsible for the entire class - that is, during
  school hours. To have sufficient time to discuss your child's progress, please schedule a
  conference with the teacher at a time convenient
  to both of you.

WE HOPE YOU ENJOYED YOUR VISIT.

PLEASE COME AGAIN SOON

D'Evelyn has developed a manual on parent conferences for teachers of young children; it is unexcelled in helps and illustrations. It should be a must in your reading. At the conclusion of her manual, D'Evelyn lists general guides for teacher-parent conferences which are worthy of much thought. They follow:[20]

Not forgetting that each parent is unique in his personality and his problems, it may be helpful to list a few guides to conferences in general.

1. Responsibility for the success or failure of a conference rests primarily with the teacher. It is well to remember that success is relative, and each conference must be judged according to its own circumstances and results.

2. It is well to arrange for no interruptions during a conference. Nothing is more disturbing to the serious efforts of trying to think through a problem than to be interrupted at a crucial moment.

3. It is easier to build a cooperative relationship if the teacher is not seated behind a desk. Behind a desk the teacher is in the place of authority, not partnership.

4. The teacher's greeting should be friendly and relaxed. If he is hurried or tense, the parent will know it. It is difficult to discuss a problem with someone who looks as if he wished you were not there, or would leave soon.

5. Listen, and then listen some more. The teacher did not invite the parent to deliver a lecture to him, but to get, as well as to give, help. Encourage the parent to talk, and then listen to what he has to say.

6. Find out how the parent is thinking and feeling about his child. This is important because the teacher cannot understand the child's behavior until he knows the parent attitude.

7. If a parent says he is worried about his child's behavior, follow through. Find out why he is worried. The teacher should not assume that he knows why. He and the parent may not feel the same way about the child.

8. If a parent gives what he thinks is the reason for a child's behavior, accept it, and lead the discussion on to the consideration of other possible causes. Behavior is the result of many causative factors, not one.

9. If a parent suggests a plan of action, accept it if it is at all possible to do so. It is better for the parent to try it than for the teacher to force one of his own. One of the goals . . . is to get the parent to take the initiative. If the parent's plan fails, it is always possible to suggest others that may strike nearer to the root of the difficulty.

10. If a parent cannot suggest reasons for a child's behavior, or plans of action to deal with it, the teacher might suggest alternatives for joint con-

[20] Katherine E. D'Evelyn, *Individual Parent-Teacher Conferences: A Manual for Teachers of Young Children* (New York, Bureau of Publications, Teachers College, Columbia University, 1952), pp. 95-97.

240

sideration. "This might be a possibility What do you think? You know all the facts of the situation better than I do." Or, "We might try this and see what happens. It may take us a while to find out the source of the difficulty." Such an approach makes the parent a participator in the final decision for tentative plans, and leads to discussion that helps him accept the plan as his own.

11. It does not help to argue with a parent. Arguing will arouse resentment and resistance.

12. It is better not to assume that a parent wants help or advice. Such an assumption usually brings resistance, because it implies a form of criticism.

13. Most parents cannot be objective about their own children. Therefore, do not critcize, either directly or indirectly. Criticism is fatal to the building of a cooperative relationship.

14. Avoid giving direct advice when the parent gives a statement of his problem and then leans back, saying, "Tell me what to do." Let any advice or suggestions grow out of mutual discussion and a growing insight on the part of the parent into the reasons for the behavior.

15. Do not get ahead of the parent in his thinking. In other words, the teacher should not try to push his thinking onto a parent before the parent is ready to see it through a process of discussion and mutual thinking.

16. Try to be aware of sensitive spots, and avoid embarrassing the parent by noting facial expressions, gestures, and voice. These all give a clue to the parent's emotion.

17. Be accepting. That is, accept anything the parent tells you without showing surprise or disapproval. If the teacher cannot do this, he will not get an honest picture of the parent's attitudes and feelings.

18. The teacher should be ready to recognize problems that are so difficult as to prevent him from giving sufficient help to the parent. Parents with complex emotional problems should be referred to the consulting psychologist or guidance specialist on the staff, who in turn will refer the individual to a psychiatrist if there is such need. . . .

19. It is helpful to try to close the conference on a constructive, a pleasant, or a forward-going note, such as plan for further consultation, a definite date for the next conference, a statement of encouragement or reassurance, a statement of a plan for cooperative action.

Records of the conference, written during or after, should be made. Data should include the date and the personnel of the conference, the points discussed, and the recommendations made. In some systems such records are made during the conference and the parent is given a carbon to take with him; in others, the record is made after the close of the conference and is confidential.

The report card, the written report to the parent, is the traditional form of reporting. Today, most schools continue this report form two, four, or six times a year even though the parent conference technique is used. A few systems use only the parent conference, having discontinued written reports. An excellent and useful study of reporting practices was made by the Office of Education. (It can be obtained by writing Dr. Gertrude Lewis[21] and requesting Brief 34.)

The form and appearance of the newer report forms differ from those used formerly. The uncolored single sheet, listing numerical grades and requiring a parent's signature, has been replaced in most systems by a colorful, four-page folder containing a message to parents, often a note regarding the program, evaluation of academic progress, data giving a picture of the child's total development, teacher's comments, and space for the parent's signature and request for a conference. Some systems use letters from the teacher as reports.

The report form today is usually developed with parent participation. Teachers, administrators, and parents co-operatively develop it. Usually report forms differ somewhat in the early elementary and upper elementary levels.

All report forms are a part of the evaluation process; evaluation (see page 233) is the total study of the child's behavior while the report card and conference are the means of keeping the parent informed on the child's total progress. Examples of outstanding report forms may be found on pages 347-414.

3. Parent participation in the school program. Parents are increasingly being involved in the school program under good professional leadership. In a democratic form of society such as ours, professional leadership with lay participation is the ideal way for us to arrive at improved and functional school programs. Illustrations of such participation throughout our country are many; a few are selected for presentation here to give an idea of the forms such participation may take (that is, beyond the teacher-parent conferences, co-operatively developed report forms, and teacher-parent education groups already cited).

Workshops for parents are becoming popular. In some areas primary teachers and supervisors are meeting with parents in workshops to develop materials for use in the children's classrooms. Not only does

[21] G. L. Lewis, *Reporting Pupil Progress to Parents,* Brief 34 (Washington, D.C., Office of Education, 1957).

this give the teacher help in the preparation of materials, but it also gives her an opportunity to acquaint the mothers and fathers with the kinds and purposes of such materials, to encourage and guide them in the types of outside materials and helps they can give their children, and to establish an excellent rapport.

Curriculum involvement of parents is widely practiced. In 1946 the ASCD (NEA) publication entitled *Laymen Help Plan the Curriculum*[22] gave national help and direction to such procedures. Strong professional guidance combined with lay participation definitely has improved curriculum planning. Illustration of this procedure through state direction is seen in the following paragraph.

In 1952-53 the Illinois school systems carried on a Curriculum Program Consensus Study[23] that had been planned and developed by professional educators from the State University, the State Department of Education, and the various levels of the school system personnel along with lay representatives from the State Association of School Boards and the State Congress of Parents and Teachers. The purpose of the study was:[24]

. . . to help parents and teachers accomplish three things:

1. To come to an agreement concerning what parents and teachers *should be doing together* in the development of a better school program.
2. To come to an agreement concerning the things parents and teachers *want to start working upon together* in order to better the school's program.
3. *To work out your own plan* for cooperation and to devise ways that parents and teachers may work together most effectively in the development of better school programs.

The Study consisted of three separate questionnaires: (*1*) "What do you think about parents and teachers working together for better schools?"; (*2*) "What kind of parent-teacher co-operation should we strengthen in our schools?"; and (*3*) "How can parents and teachers organize to improve the school's program?"

[22] Association for Supervision and Curriculum Development, *Layman Help Plan the Curriculum* (Washington ,D.C., The Association, 1946).

[23] Illinois State Department of Education, *Illinois Curriculum Program Consensus Study No. 8,* Inventory A, B, and C. (Springfield, Superintendent of Public Instruction, State of Illinois, June, 1952).

[24] *Ibid.,* Inventory A., p. 3.

Teachers were specifically defined in the Study as:[25]

Teacher: any school person who is directly and professionally concerned with the education of children. Besides classroom teachers, it should be taken to include such persons as principals, superintendents, supervisors, counselors, and school psychologists.

Teacher also includes those directly concerned with the education of children and youth regardless of the level of that education, whether nursery, kindergarten, elementary, secondary, or post-secondary as long as they are a part of the school system.

The Study defined the phrase "working together":[26]

The basic idea in this study is that parents and teachers should work together in building the understandings and relationships that will lead to a better school program. It is an attempt to help them find ways of working together more effectively in a cooperative approach to the problem of improving the local school system. This study will help you in making decisions concerning the things that parents and teachers might work upon cooperatively in improving the school's program. It may help you in making these decisions to keep in mind the distinction between 1) *what* schools do to help young people and the community and 2) *how* they do it. Parents are intimately concerned with what the school should be doing—the purposes, objectives, extent, etc. of the school program. Decisions about *how* these purposes and objectives are to be accomplished (how they are to be put into action) are, of course, the professional responsibility of the teachers and other school persons.

The inventories were filled out by parents and teachers but not signed. Inventory A, when completed, was tabulated and used by each local group in its discussion of whether the school felt teachers and parents should work together. Then Inventory B was completed and followed by group discussion regarding what problems were to be selected to begin the work. Inventory C concerned possible ways of working together on problems selected in B. Suggested ways included: panel discussion, interview meetings, demonstration meetings, debates, open forums, symposium meetings, lectures, meetings using audio-visual aids, parent-teacher discussion groups, and parent-teacher action study groups. Operating rules[27] were set for parent-teacher co-operation.

[25] *Ibid.,* p. 4.
[26] *Ibid.,* p. 5.
[27] See *ibid.,* Inventory C., pp. 8-9.

Citizen commissions and councils also participate with the profession in the improvement of schools. One important group is the National Citizens Commission for the Public Schools, organized to develop "popular interest in the public schools." State and local organizations exist as commissions co-operating with those on the national level.

More familiar to most students, however, will be parent participation through Parent-Teacher Associations; these, too, have local, state, and national groups. They also publish a journal for parents.

4. *Use of community and its resources in the learning experiences of children.* Parent-teacher-community participation is also prominent in the educational picture through the use of community agencies and resources. (See Chapter 8.) A very useful list of all community agencies, their locations, and the kinds of services they offer may be mentioned here. It is available in *Childhood Education,* Vol. 28 (March, 1952), pp. 297-304.

The Role as Citizen

The teacher in her role as citizen should know and study the community—its needs, problems, and goals. It is each teacher's responsibility to be an effective teacher-citizen: helping organize and sponsor groups when possible, contributing to groups and knowing the contributions and interests of others, and serving on planning councils and groups are all part of her job.

The NEA statement of the "teacher as a citizen"[28] effectively summarizes this concept.

Every teacher is a teacher of citizenship. Good citizenship for the teacher means not only that good citizenship qualities inherent in any teaching or supervisory position are always stressed by example of teacher as well as activities of class, but that, as an adult citizen of the community, the teacher assumes at least his equal proportion of citizenship responsibility. . . .

In the 1957 NEA research study summary[29] regarding teachers and their citizenship and community activities we find:

[28] "Teachers Are Citizens," *National Education Association Journal,* Vol. 41 (November, 1952), pp. 504-505.
[29] Research Division, NEA, *The Status of the American Public-School Teacher,* Research Bulletin, Vol. 25, No. 1 (Washington, D.C., The National Educational Association, February, 1957), pp. 32-33.

An impressive record in character-building and social-civic groups is presented by the teachers. They were asked about the extent of their active membership in churches and in nine types of civic, recreational, and social organizations. . . .

Overwhelming majorities of teachers were church members: 87.5% of the men and 93.1 of the women, 91.5 of the total. Figures in *The World Almanac* show that total church membership in 1955 equaled 60.9% of the *total* population. . . . More than a fourth of the teachers were helping in church educational programs. . . .

The five most popular community organizations (besides the church) were lodges and related groups (social); health and social welfare groups; cultural and recreational groups; business and professional service and civic-social clubs; and religious-social youth building groups. Many teachers are fulfilling their civic responsibilities!

RELATIONSHIPS WITH THE WORLD

The average citizen of today is of necessity concerned with the world and its cultures and daily happenings; the teacher, in her professional role, must be even more concerned. She must understand and appreciate the different cultures and problems of the various peoples and how they affect our living; further, she should give leadership in developing avenues of understanding, co-operation, and language communication with these peoples.

Many opportunities are open to the teacher for development in international understanding. Travel, either individually or with professional organization tours, is one of the easiest and most possible means. Study and understanding of foreign language and cultures is helpful. Acceptance of a short term assignment as an exchange teacher through the State Department, a Fulbright Grant, the International Division of the Office of Education, or some other agency is advantageous. Working in our schools and communities with foreign visitors, exchange teachers, UNESCO activities, and other international interests is advantageous to the professional growth of the teacher, and at the same time a contribution is made to international relations. Yes, many opportunities exist to help teachers grow in understanding while serving many different groups.

PROJECTS AND QUESTIONS

1. In terms of your interest in teaching at the early elementary level survey your personal needs for growth as: a person; a professional person; and a citizen.
2. Write five anecdotal records on young children (using your observations as the source of material). Evalute these in your class group.
3. Children in the first grade participate in the following activities. What does the teacher's role as guide imply as her part in each?
   a. block play
   b. outdoor free play
   c. field trip
   d. reading class
4. How would you handle the following?
   a. a parent who insists on remaining in the kindergarten because the child cries when she leaves.
   b. a primary parent who is disturbed because he says his child complains that he "doesn't get to think, only to do what he is told."
   c. a child who has an excessive dependence on another child.
   d. an individual child who is very capable but always has to succeed and be first.
5. Begin to develop for your teaching file lists of annotated references and films useful for your work with parents.
6. Evaluate the extent and kind of professional activities you engage in as a teacher education student.
7. Differentiate the teacher's role in a traditional school and a community-centered school.

GUIDE TO REFERENCES FOR FURTHER STUDY

EVALUATION

BIXBY, P. W., "Parents and Teachers Study Report Cards," *National Elementary Principal,* Vol. 5 (September, 1945), pp. 90-92.

FOREMAN, Anna B., "A Report Card for Evaluating the Progress of the Whole Child," *Elementary School Journal,* Vol. 49 (November, 1940), pp. 195-205.

KOOKER, Earl W., and WILLIAMS, Chester S., "Standards Versus Evaluation," *Educational Administration and Supervision,* Vol. 41 (November, 1955), pp. 385-389.

MICHAELIS, John U., "Current Practices in Evaluation in City School Systems," *Educational and Psychological Measurement,* Vol. 9 (Spring, 1949), pp. 15-22.

ROTHNEY, John W. M., *Evaluating and Reporting Pupil Progress,* What Research Says to the Teacher Series, No. 7 (Washington, D.C., The National Education Association, 1955).

SHANE, Harold G., "Recent Developments in Elementary School Evaluation," *Journal of Educational Research,* Vol. 44 (March, 1951), pp. 491-506.

STRANG, Ruth, *Reporting to Parents,* rev. ed. (New York, Bureau of Publications, Teachers College, Columbia University, 1954).

TODD, M. N., "Kindergarten Report Cards," *American School Board Journal,* Vol. 112 (February, 1946), pp. 82-84.

WILES, Kimball, *Teaching for Better Schools* (Englewood Cliffs, N. J., Prentice-Hall, Inc., 1952), Chs. 9, 10.

WRIGHTSTONE, J. Wayne, "Trends in Evaluation," *Educational Leadership,* Vol. 8 (November, 1950), pp. 91-95.

PARENTS

BENNETT, Mabel C., and BISHOP, Katherine V., *Sharing and Showing: Pupils and Teachers Interpret Education Through Parent Group Conferences* (Los Angeles, Education Press, 1952).

BOSSARD, James H., *The Parent and Child* (Philadelphia, University of Pennsylvania Press, 1953).

D'EVELYN, Katherine, *Individual Parent-Teacher Conferences: A Manual for Teachers of Young Children* (New York, Bureau of Publications, Teachers College, Columbia University, 1952).

DEL SOLAR, Charlotte, *Teachers and Parents View the Child* (New York, Bureau of Publications, Teachers College, Columbia University, 1951).

Department of Elementary School Principals, *Parents and the School,* 36th Yearbook (Washington, D.C., The Department, 1957).

ELDER, Franklin L., *Explorations in Parent-School Relations* (Austin, University of Texas Press, 1954).

FOX, L., and others, *All Children Want to Learn: A Guide for Parents* (New York, Grolier Society, 1954).

FRANK, Martha, *The Challenge of Children* (New York, William Morrow Company, 1957).

GILMER, Von Haller, *How to Help Your Child Develop Successfully* (Englewood Cliffs, N. J., Prentice-Hall, Inc., 1951).

HYMES, James, *Effective Home School Relations* (Englewood Cliffs, N. J., Prentice-Hall, Inc., 1953).

LANGDON, Grace, and STOUT, Irving W., *Teacher-Parent Interviews* (Englewood Cliffs, N. J., Prentice-Hall, Inc., 1954).

LEONARD, V. E., and others, *Counseling with Parents in Early Childhood Education* (New York, The Macmillan Company, 1954).

LONSDALE, Bernard J., "Parent-Teacher Conferences: An Experience in

Human Relations," *California Journal of Elementary Education,* Vol. 24 (November, 1955), pp. 78-90.

READ, C. H., and ROBERTS, D. D., "What Parents Like in the Kindergarten Interpretation Program," *Nation's Schools,* Vol. 59 (April, 1957), pp. 50-52.

RICHARDSON, S. K., and others, "How Good School-Home-Community Relations Aid the Kindergarten Program," *California Journal of Elementary Education,* Vol. 24 (August, 1955), pp. 46-61.

SMITH, Norvel L., "Primary Schools and Home-School Relationships," *Educational Administration and Supervision,* Vol. 42 (March, 1956), pp. 129-133.

COMMUNITY

American Association of School Administrators, *Public Relations in America's Schools* (Washington, D.C., The Association, 1950).

Association for Supervision and Curriculum Development, *Laymen Help Plan the Curriculum* (Washington, D.C., The Association, 1946).

CAMPBELL, R. F., and RAMSEYER, J. A., *The Dynamics of School-Community Relationships* (New York, Allyn and Bacon, Inc., 1954).

GRINNELL, J. E., and YOUNG, Raymond J., *The School and the Community* (New York, The Ronald Press Company, 1955).

National Congress of Parents and Teachers, *101 Questions About Public Education* (Chicago, The Association, 1954).

National Society for the Study of Education, *Citizen Cooperation for Better Schools,* 53rd Yearbook, Part I (Chicago, University of Chicago Press, 1954).

———, *The Community School,* 52nd Yearbook, Part II (Chicago, University of Chicago Press, 1953).

OLSEN, Edward G., *The Modern Community School* (New York, Appleton-Century-Crofts, Inc., 1953).

———, ed., *School and Community* (Englewood Cliffs, N.J., Prentice-Hall, Inc., 1954).

REEDER, Ward, *An Introduction to Public School Relations* (New York, The Macmillan Company, 1953).

THOMAS, Maurice J., *Improving Public Education Through Citizen Participation* (Pittsburgh, University of Pittsburgh Press, 1954).

YEAGER, W., *School-Community Relations* (New York, Henry Holt & Company, Inc., 1954).

Part IV

AND NOW?

CHAPTER 11

History as Foundation of Present and Future Practices

What is past is prologue.

INTRODUCTION

Education in the United States, as indicated in Chapter 1, has no national pattern to follow in contrast to that in most of the countries of the world. The curriculum for our schools is developed in the various school systems and in the individual schools within a system. Administration and direction is centered in the individual state departments of education and in the local school systems rather than in the Federal Office of Education, and hence may vary greatly. But these variations are within the framework of basic democratic guidelines and objectives of education as described in Chapter 4.

RELATIONSHIP BETWEEN PRESENT PRACTICE AND THE PHILOSOPHY AND WORK OF EARLY LEADERS IN THE EDUCATION OF YOUNG CHILDREN

The New Is Old

Looking at the over-all picture of early elementary education with its range of variations, one may ask, Is the living and learning in the classroom of the young child today closely related to the principles and psychology of the kindergarten and primary of the past, or are the practices of today peculiar to our immediate period alone? Study of our present curriculum, which is based on a functional and ever-increasing knowledge of child growth and the psychology of how young children learn, in comparison with practices of earlier periods, gives us much opportunity for thought and professional growth.

The beginnings of our modern approaches are found in the work, thought, and philosophy of educators of the past, and relate immediately to that of educators in the so-called modern education period, which began around the early seventeenth century with Comenius, and which, during the eighteenth century, included Rousseau, Pestalozzi, and Froebel. Actual beginnings of education relate indirectly to the very early period of Plato. Analysis of the classics and the history of education indicates a strong and continuous link between the present and the past in the education of young children.

Today, we provide a program centered in the child, the subject content, and the social processes; our emphasis is on him as an individual and as a member of groups. Our learning situations are planned to meet the developmental needs of his growth and maturity level. Our curricular activities are designed to involve his home and community background experiences in order to provide psychological readiness and security in new learning and to extend his knowledge, experiences, and process skills. Our psychological method is to build from the precept to the concept through the use of stimulating environment and through multiple sense approach. Our educational goals foster the development of the whole child through curriculum living in all areas of knowledge, and in experiences developing skills in the processes.

Similarly, in a form consistent with their observations, study, and evaluations, Comenius, Rousseau, Pestalozzi, and Froebel urged that emphasis be placed on the child, and that learning situations be planned in terms of children as children and *not* as small adults. These pioneer educators of earlier periods spoke strongly for the place of interest in motivation, for the need of less rigidity and formality, for the use of play as a means of learning, and for the necessity of realizing the importance of social relationships in learning and teaching. They advocated the use of the cultural background of the child in his learning experiences and stressed that we must teach the whole individual.

In methodology they believed, as we do, in moving from precept to concept, and in the use of sense objects and firsthand experiences to teach the foundation of such concepts. There is a strong tie between early elementary education today and that of the past, as the following review of educational history will show.

FOUNDATIONS OF EARLY ELEMENTARY EDUCATION IN HISTORY

Turning our attention to the history of education we find a very satisfying and fascinating story of progress in which the history of early elementary education commands a prominent place. We do *not* see, as is sometimes assumed, that interest in the education of the young is limited to or unique to our recent period of development. Rather, the study of early elementary education, necessary for our understanding of the field and effective work in it, takes us back into the history of education in America, Europe, and even ancient Greece. Here, we find the forerunners of our present programs, the educators and philosophers of vision who laid the groundwork for the presently accepted psychology, methodology, and improvement in our programs for young children today.

We see that throughout educational history the philosophy and programs for the education of young children set the pace for improvements and changes made later in the upper levels of the elementary school and on through the educational system. This trend continues today. If we look carefully at our present-day school practices we find that it is in the education of young children that the most extensive application of recent research and psychological study has been made; later, its application extended up through the elementary school and to some degree into the secondary school and higher education. An illustration of this is seen in the concentration on child growth and developmental psychology in early elementary education; this interest has moved into the elementary school but only partially to the secondary level as a major concern. Most secondary programs and much of the work at the university level (with exception of some teacher education programs) continue in the traditional pattern of academic content advocated by subject-matter specialists.

The great classics of literature and the work of the early philosophers and educators are an important part of the background of early elementary education.

Greece

Plato (428 B.C. to 348 B.C.) was the first great writer of philosophy and education in our western civilization. He believed and taught that infancy from birth to six years of age was the most important period of education for children, and that between the ages of three and six a definite curriculum should be followed. It covered play, fairy tales, rhymes, and simple amusements. Play, he believed, was the approach to learning to use with young children (though he believed in compulsory learning for older children). Through it, he believed, we gained insight into a child's abilities. This reference to the importance of early education was developed in *The Republic,* his greatest work, and in *The Laws.* In his development of an ideal state, Plato expressed his belief in community responsibility for all education beginning with the child at birth, with emphasis on the nursery school period from three to six years. He maintained that young children at an early age are most impressionable and that these beginnings are important since they determine the directions of later growth.

Plato's writings, then, were the first in our western civilization to consider the relationship of government and education, and to point out the need for all to be educated, *the importance of developing the whole personality,* and within this pattern, the foundational importance of early education.

Europe

Among the pioneers of our modern education, John Amos Comenius first commands our attention as one of the greatest, if not the greatest leader. He was the first of a long line of educationists whose vision and thought, as expressed in their writings and accomplishments, helped to influence and develop our educational system of today. Comenius, Rousseau, Pestalozzi, and Froebel turned their attention to the psychology of the teaching process, emphasizing that education be based on the nature of the child.

Comenius. John Amos Comenius was a Moravian bishop who lived from 1592 to 1670. There is much about his life that is interesting, but sufficient for us here is the consideration of those aspects of his life and work that have influenced early elementary and elementary education of today.

Comenius' greatest work was *The Great Didactic*[1] (1632). In it he developed two contributions to education which are of especial interest to us. They are: (*1*) the fourfold division of schools, and (*2*) the Mother School. Considering the period from birth to twenty-five years of age the most concentrated period of education in a person's life, Comenius divided this period into four distinct grades, each approximately six years in length and each the concern of a special school. Infancy, the first period, had the Mother's Knee as its school; Childhood had the Vernacular-School, which was comparable to our elementary school; boyhood was the concern of the Latin-School, or Gymnasium, which was the counterpart of our modern high school; the last period of youth was assigned to the University and travel. The Mother School, Comenius thought, "should exist in every house," for he did not advocate that young children enter the village school until they were six years of age.

Of especial interest to those of us in early elementary education also is the fact that Comenius was the first to develop a teaching handbook outlining duties for teachers, mothers, and nurses, and that he was the first, also, to place a picture book directly in the hands of the young child as a means of educating him. The purposes of the picture book were: (*1*) to teach through sensual perception, (*2*) to give the idea of pleasure from books, and (*3*) to aid the children in learning to read.[2]

In his *School of Infancy,* published in 1633, Comenius entitled Chapter XII, "How to Prepare Children for Public School." He stated:[3]

. . . Parents, therefore, should not carelessly hand over their children for instruction in school. They themselves should first seriously weigh what should be done and then open the eyes of their children to look forward to the same.

Modern? Yes! He continued, "As the time for sending children to school draws near, they should try to inspire them with joy."[4] Is this

[1] John Amos Comenius, trans. and ed. by M. W. Keating, *The Great Didactic* (London, Adam & Charles Black Company, 1896), Ch. 27, pp. 407-410.
[2] See *Ibid.,* pp. 416-417, points 24, 25, 26.
[3] John Amos Comenius, ed. by Ernest M. Eller, *The School of Infancy* (Chapel Hill, University of North Carolina Press, 1956), p. 119.
[4] *Ibid.,* p. 120.

not a major purpose of our visiting days and other programs planned for the kindergarten child prior to his school entrance?

And again:[5]

It will also be beneficial to tell them how excellent a thing it is to frequent school and get learning.

. . . Moreover, tell them learning is not labour but that amusement with books and pens is sweeter than honey and that of this amusement children may have a foretaste, they can be given chalk. With it they may draw on slate or paper, angles, squares, circles, little stars, horses, trees. . . .

. . . Parents should also try to form in their children confidence and love towards their future teacher. . . .

. . . With such preparation a child will easily acquire love and joyous anticipation of school and teacher. . . .

Ulich[6] states, regarding Comenius:

The Great Didactic . . . reveals in essence all those elements on which any modern system of education has to be built: a definition of a goal, a psychology of human nature as a basis for interconnecting the methods of education with the laws of mental growth, and, finally, a consideration of the role of education within human society.

Next of importance in the development of modern education is a group who lived in the eighteenth century and left a definite impact on all of education today. Included among these outstanding educators are Jean-Jacques Rousseau, Johann Heinrich Pestalozzi, and Friedrich Wilhelm Froebel. Like Comenius, they were concerned that education should begin with study of the child as a child and not as a small adult. All who are concerned with the education of young children have a deep interest in these educators, in the classics they wrote, and in the direct relation of their work to that of the school life of the young child today.

Rousseau. Jean-Jacques Rousseau was a French naturalist who lived from 1712 to 1778. He is best known for his contribution to education through his great classic, *Emile,* published in 1762. This book, written in popular style, was one of the most widely read and discussed classics. It advanced an educational theory which directly opposed that of Rousseau's period. In *Emile,* Rousseau advocated the

---

[5] *Ibid.,* pp. 119-121.

[6] Robert Ulich, *Three Thousand Years of Educational Wisdom* (Cambridge, Mass., Harvard University Press, 1950), p. 339.

development of individual personality and the right of a little child to develop as an individual and as a child, not as a small adult. This concept opposed the adaptation of the small child to his environment through forcing him to absorb organized subject matter alone; rather, it attempted to adapt learning to the child and his needs. Rousseau believed in education as living, and in the use of normal child activities as the natural means of development; he believed in freedom rather than authority; he believed in focusing on the child. Only Comenius before him had the latter concept in common with Rousseau.

In *Emile,* Rousseau advocated rearing a young child through the natural process of growth in the outdoors; his questions and needs were to be met as they arose but no positive education was to be imposed.

Rousseau, despite his inconsistent and sentimental form, wrote in a vivid and forceful manner which enabled others to put his ideas into effect in a practical and intelligent way. He himself, however, was not sound in his approach to a practical application of the theory he advanced in *Emile*.

It was left for Pestalozzi, Froebel, and at a later date John Dewey and others, to translate Rousseau's basic idea into a practical philosophy for our schools. The findings of modern psychology, anthropology, and sociology, the evolution of philosophical realism and pragmatism, and the growth of democratic institutions have all contributed to the validity of the central theme in Rousseau's writing.

Pestalozzi. Modern education, developed to this point in the eighteenth century, needed a leader who could draw together the ideas of the philosophers and educators who had preceded him in order to lay the foundation for the further development and expansion of education.

In Johann Heinrich Pestalozzi we find such a person. Pestalozzi, named the "father of modern education," gave aim and purpose to the nineteenth century elementary school. He took the best of all who had preceded him and used it to build a form that could be adapted, expanded, and extended by those who followed him. Through his work a new philosophy of elementary education took form and spread in influence, not only in his native Switzerland at that time, but throughout all Europe and especially in America where it is still a major force today. Methods and curriculum were changed and the teacher assumed a new role and a creative part in the learning process through Pestalozzi's influence.

Pestalozzi lived between 1746 and 1827. As is often true of those who are ahead of their time in vision and thought, he had a difficult life, but his contributions seem to justify the struggle that he endured.

Pestalozzi contributed two great writings to the list of educational classics. They are *Leonard and Gertrude* and *How Gertrude Teaches Her Children*. These publications give us a record of Pestalozzi's life, work, and thought. The first, *Leonard and Gertrude*, was written in story form; the second was written as an academic discussion of Pestalozzi's educational theory and his attempts in his schools to put such theory into practice. Study of these classics shows that the essential ideas which they express are as true today as when they were first advanced; one of the important contributions is the belief in sense perception as the basis of knowledge.

It is worthwhile to summarize some of the basic concepts in the two classics. They may be stated as:

1. belief in a more natural life for children.
2. belief in an education that is society-centered.
3. belief that the deepest source of development and education lies in the experience of love that a child has for his parents. (This is a core concept in early elementary education and mental heatlh today.)
4. belief in the idea of essential equality supplemented with belief in the idea of individuality.
5. belief in equality not as uniformity but as the concept that nature develops differently in different persons according to their particular abilities.
6. belief in positive experiences in early childhood to build the child's confidence.
7. belief in the organization of learning with consideration of the instincts, capacities, and power of the growing child.
8. belief that sense perception is the basis of knowledge.
9. belief that education is the harmonious development of all a child's faculties.
10. belief that subject matter should be graded and proceed from the particular to the general, from the known to the unknown, and from the simple to the complex.
11. belief that learning should be closely related to everyday living.
12. belief in development of the child as an important facet of teaching.

13. belief in early manual dexterity.
14. belief in home and school co-operation.

Thus Pestalozzi's work gave new direction to the elementary school in the nineteenth century. It introduced into the school the study of real objects. It advocated learning through the senses. It fostered individual expression of ideas. It developed child abilities through child activities. It effected changes in teacher education and philosophy, and did much to further the need for normal schools.

Froebel. Just as Pestalozzi of Switzerland stands out as one of the greatest influences in American education today, so Froebel of Germany is remembered as the founder of the great kindergarten movement and methodology in the important phase of education we know today as early elementary education.

Deeply influenced by Pestalozzi, Froebel devoted his life to the education of teachers, and especially to the education of those who taught young children. Before beginning his work, Froebel studied for two years under Dr. Gruner, who had also been a student of Pestalozzi; the methods and philosophy of the Pestalozzian school of thought became the foundation for the kindergarten movement of Froebel.

Froebel's deep belief in the development of the child and in the significance and importance of early development for all later growth, caused him to found the kindergarten and lay the foundation for the development of this important present-day educational level. Froebel developed his beliefs in his classic, *The Education of Man,* which was published in 1826 and later translated as a key source in the development of the American kindergarten.

The *Education of Man* expresses the essence of Froebel's philosophy and of the kindergarten movement. Summarized from it are the following statements:

Froebel believed

. . . that childhood was not just a transition toward adulthood but something complete and organized in itself; play was not just a preparation for the activities of the mature person. . . .
. . . in discovering laws which could be used for a scientific system of teaching and education
. . . in the interrelatedness of all growth

[7] Friedrich Froebel, trans. by W. N. Hailman, *The Education of Man* (New York, D. Appleton & Company, 1903).

. . . in a co-operative rather than a competitive education

. . . in play as an important phase of developmental activity

. . . in recognition of the natural abilities of the child

. . . in growth that is from within

. . . in knowledge as a means, not an end (the end being the development of the child's abilities)

. . . in class activities based on immediate interests and circumstances

. . . in five basic principles, namely: (1) free activity; (2) creativity; (3) social participation; (4) motor expression; and (5) symbolism

As stated above, the kindergarten was begun by Froebel, who began his first work in the education of young children in Germany in 1857. The name *kindergarten* means "children's garden."[8] Terms used in Froebel's time to designate schools for young children were Infant School, Nursery School, and House of Children; these schools were built on the philosophy that the child's mind was a blank page on which the teacher and parent wrote at will, or clay which the teacher or parent molded according to his own ideas. Froebel wanted a name that would convey his ideas of growth and self-activity. He considered among possible names, *Institute for Self-Teaching of Little Children, Play School,* and *School for the Psychological Training of Little Children by Means of Play and Occupations;* but in 1840 he chose the name of *Kindergarten* as expressing most clearly what he had in mind as an educational school for young children. He wanted the name to clearly emphasize the difference between his concept of education for young children and that of his contemporaries.

Froebel based his philosophy on democratic concepts of government and "demanded the introduction of such active processes as experiment, construction, excursions, discovery and invention"; his contemporaries believed that learning emphasized "memory, recitation, receptivity, and quiescence of both mind and body at the cost of the child's opportunity to learn through self-activity."[9]

One of the key materials provided for the self-activity of the Froebelian kindergarten is known as "The Gifts." Of interest are the following thoughts regarding the Gifts.[10]

[8] See Patty Smith Hill, *Kindergarten, Reprint* (Washington, D.C., Association for Childhood Education International, 1942), pp. 1949.

[9] *Ibid.,* pp. 1948.

[10] Kate Douglas Wiggin and Nora Archibald Smith, *Froebel's Gifts* (Boston, Houghton Mifflin Company, 1895), pp. 1-4.

A correct comprehension of external, material things is a preliminary to a just comprehension of intellectual relations. (Friedrich Froebel)

The correct perception is a preparation for correct knowing and thinking. (Friedrich Froebel)

Let us educate the senses, train the faculty of speech, the art of receiving, storing, and expressing impressions, which is the natural gift of infants, and we shall not need books to fill up the emptiness of our teaching until the child is at least seven years old. (E. Seguin)

Instruction must begin with actual inspection, not with verbal descriptions of things. From such inspection it is certain knowledge comes. What is actually seen remains faster in the memory than description or enumeration a hundred times as often repeated. (Comenius)

Observation is the absolute basis of all knowledge. The first object, then, in education, must be to lead the child to observe with accuracy; the second, to express with correctness the results of his observation. (Pestalozzi)

The Gifts, used for many years in the American kindergarten, consisted of ten parts. They may be described briefly as follows:[11]

The *First Gift* included six soft woolen balls ranging in color from red through violet; each had a string attached to the ball so it could be held and put into motion. These objects were of the same shape but differed in color.

The *Second Gift* included a wooden sphere, cube, and cylinder two inches in diameter; a rod for turning was placed on each object. In this Gift the objects differed in shape.

The *Third Gift* through the *Sixth Gift* were known as "the building Gifts." In each Gift, the form was divided into parts; the child was to see the relationship of the parts to one another, and to the whole.

The *Third Gift* was a two-inch wooden cube divided once each way across the width, breadth, and height so that there were eight smaller cubes in the big cube. The *Fourth Gift* was a similar two-inch cube, only it was divided once across the height and three times across the thickness making eight pieces two inches long, one inch wide, and one-half inch thick. In the *Fifth Gift,* a three-inch cube was divided twice in each dimension making twenty-seven one-inch cubes. Three of these were divided into halves by one diagonal cut, and three into quarters by a double diagonal cut, making a total of thirty-nine pieces. The *Sixth Gift* became more complicated still. It consisted of thirty-six pieces of various shapes and dimensions. These are the last of the solid Gifts.

[11] See *Ibid.*

The *Seventh Gift* involved plane surfaces and consisted of wood or pasteboard materials cut into squares and triangles. (Whole and half wooden circles and oblong tablets preceded the introduction of this Gift.) The *Eighth Gift* gave meaning to length as a dimension through the use of wooden slats.

The circumference of the sphere and the edge of the cylinder were illustrated through the "rings" of the *Ninth Gift*. These were whole one-, two-, and three-inch circles of silver wire.

Froebel, through these Gifts, had brought the child from introduction to the solid object, the divided object, the plane and the line, to the *Tenth Gift* which concerned "the point made concrete"; it involved the handling and use of objects in the child's environment.

Viewed in terms of present kindergarten methodology and in terms of recommendations for kinds and sizes of materials for the young child, the above *Gifts* seem far removed from our program today. But, evaluating Froebel's Gifts in terms of basic philosophy and psychology they are immediately related to our present-day thinking. They teach through objects; they begin with the simple and move to the complex; they are designed to aid learning through self-activity; and they stress the interrelatedness of learning.

Froebel's democratic philosophy was a cause of difficulty with the Prussian authorities, who were gaining power in Germany at that time; it resulted in the official closing and prohibition of kindergarten before Froebel's death. The result of this ruling was detrimental to Froebel himself and to the continued growth of the kindergarten movement in its native Germany.

Had Froebel lived longer or had the decree regarding kindergarten been made earlier in his life, he might have hoped to bring the kindergarten to America himself. He foretold that in America, where democratic principles of government and democratic education were more in accord with his own ideas, "the kindergarten would prosper as in no other country." This prophecy came true.

It is interesting to note that in 1870 John Eaton, then United States Commissioner of Education, repeated in essence what Froebel had stated. Eaton said:[12]

[12] United States Department of the Interior, Office of Education, *Report of the United States Commissioner of Education 1870* (Washington, D.C., Government Printing Office, 1872).

But to no country is the kindergarten adapted so entirely as America, where there is no hindrance of aristocratic institutions to interfere with a method which regards every human being as a subject of education, intellectual and moral as well as physical, from the moment of birth, and as heir of universal nature in co-sovereignty with all other men, endowed by their Creator with equal rights to life, liberty, and the pursuit of happiness.

Froebel contributed the kindergarten to the early elementary education field; the kindergarten, in turn, influenced the whole of American education. It involved education by doing through play, the use of music, and a milder discipline. Its principal method was social co-operation through directed self-activity focused on educational, social, and moral goals. Its aim was individual development. Its form was in motor expression and self-activity.

Other Beginnings. Europe was witnessing the beginnings of other types of preschool development prior to Froebel's work in the kindergarten and related to social and industrial causes rather than to education. Nevertheless, mention of these beginnings is of interest to the student of early elementary education history.

Because of the conditions created by the Industrial Revolution and the resulting migration of rural families into cities, the need for care of young children arose. These programs, resulting from social needs, are more directly related to the day nursery (not the nursery school, which is an educational program) than to public elementary education. The work and contributions of two leaders, Jean Frederic Oberlin and Robert Owen,[13] are of interest.

Jean Fredcric Oberlin worked in Alsace. In 1774 he established "the first school for preschool children to be taught by trained attendants outside the home and having a curriculum planned especially for the children . . . he was the first to plan a school for the young child which grew directly out of the needs of the community and child." Robert Owen of Scotland, unaware of Oberlin's work, set up a school for children of mothers working in his mill in 1800. His criteria for admission of children was "the ability to walk." His school program consisted of larger manual activities, excursions, dancing, and experiences that he believed would lead to "health and happiness for children at this early age of development."

[13] See Hill, *op. cit.,* pp. 1953-1955.

Though the work of both Oberlin and Owen were unknown to Froebel, they, like him, were arousing forces for interest in young children. Though they did not work from the philosophy of a true educational program, as did Froebel in his kindergarten movement forty years later, their work represents a real contribution.

America. The end of the nineteenth and the beginning of the twentieth centuries witnessed the start of another period in educational thought. Along with the event of compulsory education came progressive steps in educational thought through the work of such men as G. Stanley Hall, William James, John Dewey, and William Kilpatrick. A psychological understanding of the child, organization of subject matter on the psychology of how children learn, and emphasis on social setting became the core of educational thinking and planning, and the bases for our philosophy, theory, and practice of today.

On the basis of this general educational history background, it is interesting to highlight the history of early elementary education in America.

HISTORY AND DEVELOPMENT OF THE PUBLIC NURSERY SCHOOL, KINDERGARTEN, AND PRIMARY EDUCATION IN AMERICA, HIGHLIGHTING PERSONS OF INFLUENCE AND EVENTS AND WRITINGS OF IMPORTANCE

Early elementary education, as one of the phases within the pattern of growth, refers to the organized school experiences of children in the early childhood years from public nursery school through the primary level. It usually covers the chronological ages of four through eight or nine years. Its program is an integrated and co-ordinated whole, but this has not always been true. In the beginnings of education of young children, the nursery school, the kindergarten, and the primary were separate. The kindergarten grew directly out of the Froebelian movement in Germany. The primary level was a part of elementary education patterned after the usual traditional program of the intermediate and upper levels. The public nursery school did not exist for many years; the first was opened in 1924.

The concepts implied in the terms nursery school, kindergarten, and primary in the following outline will be those which are understood in the educational programs planned for children's development in the public schools. Primary will refer to the program for children usually six to nine years of age in the traditionally accepted first three grades of the elementary school. The kindergarten will apply to the program planned for growth during the fifth chronological year and prior to entrance into the primary level as such. The nursery school will indicate an organized educational program designed to meet the growth pattern of four-year-old children. It will not include day nursery, childcare, welfare, and other types of programs which have as their goal the care of children while parents are working. Such programs, while they should be and often are truly educational, are not included in public nursery school as defined herein. Though the three programs now tend to be a unit, historical perspective demands that they be considered independently in their beginnings.

STUDENT'S OUTLINE OF PUBLIC EARLY ELEMENTARY EDUCATION

This outline is a suggested beginning for the student to use in developing a history; it is *not* meant to be comprehensive.

1816-1869

Kindergarten	Primary Education
(In early concepts the term kindergarten implied a method of teaching rather than a specified age level.)	1816 Infant School begun in Boston.
1848 Carl Schurz and his wife fled from the revolution in Germany to America; they brought deep and vivid memories of Froebel's kindergarten work and teaching.	By this time the Infant School had absorbed the Dame School and become the Primary Department of the Elementary school.
1855 Mrs. Schurz established the first kindergarten in our country at Watertown, Wisconsin. It was a private, German speaking school established in her own home especially for her three-year-old daughter.	

Kindergarten	Primary Education

1856 Dr. Henry Barnard published the first article in our country on kindergarten education in *The American Journal of Education,* which he edited. It described materials and was based on his visit to England's International Exhibit of Educational Systems in 1854, where his interest in kindergarten developed.

1858 Second private kindergarten opened in Columbus, Ohio, by Miss Caroline Frankenberg, a teacher from Germany who had studied with Froebel.

1860 Miss Elizabeth Peabody, "The apostle of the kindergarten movement in the United States," established a private kindergarten in Boston. She was a member of the Concord School of Philosophy and the Brook Farm Experiment; she and her two sisters, Mrs. Horace Mann and Mrs. Nathaniel Hawthorne, interested national leaders including William T. Harris (later U.S. Commissioner of Education), the Alcotts, Ralph Waldo Emerson, and Susan E. Blow in the kindergarten movement.

1861 Dr. E. A. Sheldon opened a department for training teachers in Pestalozzian principles (in the Oswego Public Schools, New York).

Kindergarten	Primary Education
1863 Oswego Training Department became a State normal school; its Pestalozzian philosophy helped effect acceptance of kindergarten movement.	The primary school as a division level of elementary education was begun about this time; it had the traditional curriculum of the three R's.

E. Peabody published *The Kindergarten Guide,* following her article, "What Is a Kindergarten?," in the *Atlantic Monthly,* 1862.

1868 Establishment of a kindergarten training school by Madame Mathilde Kriege and her daughters. They had all studied under Froebel's great disciple, Baroness Van Maren-Buelow, and were brought to Boston by E. Peabody.

1869 Milton Bradley, of Milton Bradley Company, began an active interest and work in the kindergarten movement; his services were in materials and assisting with publication.

1870-1879

During this decade kindergartens were established and maintained largely by private funds, but the first kindergarten in a public school appeared in 1873.	In the early 70's drawing (based on geometric principles) was introduced in the Boston primary schools.
1870 Mrs. Susan Pollack opened a kindergarten in Washington, D.C.	The word method of teaching reading replaced drill on the A.B.C.'s.

The first charity kindergartens were opened in New York.

Kindergarten   Primary Education
_____   _____

The first kindergarten association began in Milwauke.

Miss Emma Marwedel (Ger-
many) came to America at
E. Peabody's invitation and
established a kindergarten
training school for teachers,
Washington, D.C.

FIRST PUBLIC SCHOOL
KINDERGARTEN
1873 Susan E. Blow (with William
      T. Harris) established the
      first public school kinder-
      garten in America at St. Louis,
      Missouri, This initiated the
      movement for the establish-
      ment of public kindergartens
      throughout the country.

      E. Peabody began *The
      Kindergarten Messenger,* a
      monthly magazine.

1874 Kindergarten movement be-
      gan in Chicago through Mrs.
      Alice H. Putnam.

1875 Kindergartens were estab-
      lished in Los Angeles and In-
      dianapolis.

1876 Philadelphia Exposition dis-
      play furthered the kinder-
      garten movement.

      Denver and San Francisco es-
      tablished kindergartens. The
      latter began the Silver Street

Kindergarten | Primary Education

Kindergarten, directed by Miss Kate Douglas Wiggin and her sister, Nora A. Smith. It laid the foundation for kindergarten education in California.

The Kindergarten Messenger became *The New England Journal of Education.*

1877 *The New England Journal of Education* became *The New Education.*

1878 The San Francisco Kindergarten Association was formed (second in the country).

1880-1889

The kindergarten began its extension into the public schools, influencing the curriculum and methods of elementary education. The public kindergarten movement was supplemented by private, social settlement, and church kindergartens. This period also saw the formation of many kindergarten associations.

1880 Status: 400 kindergartens in over 30 states; kindergarten training schools in the ten largest cities and in many small ones.

First state normal school kindergarten established at Oshkosh, Wisconsin; a few months later a kindergarten depart-

This period saw the addition of new subjects and of changing methods; it has been called "the decade of transition."

271

Kindergarten	Primary Education

ment was opened at Winona, Minnesota.

Golden Gate Kindergarten Association founded at San Francisco.

1881 Kindergarten department was added to Chatauqua school (summer) program.

Sub-Primary Society of Philadelphia was formed.

H. Barnard's "Kindergarten and Child Culture" papers were published.

1882 Des Moines Kindergarten Association was formed.

1884 Indianapolis and Portland (Ore.) formed kindergarten associations.

Commissioner William T. Harris went on record stating that he believed Froebel's principles and philosophy had to be spread through the normal schools.

1885 The kindergarten class and materials at the New Orleans Exposition drew much attention in the South.

Los Angeles kindergarten association was formed.

1886 Commissioner of Education stated: "The work of making

Kindergarten	Primary Education

the kindergarten a part of the school system is only a question of time."

1887 Louisville Kindergarten Association formed.

E. Marwedel published *Conscious Motherhood*.

1888 Albany and New Orleans began Kindergarten Associations.

The Kindergarten Magazine was founded in Chicago.

1889 Kindergarten associations appeared in Detroit, Denver, and Asheville, North Carolina.

1890-1899

Rapid spread of public school kindergarten movement. Kindergarten training departments were added in many state normal schools and in a few state universities. Legislation favoring kindergarten establishment was passed in various states. Disagreement which led to division of kindergarten leaders into two schools of thought began and lasted for approximately ten to fifteen years, after which the difficulty was permanently resolved.

1890 E. Harrison published *Child Nature;* was widely used and and translated into several languages.

Primary school influenced by the new movements in psychology, child study, and Herbartianism. Influence of Colonel Francis W. Parker was felt.

273

Kindergarten	Primary Education

The Kindergarten News magazine was established in Buffalo.

The Grand Rapids and Chattanooga Kindergarten Associations were formed.

1891 Kindergarten associations appeared in Buffalo and Minneapolis.

1892 *The Child's Garden* begun (a magazine of stories, songs, and plays).

International Kindergarten Union organized at the National Education Association Conference. It was known as IKU.

Pittsburgh, Galveston, and Charleston (S.C.) formed kindergarten associations.

1893 Associations formed in Washington, D.C. and St. Louis; also Spokane.

Kindergarten Exhibit at Columbia Exposition, Chicago.

1895 An important publication was *The Republic of Childhood,* which included three books: (*1*) S. Blow's translation of Froebel's *Mother Plays;* (*2*) Miss Jarvis' translation of *Pedagogics of the Kindergarten;* and (*3*) Wiggin and Smith's *Froebel's Gifts.*

Kindergarten	Primary Education

S. Blow's *Symbolic Education* was published; was very important in kindergarten literature.

G. Stanley Hall, leader in the child study movement, offered first workshop in kindergarten problems.

IKU affiliated with National Education Association and National Council of Women; met with both groups this year.

First formal discussion of two schools of kindergarten thought: conservative versus liberal concepts of method.

1896 IKU held its first independent meeting at Teachers College, N.Y.

Kindergarten attitude toward the child began to be accepted by primary teachers. Kindergarten influence was felt in songs, games, art methods, and in the general revision of methods. Teaching of music, nature study, and physical education training added to the program.

1897 Interest in child study stimulated by kindergarten movement; led to formation of National Congress of Mothers.

The Kindergarten News was changed to *The Kindergarten Review*.

1897-8 Status: 189 cities now maintained public kindergartens.

Kindergarten	Primary Education

1900-1909

5000 established kindergartens open. G. Stanley Hall, leader in the child study movement, contributed to kindergarten reorganization. Commissioner Claxton stated: "The kindergarten is a vital factor in American education, both for its direct work with young children in the kindergarten and its influence on the care of children in the home and on methods of teaching in the schools. It ought to become a part of the public school system of every city, town, and village in the country."

1903 Translation of Froebel's *Education of Man* (by W. N. Hailman, D. Appleton & Company), an important work for kindergarten.

Committee of Nineteen appointed to study the kindergarten training and program because of different viewpoints. (One group, under S. Blow, held to the kindergarten theory and practice of Froebel; the other favored modification on the basis of findings in child study and the growing "social" point of view with regard to curriculum.)

1905 Southern kindergarten association was formed.

1906 *The Kindergarten Magazine*

Kindergarten	Primary Education
became *The Kindergarten and Primary Magazine.*	

1908 N. Vandewalker published *The Kindergarten in American Education* (The Macmillan Company).

1910-1931

Nursery School	Kindergarten	Primary Education
	Increase in number of kindergartens and increased need for double sessions; kindergarten teacher's time was lessened for mothers' meetings and attending classes. Three large associations were working for kindergartens: The National Congress of Mothers, The National Kindergarten Association, and The International Kindergarten Union.	

1912 Status: 6563 kindergartens. Dr. Marie Montessori published *The Montessori Method* (Fred A. Stokes Company).

	Kindergarten	Primary Education
	1913 Montessori Education Association was formed in Washington, D.C.	Primary and kindergarten teachers began to be seriously interested in co-ordination of their work.

Nursery School	Kindergarten	Primary Education
	1914 Status: 7254 kindergartens. Patty Hill edited *Experimental Studies in Kindergarten Theory and Practice.*	
	1915	Thirty primary teachers at the meeting of the Superintendents, NEA, Cincinnati (Feb., 1915), formed the National Council of Primary Education. Its purposes were threefold: (*1*) greater use of activities in the primary school; (*2*) greater freedom of method for teachers; and (*3*) unification of the work done in kindergarten and the primary school.
	1916 John Dewey's *Democracy and Education* appeared.	
	1919 Kindergarten extension continued despite post-war conditions.	
Teachers College, N.Y., introduced the nursery school to America through a course taught by a specialist from	1920	

Nursery School	Kindergarten	Primary Education

Miss Macmillan's School in London.

Status: three nursery schools existed—one in a college, one private, and one philanthropic, but no public.

First public school nursery opened in Highland Park, Michigan.

1924 *Childhood Education* magazine begun.

Eleven public nursery schools existed.

1928

National Association for Nursery Education established.

1929 IKU Committee studied the possibilities of reorganizing to include nursery school and primary levels.

National Association for Nursery Education established.

1931 IKU and the Primary Council combined to form the Association for Childhood Education International (including nursery education through primary).

Status since 1930

Enrollments

1930 Federally supported nursery schools and child-care centers gave

1930—723,443   9,686,073
(2.82%)   (38.52%)

Nursery School	Kindergarten	Primary Education
impetus to growth of movement.		
	1935—604,264 (2.29%)	8,786,649 (33.29%)
White House Conference on children recommended emerging nursery school should be permanent part of public education.	1940—594,647 (2.34%)	7,683,138 (30.21%)
	1945—733,974 (3.2%)	7,320,723 (31.5%)
	1950—1,034,203 (4.1%)	8,210,954 (32.6%)
Very little growth to date.	1954—1,474,007 (5.1%)	9,871,136 (31.8%)

BRIEF OVERVIEW SHOWING RELATIONSHIP BETWEEN EARLY ELEMENTARY EDUCATION AND OTHER EDUCATIONAL LEVELS

Early Elementary Education	Elementary Education	Secondary Education	Higher Education
	1636 Latin Grammar School		1636 Harvard founded
	Reading and Writing School		1701 Yale Founded
		1750 First Academy	
			1789 First State University (North Carolina)
1816 Infant School begun in Boston			
	1821 Extended through eighth grade		

BRIEF OVERVIEW—(*Continued*)

1855 First private
kindergarten
(German)

1860 First English
kindergarten

1864 First land
grant college

1873 First public
kindergarten

1896 First junior
college at
Chicago University

Six year elementary program

1909 First junior
high school

1920 Nursery
school
teacher education begun

1924 First public
school nursery school

1930 Interest in
primary unit
begins

1950's Interest in
Multigrade
plan begins

1955 Community
college
developed

EARLY ELEMENTARY EDUCATION IN OTHER COUNTRIES

Interest in young children is universal. Recognition of the need for guidance of young children is by no means limited to our country. A downward extension of the educational program to the needs and maturity level of the four- and five-year-old child, as seen in the public nursery school and kindergarten, is our answer. Other countries of the world have given attention to the same problem; a few selected programs are cited here.

281

Great Britain[14]

The present plan of Primary Education in England is based on the Education Act of 1944. It provides for: (*1*) Nursery School for children below five years of age in which attendance is voluntary; (*2*) Infant Schools for children five to seven years-of-age; (*3*) Junior Schools for children seven to ten years of age; and on through the upper levels. Though nursery school attendance is not compulsory, the local administration or authorities must provide it wherever there is reasonable demand.

The program in the English schools, like that in American schools, stresses the development and growth of the whole child; there is much freedom and activity. The nursery school centers set their goals in the growth of health habits, social activities, and communication skills. The Infant School is a readiness program in the same sense that our kindergarten programs are. It helps the child gain background experiences and growth in all phases of personality as a foundation for later work. The Primary School is also comparable to ours. Still centering attention on the growth of the whole child, it begins instruction in the fundamentals. Meyer states regarding the curriculum:[15]

> The Ministry of Education has steadfastly declined to prescribe the curriculum, insisting that it is not possible to lay down the exact number of subjects which should be in an individual school. The choice . . . is in part determined by public opinion as expressing the needs of the community. . . .

France[16]

The education of young children in France was influenced by the work of Oberlin in Alsace (see page 265) and early developed into a national program. Today "preschool" programs exist as nursery schools and kindergartens for children from two to six years of age. Those schools which are independent are called *écoles maternelles;* those attached to the primary schools are termed *classes enfantines.* Attendance is voluntary; much attention is given to health and growth. Though

---

[14] British Information Services, *Education in Great Britain* (New York, 30 Rockefeller Plaza, n.d.), pp. 13-14.

[15] Adolph E. Meyer, *The Development of Education in the Twentieth Century* (Englewood Cliffs, N.J., Prentice-Hall, Inc., 1949), pp. 175-177.

[16] Comite-France Actuelle, *Education in France* (Paris, 1956).

some attention is given to developmental activities, these programs, like those of other levels of French education, are much more formal and inclined toward basic work in the fundamentals. The statistics of 1955 show that six out of every ten children between the ages of three and five attend the "preschool."

The primary program extends over a six-year period in contrast to our three years, and includes children between the ages of six and eleven or twelve. The program in these schools is prescribed and is the same throughout the country. It centers in academic work and requires frequent examinations even in the lower primary level.

Sweden[17]

The number of nursery schools and schools for children below six years of age (the compulsory school age) is small. Interest in such schools in Sweden is increasing but the pattern in the existing ones is closer to that in our day nursery than in our nursery schools; this is because the problem of "preschool" in Sweden is considered from the social rather than from the educational aspect.

The Netherlands[18]

Though there is no legislation establishing schools for very young children in the Netherlands, The Elementary Education Law of 1920 permits the school authorities to establish such schools locally, or through private funds. However, such schools, once established, come under the direct inspection of the State Inspectors of Education in Nursery and Infant Schools and under Public Health Inspectors.

Various national associations and municipalities have been active in setting up these schools for children. In 1948 there were 2,663 nursery and infant schools already established, eighty-six per cent of which have been provided through the work of national organizations. The majority of these schools are independent schools, but a few have been incorporated into the public elementary schools by the local districts.

Programs in the schools vary widely. A basic pattern, however, is the Froebelian system, which in many cases has been somewhat modi-

[17] The Swedish Institute, *Education in Sweden* (Stockholm, 1950), pp. 9-10.
[18] Philip J. Idenburg, *Education in the Netherlands* (Hague, Netherlands Government Information Office, 1950), pp. 11-15.

fied in procedure and in the materials used. Children attending these schools range in ages from three to six.

Norway[19]

Norway has a program for young children carried on in nursery schools and kindergartens; some are under private maintenance, others are provided through public funds. Teachers for these schools are prepared in some few institutions under the Supervision of the Ministry of Social Affairs. Norway, like Sweden, looks upon such programs as a social responsibility rather than an educational one. These schools are planned for children from three or four to seven years of age; the question has arisen as to whether or not the six- and seven-year-olds should have an educational rather than a care program.

The primary program is the equivalent of our elementary level program, as is true in most of Europe. The curriculum is uniform and academic in nature.

Russia[20]

Almost immediately after the Revolution of October, 1917, Russia established a Dictorate of Preschool Education, which continues to function today. In 1918 an Institute of Preschool education was established to direct and supervise teacher education for this level. Preschool education has been evaluated by Russia as one of the important levels and interest in it is high.

Preschool education covers nurseries and kindergartens. Children from six weeks of age through three years attend nurseries; those three to seven attend kindergarten. Both programs are conducted in the permanent year-round programs and also in part time and seasonal programs.

Nurseries in Russia compare to our day nurseries; they are established primarily for custodial service. Much attention is given to health. Kindergartens, while performing this function, also have an educational program; kindergartens are the responsibility within the Ministry

[19] Olav Hove, *An Outline of Norwegian Education* (Oslo, Royal Norwegian Ministry of Foreign Affairs, 1955), pp. 24-31.

[20] United States Office of Education, Division of International Education, *Education in the U.S.S.R.*, Bulletin 1957, No. 14 (Washington D.C., Government Printing Office, 1957), Chs. 1, 2, and 3.

of Education, whereas the nurseries are under the health ministries. Both kindergartens and nurseries are well staffed and have adequate and attractive educational toys.

The "Rules for Kindergarten" state that "the fundmental purpose of the Soviet Kindergarten is to achieve all-round development of children between the ages of three and seven," and "that such institutions should also be recognized as a means of providing mothers of young children with the opportunity to participate more actively in the productive, governmental, cultural, and socio-political life" of the country.

The kindergarten curriculum includes guided creative group and individual games and activities, music—rhythms, singing, listening, and musical games—formal drawing, play, both as an activity and as a means of education, and communist orientation. Orientation to work in the grades is provided. Classes are kept at 25 or fewer children.

Every kindergarten has a parents' corner in which "lists of recommended children's books, toys, sample pieces of children's furniture, recommended types of meals, and examples of self-made toys are displayed."

At seven, children enroll in first grade in a four-year primary school. Organization is controlled. Lessons are scheduled for forty-five minutes each. After each of the first three periods there is a ten minute break; then after the fourth lesson a thirty minute break. Much of the instruction and the framework of the program are designed to develop a socialist attitude "toward labor and work."

Mexico[21]

Mexico has given recognition to the importance of early education through both public and private education and enterprise.

Under the Secretariat of Health and Welfare day nurseries and welfare centers have been established. Many government and business offices conduct a *guarderia infantil* (day nursery) which gives medical and educational attention to young children.

More important, however, is the goal of the Secretariat of Public Education to include a kindergarten in every elementary school. *Kin-*

---

[21] Marjorie C. Johnston, *Education in Mexico,* Office of Education Bulletin (Washington, D.C., Government Printing Office, 1956), pp. 30-32.

dergartens were started in Mexico in 1904; in 1942 they were made an integral part of the educational system.

Kindergartens enroll children between the ages of four and seven. "The program consists of activities centering about the home and community in miniature with emphasis on health, recreation, and music." Though patterned after the work of Froebel and Montessori, Mexican kindergartens have been adapted to develop and express their own culture.

PROJECTS AND QUESTIONS

1. Using the data of this chapter and that from your research and outside reading, develop a presentation of the history of early elementary education showing persons of influence, and events and writings of importance.

GUIDE TO REFERENCES FOR FURTHER STUDY

BARNARD, Henry, ed., *Papers on Froebel's Kindergarten* (Hartford, Office of Barnard's American Journal of Education, 1908).

BLOW, Susan E., "Kindergarten Education," in *Monographs of Education in the United States,* N. H. Butler, ed. (New York, J. B. Lyon Company, 1900).

———, *Conservative Report of the Committee of Nineteen: The Kindergarten* (Boston, Houghton Mifflin Company, 1913).

BUTLER, N. M., *The Meaning of Education* (New York, Charles Scribner's Sons, 1915).

CLOUD, Roy, *Education in California* (Palo Alto, Stanford University Press, 1952).

COLE, Luella, *History of Education from Socrates to Montessori* (New York, Rinehart & Company, Inc., 1950).

DAVIS, Mary Dabney, *General Practice in Kindergarten Education in the United States* (Washington, D.C., National Education Association, 1925).

———, *Nursery Schools: Their Development and Current Practices in United States,* Bulletin No. 9 (Washington, D.C., Government Printing Office, 1932).

———, "Century of the Kindergarten," *School Life* (November, 1936), p. 67.

DEWEY, John, *The School and Society* (Chicago, University of Chicago Press, 1924).

FROEBEL, Friedrich, *Pedagogics of the Kindergarten,* trans. by J. Jarvis, (New York, D. Appleton & Company, Inc., 1895).

————, *Letters on the Kindergarten,* trans. by Michaelis and Moore (Syracuse, Bardeen Company, 1896).

————, *Education of Man,* trans. by W. N. Hailmann (New York, D. Appleton & Company, 1892).

————, *Mottoes and Commentaries of Friedrich Froebel's Mother-Play,* trans. by H. R. Eliot (New York, D. Appleton & Company, 1908).

————, *Education by Development,* trans. by J. Jarvis (New York, D. Appleton & Company, 1902).

GESELL, A., *The Preschool Child from the Standpoint of Public Hygiene and Education* (Boston, Houghton Mifflin Company, 1932).

GOODYKOONTZ, B., "Recent History and Present Status of Education for Young Children," in *Early Childhood Education,* 46th Yearbook, Part II, National Society for the Study of Education (Chicago, University of Chicago Press, 1947).

GRAVES, Frank, *Great Educators of Three Centuries* (New York, The Macmillan Company, 1912).

HALL, G. Stanley, "Some Defects of the Kindergarten in America," *Forum* (January, 1900).

HILL, Patty, *Kindergarten,* American Educational Encyclopedia Reprint (Washington, D.C., Association for Childhood Education International, 1942).

————, "Changes in Curriculum and Method in Kindergarten Education," *Childhood Education,* Vol. 2 (November, 1925), pp. 99-106.

————, *A Conduct Curriculum for the Kindergarten and First Grade* (New York, Charles Scribner's Sons, 1927).

International Kindergarten Union, Committee of Nineteen, *Pioneers of the Kindergarten in America* (New York, The Century Co., 1924).

————, Committee of Nineteen, *The Kindergarten* (Boston, Houghton Mifflin Company, 1913).

JOHNSON, Harriet, *Children in the Nursery School* (New York, The John Day Company, 1928).

KANDEL, I. L., Comparative Education (Boston, Houghton Mifflin Company, 1933).

KILPATRICK, William H., *Froebel's Kindergarten Principles Critically Examined* (New York, The Macmillan Company, 1916).

KNIGHT, Edgar, *Education in the United States* (Boston, Ginn and Company, 1929).

————, *Twenty Centuries of Education* (Boston, Ginn and Company, 1940).

————, and HALL, R., *Readings in American Educational History* (New York, Appleton-Century-Crofts, Inc., 1951).

MCMILLAN, Margaret, *The Nursery School* (New York, E. P. Dutton & Company, 1921).

MINOR, RUBY, *Early Childhood Education: Its Principles and Practices* (New York, Appleton-Century-Crofts, Inc., 1937).

MONROE, PAUL, *Textbook in the History of Education* (New York, The Macmillan Company, 1930), pp. 643-673.

MONTESSORI, MARIE, *The Montessori Method* (New York, Frederick A. Stokes Company, 1912).

PARKER, S. C., *Textbook in the History of Modern Elementary Education* (Boston, Ginn & Company, 1912).

SNIDER, D. J., *Froebel's Mother-Play Songs* (Chicago, Sigma Publishing Company, 1895).

TEMPLE, Alice, *Unified Kindergarten and First Grade Teaching* (Boston, Ginn and Company, 1925).

ULRICH, Robert, *History of Educational Thought* (New York, American Book Company, 1945).

————, *Three Thousand Years of Educational Wisdom* (New York, The Macmillan Company, 1950).

CHAPTER 12

And Now?

Education must become increasingly effective in influencing the behavior of students.[1]

Two major concerns are uppermost in the thinking of those concerned with the early elementary education level and its importance as a period of development for the young child. The first is the provision of more and better educational programs for young children; the second is the preparation of teachers who are qualified to understand and plan learning experiences for the maximum development of children at the early age where the foundation for all later development is laid.

THE EARLY ELEMENTARY EDUCATION PROGRAM

As already indicated, the education of young children is increasingly becoming a major concern of those within the related disciplines such as psychology, sociology, and anthropology, as well as for many lay persons and groups. The study of growth and development has caused us to move forward toward a co-ordinated program in early elementary education extending from the nursery school through the primary level as a phase of the total elementary program. Basing our thinking on scientific research and data, and on recognition of educational needs in our current society, there is only one sound conclusion. We must accept in practice as well as in theory the early elemen-

[1] Hollis L. Caswell, "What Kind of School Program Will Best Serve Our People and Our Country in the Decades Ahead?," Speech, National Education Association Centennial (Philadelphia, July 4, 1957).

tary program as a co-ordinated, publicly supported phase of the elementary school program.

General Trends

The intensive and extensive studies of the various disciplines concerned with the development of young children have given rise to real concern for and interest in educational programs designed for early elementary education levels. Realization of the far-reaching values and effects of guided learning experiences in the early years when the foundation of personality is laid, and when parent guidance and education in child development is needed, is fostering public as well as professional acceptance of responsibility for extended early elementary education as an integral part of public elementary education.

The National Society for the Study of Education in its 46th Yearbook states:[2]

. . . It is evident that the nursery school and kindergarten should be considered as a sequential unit and that this preschool unit should be completely integrated with the primary—and elementary—school programs which follow. The most logical, constructive, and workable pattern which seems to emerge from a study of existing facilities and their basic values in ultimate child growth would appear to be that of an early childhood educational unit. Such a unit, whether it be developed as a primary school sufficient unto itself or whether it be developed as an extension of the elementary school downward, offers the finest opportunity for sequential growth throughout the early years of childhood.

The kindergarten unit has been generally accepted as a part of the elementary education program, but the nursery school is just making a beginning in this respect. The same Society comments:[3]

Some regard nursery education as distinct and separate from public education. It is largely an historic accident that schools for young children developed outside of public auspices. But with the demonstration of their value, the logical place for them is in the public school system. Since society has already established the agencies for educating children and has entrusted the responsibility for them to a particular group of people, any consideration of future developments must recognize the purpose of the public educational system and seek to include the program for educating young children

---

[2] National Society for the Study of Education, *Early Childhood Education,* 46th Yearbook, Part II (Chicago, University of Chicago Press, 1947), pp. 369-370.

[3] *Ibid.,* p. 97.

with that system. Further, although custodial institutions, such as day nurseries for young children, have existed for some time to meet special needs, as time passes they will be forced to develop an "educational" rather than a "service" point of view, in exactly the same way as the custodial institutions for older children are being replaced by institutions with remedial, preventive, and educational philosophies.

Thus, the general trend of movement for education of young children today is toward a co-ordinated early elementary unit including the nursery school, the kindergarten, and the primary level as part of public elementary education.

Specific Trends

Within the general trend toward a continuous program of education extending downward to include the four-year-old child, we note more specific trends. Since these have been developed at length throughout this book, we can summarize them briefly as follows:

1. increasing realization of the importance and influence of guided experiences at an early age level
2. attention to early development as a foundation for learning, social adjustment, and personality.
3. greater emphasis on individual needs and potentialities
4. increased co-ordination in the work of professional people concerned with young children
5. emphasis on activities and experiences that build readiness for formal learning
6. increased use of community and its resources
7. more extended use of resources and resource people
8. extension of parent-child-teacher-community relationships
9. development of administrative plans, such as the primary unit and multigrade grouping, to foster continuous growth
10. statistical increase in the number of public nursery schools and kindergartens
11. increased attention to and interest in the early elementary level by administrators in their background education
12. increase in the number of men teaching at the primary level
13. extension of more graduate level programs into early elementary education

TEACHER EDUCATION FOR EARLY ELEMENTARY EDUCATION

And what about the teacher education programs to prepare teachers to work with and guide young children in the emerging early elementary program? Can they remain static? How should they be changed and what directions should be taken? Just as the early elementary level is an integral part of the elementary school and of the total educational program, so teacher education for this specific level must be an integral part of the total process of teacher preparation. Let us look first at the total educational needs in our country, then at the teacher education programs for elementary and early elementary education in particular.

Overview of the American Educational Picture

Dean Quillen, in his address to the Council on Cooperation in Teacher Education in 1956, stated:[4]

We are approaching the end of the period in American education when the major aim was to provide all children and youth with an elementary and high school education because this ideal has been almost reached. . . . We are truly entering a period of great vitality and change in education at all levels.

Now is the time for a thorough reappraisal of our whole educational system in the light of the demands of our changing society and the values we want to achieve. . . .

The emerging emphasis in American education is quality . . . The quality of American education can be improved only by improving the quality of the teacher . . . But in order to identify some of the goals, content, and practices in the teacher education of the 60's it is necessary to identify the emerging character of the American educational system and the special educational needs that social and economic changes are producing.

In the 1960's the American educational system will be greatly expanded and extended. In many parts of the country the nursery school will be an integral part of public education as the kindergarten is today . . . and in a generation we can expect a common school system . . . from the ages of three to twenty.

There is a need for more solid and up-to-date content throughout the school program . . . needs in mathematics and sciences . . . but needs are equally great, if not greater, in the social sciences and the humanities.

[4] James Quillen (Dean, School of Education, Stanford University) Address: "What Developments Should Be Anticipated as We Plan Teacher Preparation Programs? . . . In the Specialized Education of Teachers," delivered at 15th Annual Meeting, Council on Cooperation in Teacher Education (Washington, D.C., November 8-10, 1956).

The complexity of the modern world requires a much higher level of effectiveness in basic communication skills. . . .

The many problems produced by the rapidity and incoordination in change in the modern world means that the schools need to place more emphasis on problem-solving and reflective thinking at all levels. And emphasis on problem solving also means emphasis on values . . . some conceptions of what is good and desirable as a basis for making choices . . . Finally, a time of rapid change means that education in the future will need to put more emphasis on the development of abiding interests, self-discipline, and self direction in learning . . . the principal function of formal education is to lay the foundation of a life-time of self learning.

We have seen that the program of early elementary education is a program that strives for early and foundational training in the goals of American education, that is, in functional content, effective communication skills, process skills of thinking and problem solving, and increasing self direction. Consideration of the teacher education programs designed to prepare candidates for the teaching profession follows.

Teacher Education Programs

Teacher education programs and teacher certification have tended in the past (and to a considerable degree even at the present time) to differentiate among the amount and types of preparation required for teaching at the various levels of the school system. Preparation for the secondary school major follows a pattern quite different from that for the elementary major in most colleges. Preparation for the teaching of young children in the nursery school and kindergarten follows various patterns. Certification for the secondary level differs from that of the elementary in most states; elementary certification in many differs from that for the Kindergarten-Primary. Certification for teaching the very young child is non-existent in most places.

At an earlier period kindergarten and primary teachers not only were prepared in separate, specialized programs (or even schools), but were supervised in the field after graduation by personnel from the two separate groups. This lack of relationship between the education and work of the kindergarten and primary teachers resulted in a distinct difference in the kindergarten and primary curricula, and made the transition from kindergarten to first grade difficult for the child (whose growth and needs are a continuing pattern). Thus the school, in direct opposition to the developmental growth patterns of children, marked off these two areas as being vastly different from each other.

Gradually, adaptations and changes within the educational programs, supervision, teacher education, and certification concerned with these levels were made on the basis of our research and knowledge of how a child develops, and the increasing attention to social processes. These changes effected a wholehearted co-operation and interest on the part of those concerned with the young child's development. They resulted in a more closely co-ordinated curriculum pattern of *continuous* learning experiences. They stimulated teachers and supervisors to plan transitional activities to help the child move easily and gradually from the nursery school to the kindergarten and on through the primary level, less disturbed by the changes in types of experiences and program provided at the different levels. Recently, these changes made possible the development of the primary unit, which places even more emphasis on continuous development (see Chapter 7).

We have moved forward in teacher education. What further planning should be done in terms of our "entering another period of change," and in the extended responsibility of public education for young children?

WHAT DIRECTION SHOULD BE TAKEN IN EARLY ELEMENTARY TEACHER EDUCATION?

The teacher of early elementary education is a part of the total elementary program; therefore, her field must be a specialization *within* the whole of elementary education. Her preservice education should be broad and basic: it should give her a thorough and functional understanding of democratic philosophy, values, and goals in elementary education; it should give her a specific and scientific knowledge and understanding of the continuous developmental pattern of children; it should give her understanding of and functional skills in the social and thinking processes; it should equip her with a solid foundation in general and cultural knowledge; and it should develop in her all the understanding and competence that would enable her to teach effectively at any level in the elementary program.

But, on this foundation and within the elementary education framework, the teacher preparing for teaching and guiding young children should be given *further* specialized training in understanding the young child and effectively working with him and his parents. Only as she works from the total picture can she effectively guide the young child's development. She views her particular educational level with very special interest and understanding; but she sees it also as an integral phase of the child's whole living, and *not* as an isolated field. How can the teacher of young children guide the child for total development if she is prepared and specialized in only one phase of his growth? There are nursery school and kindergarten teachers who feel that all work for their level should be completely planned for that level only in such courses as growth and development, music, science, and methods. Levels of ability and even physical maturity vary widely for any chronological year; a teacher must understand these ranges and provide for them. Can you find a nursery school class of four-year-olds that doesn't have children of three- and five- and even six-year maturity? Or, a kindergarten where the range of maturity doesn't extend from three or four to six or even older? How many primary and upper level elementary classes could you find without a range span of three to five years within the one chronological age group? No, isolation of special years or levels is not sound! Even within specialization for early elementary education the teacher must have the understanding and preparation for working with a range of several chronological years.

In summary, the preparation of the early elementary education teacher should include:

1. in common with all elementary education students:
    a. a general and cultural education program
    b. an active interest in and understanding of our society and our close interrelationships with other cultures
    c. a knowledge and understanding of the impact of current happenings on our culture and on our educational program
    d. a scientific knowledge and understanding of the child at all growth levels from infancy through maturity
    e. functional learning in broad areas through skills in thinking processes
    f. skills in mature human relationships

295

    g. a program combining an immediate knowledge of children with the theory, philosophy, and study of educational processes

    h. participation in professional organizations for preservice teacher candidates

2. in specialized study:

    a. understanding of the role of the teacher in bringing into the functional learning of the *young* child an understanding and appreciation of our culture and its values

    b. skills in guiding and working with parents of young children in their special problems concerning young children

    c. participation and responsibility in professional organizations especially concerned with young children

    d. knowledge of the research and helps in the various disciplines as they relate to the young child, that is, in sociology, pediatrics, child development, psychology, psychiatry, and play therapy

    e. psychological insight into problems of young children

    f. understanding of the ways young children learn; the place of play, real experiences, freedom, and creative expression in such learning

    g. development of flexibility and creativity in thought and practice in working with young children

    h. opportunity for study of individual children including the gifted, the slow, and the problem child; also opportunity to learn how to detect and correct remedial problems

    i. knowledge and skill in family life problems

    j. *much* practical experience with young children in learning situations

    k. content materials taught in functional learning experiences of young children

Before closing, a word regarding certification. It is interesting to note that forward-looking states are paralleling their work in the improvement of teacher education programs with work on certification requirements. Constructive work on certification as well as teacher education programs merits close attention in the next years.

GUIDE TO REFERENCES FOR FURTHER STUDY

Association for Supervision and Curriculum Development, "Education and the Future: Appraisal and Planning," *Educational Leadership,* Vol. 15 (February, 1957), entire issue.

————, "Education for the Foreseeable Future," *Educational Leadership,* Vol. 15 (October, 1957), entire issue.

CARR, William G., "The View Ahead," *National Education Association Journal,* Vol. 46 (March, 1957), p. 167.

CHASE, Francis S., "The Schools I Hope to See," *National Education Association Journal,* Vol. 46 (March, 1957), pp. 164-166.

CHILDS, John L., "The Future of the Common School," *Educational Forum,* Vol. 21 (January, 1957), pp. 133-141.

Department of Elementary School Principals, *The Flexible School* (Washington, D.C., The Department, 1957).

STODDARD, Alexander J., *Schools for Tomorrow: An Educator's Blueprint* (New York, The Fund for the Advancement of Education, 655 Madison Ave., January, 1957).

APPENDIX

General Bibliography

Guidance in the use of this bibliography will be given by the instructor at the beginning of the course and at the beginning of each unit as it is studied.

The bibliography contains a cross section of the excellent materials and research available for study. It covers publications concerning foundations, growth and development, psychology of learning, theory and principles, curriculum and program, and parent and community relationships. Early elementary education materials for specialization, and elementary education materials for broad background thinking are included.

The student will find that many of the references are publications of professional organizations. This has been planned not only to give the student the benefit of the best professional thought on the various subjects, but also to develop an appreciation and use of such materials.

Basic references sources in library work with which the student should become familiar and use frequently are:

ALEXANDER, C., and BURKE, A., *How to Locate Educational Information and Data* (New York, Teachers College, Columbia University, 1950).
The Education Index
GOOD, C. V., *Dictionary of Education*
MONROE, W. S., ed., *Encyclopedia of Educational Research*
Reader's Guide to Periodical Literature
Review of Educational Research

The student should also have a beginning acquaintance with the following periodicals:

American School Board Journal
Architectural Forum
Architectural Record
Child Development

Child Study
Childhood Education
Children
Educational Leadership
National Education Association Journal
National Elementary Principal
National Parent-Teacher
Nation's Schools
Parents Magazine
Review of Educational Research
Understanding the Child
Journal of the State Organization

ADAMS, Fay, *Educating America's Children* (New York, The Ronald Press Company, 1954).

ADAMS, Grace, and others, "Kindergarten Equipment and Materials," *California Journal of Elementary Education,* Vol. 17 (February, 1949), pp. 195-204.

ADLERBLUM, Evelyn D., "Mental Hygiene in the Kindergarten," *National Education Association Journal,* Vol. 44 (February, 1955), pp. 80-81.

AINSWORTH, Irene, "Today's Library Becomes a Materials Center," *Library Journal,* Vol. 80 (February 15, 1955), pp. 473-475.

ALMY, Millie C., "Are They Too Young for Problem Solving?" *Progessive Education,* Vol. 27 (March, 1950), pp. 143-148.

———, *Child Development* (New York, Henry Holt & Company, Inc., 1955).

———, *Children's Experiences Prior to First Grade and Success in Reading,* Contributions to Education, No. 954 (New York, Bureau of Publications, Teachers College, Columbia University, 1949).

———, "Principles and Practices of Nursery Education," *Exceptional Children,* Vol. 21 (October, 1954), pp. 18-21.

———, "Programs for Young Children," *Educational Leadership,* Vol. 8 (February, 1951), pp. 270-275.

———, "Six Is a Magic Age," *National Education Association Journal,* Vol. 39 (December, 1951), pp. 694-696.

ALSCHULER, Rose H., ed., *Children's Centers, a Guide for Those Who Care For and About Young Children* (New York, William Morrow & Company, 1942).

———, *Painting and Personality* (Chicago, University of Chicago Press, 1947).

——— and HATTWICK, LaB., "Easel Painting as an Index to Personality in Preschool Children," *American Journal of Orthopsychiatry,* Vol. 13, No. 6 (1943), pp. 616-626.

American Association of School Administrators, NEA, *American School Buildings,* 27th Yearbook (Washington, D.C., The Association, 1949).

———, *American School Curriculum,* 31st Yearbook (Washington, D.C., The Association, 1953).

———, *Choosing Free Materials for Use in the School* (Washington, D.C., The Association, 1955).

————, *Educating for American Citizenship,* 32nd Yearbook (Washington, D.C., The Association, 1954).

————, *Expanding Role of Education,* 26th Yearbook (Washington, D.C., The Association, 1948).

————, *Public Relations for American Public Schools,* 28th Yearbook (Washington, D.C., The Association, 1950).

American Educational Research Association, NEA, *Curriculum Organization and Development* (Washington, D.C., The Association, 1954).

————, *Educational Program: Early and Middle Childhood* (Washington, D.C., The Association, 1953).

————, *Growth, Development, and Learning* (Washington, D.C., The Association, 1955).

————, *School Plant and Equipment* (Washington, D.C., The Association, 1951).

————, *Social Framework of Education* (Washington, D.C., The Association, 1955).

AMES, L. B., "The Sense of Self in Nursery School Children as Manifested by Their Verbal Behavior," *Journal of Genetic Psychology,* Vol. 81 (1952), pp. 193-232.

ANDERSON, Robert H., "Ungraded Primary Classes: An Administrative Contribution to Mental Health," *Understanding the Child,* Vol. 24 (June, 1955), pp. 66-72.

ASHBY, Lyle W., "The Teacher Shapes Tomorrow," *National Parent-Teacher,* Vol. 50 (February, 1956), p. 8.

Association for Childhood Education International, *Continuous Learning,* Bull. 87 (Washington, D.C., The Association, 1951).

————, *Creating with Materials for Work and Play Portfolio* (Washington, D.C., The Association, 1957).

————, "Experiments in Reorganizing the Primary School, a Symposium," *Childhood Education,* Vol. 15 (February, 1939), pp. 262-271.

————, *Grouping: Problems and Satisfactions,* Bull. 26 (Washington, D.C., The Association, 1953-4).

————, *Kindergarten Teachers Portfolio,* No. 2 (Washington, D.C., The Association, 1951).

————, *Nursery School Portfolio,* No. 1 (Washington, D.C., The Association, 1953).

————, *Pictures of Children Living and Learning* (Washington, D.C., The Association, 1951).

————, *Primary School Portfolio,* No. 3 (Washington, D.C., The Association, 1956).

————, *Recommended Equipment and Supplies for Nursery, Kindergarten, Primary, and Intermediate Grades,* Bull. 39 (Washington, D.C., The Association, 1958).

————, *Reporting on the Growth of Children,* Bull. 62 (Washington, D.C., The Association, 1953).

————, "What (Community) Agencies Are Available?" *Childhood Education,* Vol. 28 (March, 1952), pp. 297-304.

Association for Supervision and Curriculum Development, "A Good Environment for Learning," *Educational Leadership,* Vol. 5 (March, 1948), entire issue.

————, *Continuity in the School Program,* 1958 Yearbook (Washington, D.C., The Association, 1958).

————, NEA, *Creating a Good Environment for Learning,* 1954 Yearbook (Washington, D.C., The Association, 1954).

————, "Creativity and the School," *Educational Leadership,* Vol. 14 (October, 1956), entire issue.

————, *Curriculum Materials for Creative Thinking, Living, and Teaching* (Washington, D.C., The Association, 1956).

————, "Education and the Foreseeable Future," *Educational Leadership,* Vol. 15 (October, 1957), entire issue.

————, "Education and the Future: Appraisal and Planning," *Educational Leadership,* Vol. 15 (February, 1957), entire issue.

————, *Forces Affecting American Education,* 1953 Yearbook (Washington, D.C., The Association, 1953).

————, *Fostering Mental Health in Our Schools,* 1950 Yearbook (Washington, D.C., The Association, 1950).

————, *Group Planning in Education,* 45th Yearbook (Washington, D.C., The Association, 1945).

————, *Growing Up in an Anxious Age,* 1952 Yearbook (Washington, D.C., The Association, 1952).

————, *Large Was Our Bounty,* 1948 Yearbook (Washington, D.C., The Association, 1948).

————, *Laymen Help Plan the Curriculum* (Washington, D.C., The Association, 1946).

————, *Organizing the Elementary School for Living and Learning,* 1947 Yearbook (Washington, D.C., The Association, 1947).

————, *Toward Better Teaching,* 1949 Yearbook (Washington, D.C., The Association, 1949).

————, "Trends in Meeting Individual Differences," *Educational Leadership,* Vol. 15 (December, 1957), entire issue.

————, *Using Free Materials in the Classroom* (Washington, D.C., The Association, 1953).

AXLINE, Virginia M., *Play Therapy* (Boston, Houghton Mifflin Company, 1947).

BACMEISTER, Rhoda W., *Your Child and Other People* (Boston, Little, Brown & Company, 1950).

————, *Growing Together* (New York, Appleton-Century-Crofts, Inc., 1947).

BALDWIN, A. L., *Behavior and Development in Childhood* (New York, Henry Holt & Company, Inc., 1955).

BALDWIN, Louise, and others, "Reducing the Gap Between Kindergarten and First Grade," *The Nation's Schools,* Vol. 54 (August, 1954), pp. 38-41.

BARKER, R. G., KOUNIN, J. S., and WRIGHT, H., eds., *Child Behavior and Development* (New York, McGraw-Hill Book Company, Inc., 1943).

BARNARD, Henry, ed., *Papers on Froebel's Kindergarten* (Hartford, Office of Barnard's American Journal of Education, 1908).

BARNETT, Glenn E., "The Educational Setting of Early Childhood Education," *California Journal of Elementary Education,* Vol. 17 (February, 1949), pp. 134-138.

BARUCH, Dorothy, *Understanding Young Children* (New York, Bureau of Publications, Teachers College, Columbia University, 1953).

————, *Parents and Children Go to School* (Chicago, Scott, Foresman & Company, 1939).

BATHURST, Effie G., *Where Children Live Affects Curriculum,* Bull. 1950, No. 7 (Washington, D.C., Government Printing Office, 1950).

————, and HILL, Wilhelmina, *Conservation Experience for Children,* Bull. 1957 (Washington, D.C., Government Printing Office, 1957).

BAYLEY, Nancy, *Studies in the Development of Young Children* (Berkeley, University of California Press, 1940).

BEAUCHAMP, George A., *Planning the Elementary School Curriculum* (Boston, Allyn and Bacon, Inc., 1956).

BENNETT, Mabel C., and BISHOP, Katherine V., *Showing and Sharing: Pupils and Teachers Interpret Education Through Parent Group Conferences* (Los Angeles, Education Press, 1952).

BENT, Rudyard K., "Contributions of Student Organizations to the Professional Growth of Teachers," *Journal of Teacher Education,* Vol. 8 (September, 1957), pp. 276-277.

BERGAMINI, Yolanda, and SWANSON, Walter, "Does Kindergarten Make a Difference?" *School Executive,* Vol. 74 (December, 1954), pp. 54-55.

BERKSON, I. B., *Education Faces the Future* (New York, Harper & Brothers, 1943).

BIBER, Barbara, and LEWIS, Claudia, "An Experimental Study of What Young Children Expect from Their Teachers," *Genetic Psychology Monographs,* Vol. 60, No. 1 (1948), pp. 3-97.

BIXBY, P. W., "Parents and Teachers Study Report Cards," *National Elementary Principal,* Vol. 25 (September, 1945), pp. 90-92.

BLACKWELL, Gordon W., *Toward Community Understanding* (Washington, D.C., American Council on Education, 1943).

BLATZ, W. E., *Understanding the Young Child* (New York, William Morrow & Company, 1944).

BLOW, Susan, "Kindergarten Education," in N. H. Butler, ed., *Monographs on Education in United States* (New York, J. B. Lyons Company, 1900).

————, *Conservative Report of the Committee of Nineteen: The Kindergarten* (Boston, Houghton Mifflin Company, 1913).

BOARDMAN, B. W., and others, "Value Experiences with Children," *Educational Leadership,* Vol. 8 (May, 1951), pp. 485-487.

BOSSARD, James H., *The Sociology of Child Development* (New York, Harper & Brothers, 1954).

————, *The Parent and Child* (Philadelphia, University of Pennsylvania Press, 1953).

BOSTWICK, Prudence, and others, *One Hundred Years of Curriculum Improve-*

ment, 1857-1957 (Washington, D.C., Association for Supervision and Curriculum Development, 1957).

BOTTRELL, Harold R., ed., *Introduction to Education* (Harrisburg, Pa., The Stackpole Co., 1955).

BOTTRELL, Helen K., "Textbooks Can Be Creative Resources," *Educational Leadership,* Vol. 12 (April, 1955), pp. 418-422.

BRECHENRIDGE, Marion E., and VINCENT, E. Lee, *Child Development* (Philadelphia, W. B. Saunders Company, 1955).

British Information Services, *Education in Great Britain* (New York, 30 Rockefeller Plaza, n.d.).

BRODERICH, Catherine M., "Research in the Use and Purpose of Instructional Materials," *Educational Leadership,* Vol. 13 (April, 1956), pp. 418-422.

BROGAN, Peggy, and FOX, Lorene K., *Helping Children Learn: A Concept of Elementary-School Method* (Yonkers, N.Y., World Book Co., 1955).

BROOKOVER, Wilbur B., *A Sociology of Education* (New York, American Book Company, 1955).

BROWN, James, "First a Person, Then a Teacher," *Educational Leadership,* Vol. 13 (February, 1956), pp. 299-302.

BROWNELL, Baker, *The Human Community* (New York, Harper & Brothers, 1950).

BUFORD, Florence, "We Looked at Our Schools," *National Elementary Principal,* Vol. 34 (December, 1954), pp. 20-22.

BUROS, Oscar K., *The Fourth Mental Measurement Yearbook* (Highlands Park, N.J., The Gryphon Press, 1953).

BURTON, William H., *The Guidance of Learning Activities* (New York, Appleton-Century-Crofts, Inc., 1952).

————, *Introduction to Education* (New York, D. Appleton-Century Company, Inc., 1934).

BUTLER, N. H., *The Meaning of Education* (New York, Charles Scribner's Sons, 1915).

————, *California Looks at the Elementary School,* 27th Yearbook (San Francisco, The Association, 1955).

California Elementary School Administrators' Association, *The Characteristics of the Good Elementary School* (San Francisco, The Association, 1955).

————, *The Elementary School at Midcentury,* 23rd Yearbook (San Francisco, The Association, 1951).

————, *Instructional Supplies and Equipment for the Five- and Six-Year-Olds of the Good Elementary School* (San Francisco, The Association, 1956).

————, *Instructional Supplies and Equipment for the Four- and Five-Year-Olds of the Good Elementary School* (San Francisco, The Association, 1956).

————, *A Study of Early Childhood Education in California,* Vol. 18, No. 5 (Sacramento, The Department, 1949).

California State Department of Education, *A Teachers Guide to Education in Early Childhood* (Sacramento, The Department, 1956).

————, *California Cumulative Record, Kindergarten Through Grade 14* (Sacramento, The Department).

————, *Evaluating Pupil Progress,* Vol. 21, No. 6 (Sacramento, The Department, 1952).

————, *Guidance in the Elementary School,* Bull. 23, No. 4 (Sacramento, The Department, 1954).

———— —, *Handbook of Parent Education,* Vol. 19, No. 5 (Sacramento, The Department, 1950).

————, *Home and School Work Together for Young Children,* Vol. 13, No. 1 (Sacramento, The Department, 1949).

————, The Kindergarten Issue, *California Journal of Elementary Education,* Vol. 24 (August, 1955), entire issue.

————, *Preparation of Teachers for Home, School, Community Relations,* Bull. No. 8 (Sacramento, The Department, 1953).

————, Reporting to Parents Issue, *California Journal of Elementary Education,* Vol. 24 (November, 1955), entire issue.

California State Supervisors Association, Helen Heffernan, ed., *Guiding the Young Child* (Boston, D. C. Heath & Company, 1958).

CAMPBELL, R. F., and RAMSEYER, J. A., *The Dynamics of School-Community Relationships* (Boston, Allyn and Bacon, Inc., 1954).

————, and others, "Growth and Development of Children of Kindergarten Age," *California Journal of Elementary Education,* Vol. 24 (August, 1955), pp. 5-10.

CANTOR, Nathaniel, *The Teaching-Learning Process* (New York, Henry Holt & Company, Inc., 1953).

CAPPA, D., "Implications of Child Development for the Primary Social Studies Teacher," *Social Studies,* Vol. 48 (December, 1957), pp. 286-288.

CARMICHAEL, Leonard, ed., *Manual of Child Psychology* (New York, John Wiley & Sons, Inc., 1954).

CARR, William G., "The View Ahead," *National Education Association Journal,* Vol. 46 (March, 1957), p. 167.

CASWELL, Hollis L., "A Curriculum Viewpoint on Educational Television," *Educational Leadership,* Vol. 14 (November, 1957), p. 107.

————, *Non-Promotion in Elementary Schools* (Nashville, Tenn., Division of Surveys and Field Studies, George Peabody College for Teachers, 1933).

————, and FOSHAY, Arthur W., *Education in the Elementary School,* 3rd ed. (New York, American Book Company, 1957).

————, and others, *Curriculum Improvement in Public School Systems* (New York, Bureau of Publications, Teachers College, Columbia University, 1950).

CHAMBERLAIN, O. R., and CHAMBERLAIN, R. R., "Do Children Need Preschool Experiences?" *Childhood Education,* Vol. 32 (April, 1956), pp. 371-373.

CHASE, Francis S., "The Schools I Hope to See," *National Education Association Journal,* Vol. 46 (March, 1957), pp. 164-166.

CHILDS, John L., "The Future of the Common School," *Educational Forum,* Vol. 21 (January, 1957), pp. 133-141.

Cincinnati Board of Education, *Primary Manual* (Cincinnati, Board of Education, 1948).

CLAPP, Elsie R., *The Use of Resources in Education* (New York, Harper & Brothers, 1950).

CLOUD, Roy, *Education in California* (Palo Alto, Stanford University Press, 1952).

COFFIELD, William H., and BLOMMERS, Paul, "Effects of Non-Promotion on Educational Achievement in the Elementary School," *Journal of Educational Psychology,* Vol. 47 (April, 1956), pp. 235-250.

COLE, Luella, *History of Education from Socrates to Montessori* (New York, Rinehart & Company, Inc., 1950).

COMENIUS, John Amos, trans. and ed. by M. W. Keating, *The Great Didactic* (London, A. & C. Black, Ltd., 1896).

————, ed. by Ernest M. Eller, *The School of Infancy* (Chapel Hill, University of North Carolina Press, 1956).

Comité-France Actuelle, *Education in France* (Paris, The Comite, 1956).

Commission on Teacher Education, *Helping Teachers Understand Children* Washington, D.C., American Council on Education, 1945).

Connecticut State Board of Education, *How Is Our School Growing?* (Hartford, State Board of Education, 1955).

COOK, Walter W., *Grouping and Promotion in the Elementary School,* College of Education Series on Individualization, No. 2 (Minneapolis, University of Minnesota Press, 1941).

COREY, Stephen M., *Action Research to Improve School Practices* (New York Bureau of Publications, Teachers College, Columbia University, 1957).

————, *Audio-Visual Materials of Instruction* (New York, Bureau of Publications, Teachers College, Columbia University, 1949).

————, "Interpersonal Relations and the Work of the School," *Baltimore Bulletin of Education,* Vol. 29 (March-June, 1952), pp. 16-22.

COUNTS, George S., *Education and American Civilization* (New York, Bureau of Publications, Teachers College, Columbia University, 1952).

COWIN, Shirley H., "Reading Readiness Through Kindergarten Experience," *Elementary School Journal,* Vol. 52 (October, 1951), pp. 96-99.

Creative Playthings, Inc., *Equipment and Materials for Early Childhood* (New York, Creative Playthings, Inc., 5 University Place, n.d.).

CREMIN, L., and BORROWMAN, M., *Public Schools in Our Democracy* (New York, The Macmillan Company, 1956).

CRONBACH, Lee J., *Educational Psychology* (New York, Harcourt, Brace & Company, Inc., 1954).

CUBBERLY, Elwood P., *The History of Education* (Boston, Houghton Mifflin Company, 1948).

CULKIN, Mary Louise, *Teaching the Youngest* (New York, The Macmillan Company, 1949).

CUNNINGHAM, Ruth, and others, *Understanding Group Behavior of Boys and Girls* (New York, Bureau of Publications, Teachers College, Columbia University, 1951).

CURTIS, Dwight K., "The Contribution of the Excursion to Understanding," *Journal of Educational Research,* Vol. 38 (November, 1944), pp. 201-212.

DAVIS, Allison, and HAVIGHURST, Robert J., *Father of the Man: How Your Child Gets His Personality* (Boston, Houghton Mifflin Company, 1947).

Davis, Mary Dabney, *Nursery Schools, Their Development and Current Practice in the United States*, Bull. No. 9 (Washington, D.C., Government Printing Office, 1932).

———, *General Practice in Kindergarten Education in the United States* (Washington, D.C., National Education Association, 1925).

———, "Century of the Kindergarten," *School Life* (November, 1936), p. 67.

Davis, W. A., *Social-Class Influences upon Learning,* Inglis Lecture (Cambridge, Harvard University Press, 1948).

Dawe, Helen C., "A Study of the Effect of an Educational Program upon Language Development and Related Mental Functions in Young Children," *Journal of Experimental Education,* Vol. 2 (1942), pp. 200-209.

Del Solar, Charlotte, *Parents and Teachers View the Child: A Comparative Study of Parents' and Teachers' Appraisals of Children* (New York, Bureau of Publications, Teachers College, Columbia University, 1951).

Dennis, Wayne, ed., *Readings in Child Psychology* (Englewood Cliffs, N.J., Prentice-Hall, Inc., 1951).

Department of Elementary School Principals, NEA, *Bases for Effective Learning,* 31st Yearbook (Washington, D. C., The Department, 1952).

———, "Communication," *The National Elementary Principal,* Vol. 27 (February, 1958), entire issue.

———, *Contemporary Society-Background for the Instructional Program* (Washington, D.C., The Department, 1957).

———, *The Flexible School,* (Washington, D.C., The Department, 1957).

———, *Instructional Materials for Elementary Schools* (Washington, D.C., The Department, 1956).

———, *Parents and the Schools* (Washington, D.C., The Department, 1957).

"The Development of the Teaching Space Divider," *American School and University Journal,* Vol. 26 (1954-55), p. 435.

D'Evelyn, Katherine E., *Individual Parent Teacher Conferences: A Manual for Teachers of Young Children* (New York, Bureau of Publications, Teachers College, Columbia University, 1952).

———, *Meeting Children's Emotional Needs: A Guide for Teachers* (Englewood Cliffs, N.J., Prentice-Hall, Inc., 1957).

Dewey, John, *The School and Society* (Chicago, University of Chicago Press, 1924).

De Young, Chris, *American Public Education* (New York, McGraw-Hill Book Company, Inc., 1955).

Dillon, Ina K., *Firmer Boundaries for Greater Freedom,* reprint, Association for Nursery Education, Southern California (Los Angeles, Office of Consulting Service, 1955).

Dimond, Stanley E., *Schools and the Development of Good Citizens: The Final Report of the Citizenship Education Study* (Detroit, Wayne University Press, 1953).

Doak, Elizabeth, *What Does the Nursery School Teacher Teach?* (Kingston, R.I., National Association for Nursery Education, Distribution Center, University of Rhode Island, 1951).

309

DRACOULIDES, N. M., "Preschool Education and Mental Health," *Understanding the Child,* Vol. 25 (June, 1956), pp. 84-85.

DRISCOLL, Gertrude P., *How to Study the Behavior of Children,* 7th ed. (New York, Bureau of Publications, Teachers College, Columbia University, 1954).

DURR, William K., *The First Day of School,* Professional Series Bulletin No. 28, Bureau of Educational Research, College of Education (East Lansing, Michigan State University, 1957).

EAST, J. K., "Kindergarten Is a Good Investment," *School Executive,* Vol. 72 (May, 1953), pp. 52-53.

EAST, Marjorie, *Display for Learning: Making and Using Visual Materials* (New York, Henry Holt & Company, Inc., 1952).

Educational Policies Commission, NEA, *Education for All American Children* (Washington, D.C., The Commission, 1948).

———, *Moral and Spiritual Values in the Public Schools* (Washington, D.C., The Commission, 1951).

———, *The Purposes of Education in American Democracy* (Washington, D.C., The Commission, 1938).

———, *Strengthening Community Life: Schools Can Help* (Washington, D.C., The Commission, 1956).

ELDER, Franklin L., *Explorations in Parent-School Relations* (Austin, University of Texas Press, 1954).

ELSBREE, Willard S., *Pupil Progress in the Elementary School* (New York, Bureau of Publications, Teachers College, Columbia University, 1943).

———, and McNALLY, Harold J., *Elementary School Administration and Supervision* (New York, American Book Company, 1951).

ENGLEHARDT, N. L., Jr., "The Home-School Unit," *The School Executive,* Vol. 68 (January, 1949), pp. 42-43.

ENGLEHARDT, N. L., ENGLEHARDT, N. L. Jr., and LEGGETT, Stanton, *Planning for Elementary School Buildings* (New York, F. W. Dodge Corporation, 1953).

Field Enterprises, Educational Division, *Sources of Free and Inexpensive Educational Materials* (Chicago, Field Enterprises, 1955).

FOREMAN, Anna B., "A Report Card for Evaluating the Progress of the Whole Child," *Elementary School Journal,* Vol. 49 (November, 1940), pp. 195-205.

———, *Child Development* (New York, McGraw-Hill Book Company, Inc., 1954).

FOREST, Ilse, *Early Years at School* (New York, McGraw-Hill Book Company, Inc., 1949).

FORREST, William B., STEELE, Marion G., and FOSTER, Lester I., *The Group Conference* (Torrance, California, Torrance Unified School District, 1957).

FOSHAY, Arthur W., and others, *Children's Social Values: An Action Research Study* (New York, Bureau of Publications, Teachers College, Columbia University, 1954).

FOSTER, Josephine C., and HEADLEY, Neith E., *Education in the Kindergarten* (New York, American Book Company, 1948).

FOSTER, Josephine C., and MATTSON, Marion, *Nursery School Education* (New York, Appleton-Century-Crofts, Inc., 1939).

Fox, L., and others, *All Children Want to Learn: A Guide for Parents* (New York, Grolier Society, 1954).

Frank, Lawrence K., "Play in Personality Development," *American Journal of Orthopsychiatry,* Vol. 25 (1955), pp. 576-590.

————, and Frank, Mary, *How to Help Your Child in School* (New York, Viking Press, Inc., 1950).

Frank, Martha, *The Challenge of Children* (New York, William Morrow & Company, 1957).

Franklin, Adele, "Blocks, a Tool of Learning," *Childhood Education,* Vol. 26 (January, 1950), pp. 209-213.

Froebel, Friedrich, *Pedagogics of the Kindergarten,* trans. by J. Jarvis (New York, D. Appleton & Company, 1895).

————, trans. by Michaelis and Moore, *Letters on the Kindergarten* (Syracuse, N.Y., Bardeen Company, 1896).

————, trans. by W. N. Hailmann, *Education of Man* (New York, D. Appleton & Company, 1892).

————, trans. by H. R. Eliot, *Mottoes and Commentaries of Friedrich Froebel's Mother-Play* (New York, D. Appleton & Company, 1908).

————, trans. by J. Jarvis, *Education by Development* (New York, D. Appleton & Company, 1902).

Gans, Roma, Stendler, Celia Burns, and Almy, Millie C., *Teaching Young Children* (Yonkers, N.Y., World Book Co., 1952).

Garrison, Noble Lee, *The Improvement of Teaching: A Two-Fold Approach* (New York, Henry Holt & Company, Inc., 1955).

Garry, Ralph, "Psychological Tools Assist the Teacher," *Educational Leadership,* Vol. 12 (April, 1955), pp. 402-406.

George Peabody College for Teachers, *Free and Inexpensive Learning Materials* (Nashville, Tenn., Division of Surveys and Field Services, The College, 1952).

Gesell, Arnold, *The Preschool Child from the Standpoint of Public Hygiene and Education* (Boston, Houghton Mifflin Company, 1932).

————, and Ilg, Frances, *Child Development: An Introduction to the Study of Human Growth* (New York, Harper & Brothers, 1949).

Gilmer, Von Haller, *How to Help Your Child Develop Successfully* (Englewood Cliffs, N.J., Prentice-Hall, Inc., 1951).

Glennon, Vincent J., ed., "The Ungraded Primary School as a Contribution to Improved School Practices," *Frontier of Elementary Education II* (Syracuse, N.Y., Syracuse University Press, 1955), pp. 28-29.

Glennon, V. S., and Vandereof, T., "Essential Characteristics of a Modern Classroom," *Educational Leadership,* Vol. 9 (December, 1951), pp. 200-201.

Goodlad, John I., "Some Effects of Promotion and Non-Promotion upon Social and Personal Adjustments of Children," *Journal of Experimental Psychology,* Vol. 22 (June, 1954), pp. 301-328.

————, "Ungrading the Elementary Grades," *National Education Association Journal,* Vol. 44 (March, 1955), pp. 170-171.

————, and Anderson, Robert H., "The Nongraded Elementary School," *NEA Journal,* Vol. 47 (December, 1958), pp. 642-643.

GOODYKOONTZ, Bess., "Recent History and Present Status of Education for Young Children," in National Society for Study of Education, *Early Childhood Education,* 46th Yearbook, Part II (Chicago, University of Chicago Press, 1947).

GRAVES, Frank, *Great Educators of Three Centuries* (New York, The Macmillan Company, 1912).

GRIEDER, C., and ROMAINE, S., *American Public Education: An Introduction* (New York, The Ronald Press Company, 1955).

GRINNELL, J. E., and YOUNG, Raymond J., *The School and the Community* (New York, The Ronald Press Company, 1955).

GOULD, G., and YOAKAM, G. A., *The Teacher and His Work* (New York, The Ronald Press Company, 1955).

GUTTERIDGE, Mary V., "Nursery School in the Public School," *School and Society,* Vol. 73 (May 19, 1951), pp. 309-312.

HAGGARD, Ernest A., "Learning: A Process of Change," *Educational Leadership,* Vol. 12 (December, 1955), pp. 149-156.

HALL, G. Stanley, "Some Defects of the Kindergarten in America," *Forum* (January, 1900).

HAMILTON, Warren W., "By Their Differences They Learn," *The National Elementary School Principal,* Vol. 26 (December, 1957), pp. 27-29.

———, "Why Group by Grade Level? *The Grade Teacher,* Vol. 76 (September, 1958), pp. 18-19.

HANNA, L. A., POTTER, G. L., and HAGAMAN, N. C., *Unit Teaching in the Elementary School* (New York, Rinehart & Company, Inc., 1956).

HARAP, Henry, "Use of Free and Inexpensive Learning Materials in the Classroom," *School Review,* Vol. 63 (October, 1955), pp. 378-383.

HARRIS, Fred E., "Three Persistent Educational Problems: Grading, Promoting, and Reporting to Parents," *Bulletin of the Bureau of School Services,* University of Kentucky, Vol. 26 (September, 1953).

HARTLEY, R. E., FRANK, L. K., and GOLDENSON, R. M., *Understanding Children's Play* (New York, Columbia University Press, 1952).

HASKELL, Douglas, "The Modern Nursery School, *Architectural Record,* Vol. 83 (March, 1938), pp. 84-100.

HASKEW, Laurence D., This Is Teaching (Chicago, Scott, Foresman and Company, 1956).

HATTWICK, B. W., "The Influence of Nursery School Attendance upon the Behavior and Personality of the Preschool Child," *Journal of Experimental Education,* Vol. 5. (1936), pp. 180-190.

HAVIGHURST, Robert J., *Developmental Tasks and Education,* rev. ed., (New York, Longmans, Green & Company, 1953).

———, *Human Development and Education* (New York, Longmans, Green & Company, 1953).

———, and NEUGARTEN, Bernice L., *Society and Education* (Boston, Allyn and Bacon, Inc., 1957).

HAWKINS, Reginald R., *Easy-to-Make Outdoor Play Equipment* (New York, The Macmillan Company, 1957).

HEADLY, Neith E., "The Kindergarten Comes of Age," *National Education Association Journal,* Vol. 43 (March, 1954), pp. 153-154.

———, "Good Education for Five-Year-Olds," *Childhood Education,* Vol. 30 (March, 1954), pp. 314-316.

HEFFERNAN, Helen, "The Organization of the Elementary School and the Development of Personality," *California Journal of Elementary Education,* Vol. 20 (February, 1952), pp. 129-153.

———, "Grouping Pupils for Well-Rounded Growth and Development," *California Journal of Elementary Education,* Vol. 21 (August, 1952), pp. 42-50.

———, "Freedom for Development of Individuality," *National Education Association Journal,* Vol. 44 (May, 1955), pp. 282-284.

———, "Space for Learning," *National Education Association Journal,* Vol. 44 (March, 1955), pp. 142-145.

———, "Stimulation for Learning," *National Education Association Journal,* Vol. 44 (April, 1955), pp. 218-221.

———, "Teach Reading in Kindergarten?" *The Grade Teacher,* Vol. 75, September, 1957), p. 16.

———, "Block Play in the Kindergarten," *The Grade Teacher,* Vol. 75 (January, 1958), p. 14.

———, "Dramatic Play in Kindergarten," *The Grade Teacher,* Vol. 75 (February, 1958), p. 14.

———, and BURSCH, Charles, *Curriculum and the Elementary School Plan* (Washington, D.C., Association for Supervision and Curriculum Development, 1958).

HELMHOLZ, Henry F., *The Function of the P.T.A. in Continued Health Supervision of Children* (Chicago, National Congress of Parents and Teachers, February, 1957).

HERRICK, Virgil E., "Design of the Curriculum," *Review of Educational Research,* Vol. 27, No. 3 (June, 1957), pp. 270-276.

———, and others, *The Elementary School* (Englewood Cliffs, N.J., Prentice-Hall, Inc., 1956).

HILDRETH, Gertrude H., *Readiness for School Beginners* (Yonkers, N. Y., World Book Co., 1950).

———, *Child Growth Through Education* (New York, The Ronald Press Company, 1948).

———, "Hazards of Straight Promotions," *Educational Administration and Supervision,* Vol. 32 (January, 1946), pp. 19-26.

HILGARD, Josephine R., "Learning and Maturation in Preschool Children," *Journal of Genetic Psychology,* Vol. 41 (1932), pp. 40-53.

HILL, Patty, *A Conduct Curriculum for Kindergarten and First Grade* (New York, Charles Scribner's Sons, 1927).

———, "Experimental Studies in Kindergarten Theory and Practice," *Teachers College Record,* Vol. 15, No. 1 (January, 1914).

———, *Kindergarten,* reprint (Washington, D.C., Association for Childhood Education International, 1942).

————, "Changes in Curriculum and Method in Kindergarten Education," *Childhood Education,* Vol. 2 (November, 1925), pp. 99-106.

HILL, Wilhelmina, *Social Studies in Elementary Schools,* Brief No. 29 (Washington, D.C., Office of Education, 1954).

HILLIS, Charity, *Preparation and Evaluation of Instructional Materials on Community Agencies,* Bulletin of the Bureau of School Service, Vol. 21, No. 2 (Lexington, University of Kentucky, 1948).

HOLDEN, McLaughlin, and others, "Model Center for Child Care," *Architectural Record* (May, 1946), pp. 108-109.

HOOPER, Laura, "The Child—The Curriculum—The World of Materials," *Childhood Education,* Vol. 51 (May, 1955), pp. 443-445.

HOPKINS, L. T., *Interaction: The Democratic Process* (Boston, D. C. Heath & Company, 1941).

————, "Continuity in Learning," *Childhood Education,* Vol. 31 (January, 1955), pp. 214-217.

HORACE MANN-LINCOLN Institute of School Experimentation, *How to Construct a Sociogram* (New York, Bureau of Publications, Teachers College, Columbia University, 1951).

HOVE, Olav, *An Outline of Norwegian Education* (Oslo, Royal Norwegian Ministry of Foreign Affairs, 1955).

HUNNICUT, Clarence W., *Answering Children's Question* (New York, Bureau of Publications, Teachers College, Columbia University, 1954).

HURLOCK, Elizabeth, *Developmental Psychology* (New York, McGraw-Hill Book Company, Inc., 1953).

HUTCHINS, Clayton, and MUNSE, Albert R., *Public School Finance Programs of the United States* (Washington, D.C., Government Printing Office, 1956).

HYMES, James L., Jr., *A Child Development Point of View* (Englewood Cliffs, N.J., Prentice-Hall, Inc., 1955).

————, *Before the Child Reads* (Chicago, Row Peterson & Co., 1958).

————, *Effective Home-School Relations* (Englewood Cliffs, N.J., Prentice-Hall, Inc., 1953).

IDENBURG, Philip J., *Education in the Netherlands* (Hague, Netherlands Government Information Office, 1950).

ILG, Frances, and AMES, Louise B., *Child Behavior* (New York, Harper & Brothers, 1955).

Illinois State Department of Education, *School Begins with Kindergarten,* Illinois Curriculum Program Publication, Subject Field Service, Bulletin # C-1 (Springfield, The Department, September, 1957).

————, *Illinois Curriculum Program Consensus Study No. 8,* Inventories A, B, and C (Springfield, Superintendent of Public Instruction, State of Illinois, June 1952).

IMHOFF, Myrtle M., "The Teacher Sets the Sights," *Childhood Education,* Vol. 33 (October, 1956), pp. 60-62.

————, *Early Elementary Education,* Selected References, No. 6 (Washington, D.C., Office of Education, February, 1957).

————, *The Primary Unit,* Selected References, No. 1 (Washington, D.C., Office of Education, May, 1957).

Institute of Child Study, University of Maryland, "Child Growth and Development," *National Education Association Journal,* Vol. 47 (December, 1957), pp. 571-580.

International Kindergarten Union, Committee of Nineteen, *Pioneers of the Kindergarten in America* (New York, The Century Co., 1924).

————, *The Kindergarten* (Boston, Houghton Mifflin Company, 1913).

ISAACS, Susan, *Social Development in Young Children* (New York, Harper & Brothers, 1946).

————, *Intellectual Growth in Young Children* (Baltimore, Routledge Publishing Company, 1930).

JACKSON, Margaret M., "Understanding It Better with Felt Boards," *Instructor,* Vol. 64 (June, 1955), pp. 18, 20.

JENKINS, Gladys, SHACTER, Helen, and BAUER, William, *These Are Your Children* (Chicago, Scott, Foresman and Company, 1953).

JENNINGS, Helen H., *Sociometry in Group Relations* (Washington, D.C., American Council on Education, 1948).

JERSILD, Arthur T., *Child Development and the Curriculum* (New York, Bureau of Publications, Teachers College, Columbia University, 1956).

————, *Child Psychology,* 4th ed. (Englewood Cliffs, N.J., Prentice-Hall, Inc., 1954).

————, *In Search of Self* (New York, Horace Mann-Lincoln Institute of School Experimentation, Teachers College, Columbia University, 1952).

————, *When Teachers Face Themselves* (New York, Bureau of Publications, Teachers College, Columbia University, 1955).

————, and FITE, Mary D., "Children's Social Adjustment in Nursery School," in Wayne Dennis, ed., *Readings in Child Psychology* (Englewood Cliffs, N.J., Prentice-Hall, Inc., 1951), pp. 567-576.

JERSILD, Arthur T., and TASCH, R., *Children's Interests and What They Suggest for Education* (New York, Bureau of Publications, Teachers College, Columbia University, 1951).

JOHNSON, Earl A., and MICHAEL, E. Eldon, *Principles of Teaching* (Boston, Allyn and Bacon, Inc., 1958).

JOHNSON, Harriet, *Children in the Nursery School* (New York, The John Day Company, Inc., 1928).

JOHNSON, June, *Home Play for the Preschool Child* (New York, Harper & Brothers, 1957).

JOHNSTON, Marjorie C., *Education in Mexico,* Office of Education Bulletin (Washington, D.C., Government Printing Office, 1956).

KENDEL, I. L., *Comparative Education* (Boston, Houghton Mifflin Company, 1933).

KAWIN, Ethel, *The Wise Choice of Toys* (Chicago, University of Chicago Press, 1938).

KEARNEY, Nolan C., ed., *Elementary School Objectives,* Report Prepared by the Mid-Century Committee on Outcomes in Elementary Education (New York, Russell Sage Foundation, 1953).

KELIHER, Alice V., *A Critical Study of Homogeneous Grouping in Elementary*

Schools Contribution to Education No. 452 (New York, Bureau of Publications, Teachers College, Columbia University, 1931).

KELLOGG, Rhoda, *Nursery School Guide: Theory and Practice for Teachers and Parents* (Boston, Houghton Mifflin Company, 1949).

KELLY, Florence C., "Ungraded Primary Schools Make the Grade in Milwaukee," *National Education Association Journal,* Vol. 40 (December, 1941), pp. 645-646.

KILPATRICK, William H., *Froebel's Kindergarten Principles Critically Examined* (New York, The Macmillan Company, 1916).

KINNEY, L., and DRESDEN, K., *Better Learning Through Current Materials* (Palo Alto, Stanford University Press, 1949).

KNIGHT, Edgar, *Education in the United States* (Boston, Ginn and Company, 1929).

———, *Twenty Centuries of Education* (Boston, Ginn and Company, 1940).

———, and HALL, R., *Readings in American Educational History* (New York, Appleton-Century-Crofts, Inc., 1951).

KOOKER, Earl W., and WILLIAMS, Chester S., "Standards Versus Evaluation," *Educational Administration and Supervision,* Vol. 41 (November, 1955), pp. 385-389.

KOOPMAN, G. Robert, and SNYDER, Edith R., "Living Room for Learning—A Self Contained Unit," *National Education Association Journal,* Vol. 47 (January, 1958), pp. 18-20.

KOSKEY, Thomas A., *Baited Bulletin Boards: Handbook for Teachers* (San Francisco, Fearon Publishing Company, 1954).

KUHLEN, Raymond G., and THOMPSON, George G., *Psychological Studies of Human Development* (New York, Appleton-Century-Crofts, Inc., 1952).

LAMBERT, Hazel M., *Teaching the Kindergarten Child* (New York, Harcourt, Brace and Company, Inc., 1958).

LANDREDTH, Catherine, *Education of the Young Child* (New York, John Wiley & Sons, Inc., 1942).

———, *The Psychology of Early Childhood* (New York, Alfred A. Knopf, Inc., 1958).

LANE, Howard, and BEAUCHAMP, Mary, *Human Relations in Teaching* (Englewood Cliffs, N.J., Prentice-Hall, Inc., 1955).

LANGDON, Grace, *Children Need Toys* (New York, American Toy Institute, 200 Fifth Avenue, n.d.).

———, and STOUT, Irving, *Teacher Parent Interviews* (Englewood Cliffs, N.J., Prentice-Hall, Inc., 1954).

LAWLER, Marcella R., and others, "Free and Inexpensive Materials," *Review of Educational Research,* Vol. 26 (April, 1956), pp. 175-176.

LAWS, Gertrude, "Early Childhood Education and Parent Education," *California Journal of Elementary Education,* Vol. 17 (February, 1949), pp. 190-194.

LAYMAN, A. E., "Block Play an Essential," *Elementary School Journal,* Vol. 40 (April, 1940), pp. 607-613.

LEAVITT, Jerome E., ed., *Nursery-Kindergarten Education* (New York, McGraw-Hill Book Company, Inc., 1958).

LeBaron, Walter A., "Some Practical Techniques in Developing a Program of Continuous Progress in the Elementary School," *Elementary School Journal,* Vol. 46 (October, 1945), pp. 89-96.

Lee, Doris May, "What Should We Expect in Our Kindergarten?" *Education,* Vol. 74 (February, 1954), pp. 362-368.

Lee, J. Murray, and Lee, Dorris May, *The Child and His Development* (New York, Appleton-Century-Crofts, Inc., 1958).

————, *The Child and His Curriculum,* 2d ed. (New York, Appleton-Century-Crofts, Inc., 1957).

Leonard, Edith and others, *Counseling with Parents in Early Childhood Education* (New York, The Macmillan Company, 1954).

Leonard, George B., Jr., "What Is a Teacher?" *Look,* Vol. 20 (February 21, 1956), pp. 29-39.

Lewis, Gertrude L., *Reporting Pupil Progress to Parents,* Brief 34 (Washington, D.C., Office of Education, 1957).

————, and Imhoff, Myrtle, *Teaching in the Elementary School,* Brief 6 (WOC, Office of Ed., (1958).

Lindberg, Lucile, *The Democratic Classroom: A Guide for Teachers* (New York, Bureau of Publications, Teachers College, Columbia University, 1955).

Lindgren, Henry Clay, *Psychology of Personal and Social Adjustment* (New York, American Book Company, 1953).

Lippitt, Ronald, "An Experimental Study of Authoritarian and Democratic Group Atmosphere, Studies in Topological and Vector Psychology I," *University of Iowa Studies in Child Welfare,* Vol. 16 (1940), pp. 44-195.

Lloyd, Elizabeth C., "Nursery Education, Our Responsibility," *Journal of Education,* Vol. 137 (May, 1955), pp. 2-4.

Long Beach Public Schools, *Kindergarten Guide* (Long Beach, Board of Education, 1955).

————, *Handbook for Parent-Teacher Conferences* (Long Beach, Board of Education, 1955).

Lonsdale, Bernard J., "Parent-Teacher Conferences: An Experience in Human Relations," *California Journal of Elementary Education,* Vol. 24 (November, 1955), pp. 78-90.

Lowenfeld, Viktor, *Creative and Mental Growth* (New York, The Macmillan Company, 1957).

Maccoby, Eleanor E., "Parental Attitudes and Methods Affect Preschool Children," *Educational Leadership,* Vol. 10 (April, 1953), pp. 419-422.

Macomber, Freeman Glenn, *Guiding Child Development in the Elementary School* (New York, American Book Company, 1948).

————, *Principles of Teaching in the Elementary School* (New York, American Book Company, 1954).

Malby, Clara M., "School and Home Assist in Kindergarten Induction," *Educational Leadership,* Vol. 12 (March, 1955), pp. 350-351.

Martin, William E., and Stendler, Celia Burns, eds., *Readings in Child Development* (New York, Harcourt, Brace & Company, 1954).

Massei, Renato, "Desirable Traits of Successful Teachers," *Journal of Teacher Education,* Vol. 2 (December, 1951), pp. 291-294.

McAuley, J. D., "Qualities of a Good Teacher," *Peabody Journal of Education,* Vol. 32 (July, 1954), pp. 22-25.

McHugh, Gelolo, *Developing Your Child's Personality* (New York, D. Appleton-Century Company, Inc., 1947).

McLean, Dorothy, "Child Development: A Generation of Research," *Child Development,* Vol. 25, No. 1 (1954), pp. 3-8.

McMillan, Margaret, *The Nursery School* (New York, E. P. Dutton & Company, Inc., 1921).

Mead, Margaret, *The School in American Culture* (Cambridge, Mass., Harvard University Press, 1951).

Meek, Lois H., *Your Child's Development and Guidance Told in Pictures* (Philadelphia, J. B. Lippincott, 1951).

Mercille, Margaret G., "The Primary School Unit: Suggestions with Regard to Some Persistent Elementary School Problems," *Bulletin of the School of Education,* Indiana University, Vol. 25 (January, 1949), pp. 13-17.

Merrit, Eleanor, and Harap, Henry, *Trends in the Production of Curriculum Guides* (Nashville, Tenn., Division of Surveys and Field Services, George Peabody College for Teachers, 1955).

Merry, Frieda K., and Merry, Ralph, *The First Two Decades of Life* (New York, Harper & Brothers, 1950).

Meyer, Adolph E., *The Development of Education in the Twentieth Century* (Englewood Cliffs, N.J., Prentice-Hall, Inc., 1949).

Michaelis, John U., "Current Practices in Evaluation in City School Systems," *Educational and Psychological Measurement,* Vol. 9 (Spring, 1949), pp. 15-22.

Mid-Century White House Conference on Children and Youth, *A Healthy Personality for Every Child,* Publication No. 357 (Washington, D.C., Government Printing Office, n.d.).

Miel, Alice, "Planning for Continuity in the Curriculum," *Teachers College Record,* Vol. 54 (December, 1952), pp. 131-138.

————, *Changing the Curriculum: A Social Process* (New York, D. Appleton-Century Company, Inc., 1946).

————, "When Resources Are for Children," *National Education Association Journal,* Vol. 45 (October, 1956), pp. 401-403.

————, and Brogan, Peggy, *More Than Social Studies* (Englewood Cliffs, N.J., Prentice-Hall, Inc., 1957).

Miel, Alice, and others, *Cooperative Procedures in Learning* (New York, Bureau of Publications, Teachers College, Columbia University, 1957).

Millard, Cecil V., *Child Growth and Development in the Elementary School Years* (Boston, D. C. Heath & Company, 1951).

————, *School and Child: A Case History* (East Lansing, Michigan State University Press, 1954).

————, and Rothney, John W. M., *The Elementary School Child: A Book of Cases* (New York, Henry Holt & Company, Inc., 1957).

Miller, Bruce, *Sources of Free and Inexpensive Pictures* (Riverside, California, Bruce Miller, Box 369, 1952).

————, *So You Want to Start a Picture File* (Riverside, California, Bruce Miller, Box 369, 1954).

MILLER, Edith, "Two Years with the Same Teacher," *Elementary School Journal,* Vol. 49 (May, 1949), pp. 531-535.

MINKLAR, Rachael, "A Thought on Classroom Climate," *Bulletin of the Institute of Child Studies,* Vol. 17, No. 1 (Toronto, The Institute, 1955), pp. 15-16.

MINOR, Ruby, *Early Childhood Education: Its Principles and Practices* (New York, Appleton-Century-Crofts, Inc., 1937).

MITCHELL, Lucy S., *Our Children and Our Schools* (New York, Simon & Schuster, Inc., 1950).

MITCHELL, Morrie R., "The Whole Teacher in a Divided World," *Childhood Education,* Vol. 30 (February, 1954), pp. 267-269.

MONROE, Marion, *Growing into Reading* (Chicago, Scott, Foresman and Company, 1951).

MONROE, Paul, *Textbook in the History of Education* (New York, The Macmillan Company, 1930).

MONTESSORI, Marie, *The Montessori Method* (New York, Frederick A. Stokes Company, 1912).

MORRISON, J. C., "Influence of Kindergarten on Age-Grade Progress of Children Entering School Under Six Years of Age," *Official Report,* American Educational Research Association (Washington, D.C., The Association, 1937).

MORT, Paul R., and VINCENT, William S., *Introduction to American Education* (New York, McGraw-Hill Book Company, Inc., 1954).

MOUSTAKAS, Clark E., *The Teacher and the Child* (New York, McGraw-Hill Book Company, Inc., 1956).

————, and BERSON, Minnie P., *The Young Child in School* (New York, Whiteside, Inc. and William Morrow & Company, 1956).

MURCHISON, Carl, ed., *A Handbook of Child Psychology* (New York, Oxford University Press, 1931).

MURPHY, L. B., *Social Behavior and Child Personality* (New York, Columbia University Press, 1937).

————, and others, *Personality of the Young Child* (New York, Basic Books, Inc., 1956).

MURRA, Wilbur F., "The First Century of the National Education Association," *School and Society* (May 11, 1957), pp. 157-158.

MURSELL, James L., *Principles of Democratic Education* (New York, W. W. Norton & Company, Inc., 1955).

————, *Successful Teaching: Its Psychological Principles* (New York, McGraw-Hill Book Company, Inc., 1954).

National Citizens Commission for the Public Schools, *How Can We Discuss School Problems? A Guide to Conferences on School Problems* (New York, The Commission, 2 West 45th Street, 1956).

————, "Our Schools: The Program of the National Citizen's Commission for Public Schools," *School Executive* (February, 1950), pp. 11-14.

National Citizens Council for Public Schools, "Nursery Schools—The Part They Play," *Better Schools* (June, 1957).

————, "Kindergartens—What Part Do They Play?" *Better Schools* (June, 1957).

National Commission on Teacher Education and Professional Standards, *The Teacher and Professional Organizations* (Washington, D.C., The Commission, 1956).

National Committee on Cumulative Records, *Handbook of Cumulative Records*, Bull. No. 5 (Washington, D.C., Government Printing Office, 1945).

National Congress of Parents and Teachers, *101 Questions about Public Education* (Chicago, The Association, 700 N. Rush Street, 1954).

National Council on Schoolhouse Construction, *Guide for Planning School Plants* (Nashville, Tenn., Peabody College for Teachers, The Council, 1958).

National Council for State Consultants in Elementary Education, *Planning for America's Children: Education for Children Below Six* (Washington, D.C., The Council, care of Dr. Gertrude Lewis, 1711 Massachusetts Avenue, N.W., 1955).

National Education Association, *NEA Handbook* (Washington, D.C., The Association, annually).

————, Ethics Committee, *Code of Ethics of the NEA of the United States* (Washington, D.C., The Association, 1952).

————, Kindergarten Primary Department, *Kindergarten-Primary Education* Washington, D.C., The Association, 1955).

————, Research Division, *Status of the American Public School Teacher* (Washington, D.C., The Association, 1957).

————, Teacher Education and Professional Standards Commission, *Manual on Certification Requirements for School Personnel in the United States* (Washington, D.C., The Association, 1957).

————, Teacher Education and Professional Standards Commission, *Teacher and Professional Organizations* (Washington, D.C., The Association, 1956).

————, *Selections from the NEA Journal for the Beginning Teacher* (Washingington, D.C., The Association, n.d.).

National Society for the Study of Education, *Early Childhood Education*, 46th Yearbook, Part II (Chicago, University of Chicago Press, 1947).

————, *Citizen Cooperation for Better Schools*, 53rd Yearbook, Part I (Chicago, University of Chicago Press, 1954).

————, *The Community School*, 52nd Yearbook, Part II (Chicago, University of Chicago Press, 1953).

————, *Mental Health in Modern Education*, 54th Yearbook, Part II (Chicago, University of Chicago Press, 1955).

————, *Modern Philosophies and Education*, 54th Yearbook, Part I (Chicago, University of Chicago Press, 1955).

NAVARRA, John G., *The Development of Scientific Concepts in a Young Child: A Case Study* (New York, Bureau of Publications, Teachers College, Columbia University, 1955).

NESBITT, Marion, *A Public School for Tomorrow* (New York, Harper & Brothers, 1953).

New England School Development Council, *A Kindergarten Study* (Cambridge, Mass., 20 Oxford Street, May, 1953).

GENERAL BIBLIOGRAPHY

New York State Council for Early Childhood Education, *Good Education for Young Children* (Flushing, N.Y., The Council, Box 98, Queens College, March, 1950).

Ohio State University, School Staff, *How Children Develop*, University School Series No. 3 (Columbus, Ohio State University, 1949).

———, *Studies in the Elementary Grades* (Columbus, Ohio State University, 1955).

OLSEN, Edward G., ed. *The Modern Community School* (New York, Appleton-Century-Crofts, Inc., 1953).

———, ed., *School and Community* (Englewood Cliffs, N.J., Prentice-Hall, Inc., 1954).

OLSON, Clara, and BHARNURATNA, Sai, "Community Resources," *Review of Educational Research,* Vol. 26 (April, 1956), pp. 157-170.

OLSON, Willard C., *Child Development* (Boston, D. C. Heath & Company, 1949).

OTTO, Henry, *Social Education in the Elementary Schools* (New York, Rinehart & Company, Inc., 1956).

———, *Elementary School Organization and Administration* (New York, Appleton-Century-Crofts, Inc., 1954).

———, and others, *Principles of Elementary Education* (New York, Rinehart & Company, Inc., 1955).

OVERSTREET, Henry, and OVERSTREET, Bonaro, *Where Children Come First: A Study of the PTA Idea* (Chicago, National Congress of Parents and Teachers, 1949).

PARKER, Samuel Chester, *General Methods of Teaching in Elementary Schools* (Boston, Ginn and Company, 1922).

PECK, Leigh, *Child Psychology* (Boston, D. C. Heath & Company, 1953).

PERKINS, Lawrence B., *Workplace for Learning* (New York, Reinhold Publishing Corporation, 1956).

PERRIN, Della M., "The School Environment for Young Children in the Kindergarten and Primary Grades," *California Journal of Elementary Education,* Vol. 15 (November, 1947), pp. 120-128.

PETTY, Mary C., *Interclass Grouping in the Elementary School* (Austin, University of Texas Press, 1953).

POLKINGHORNE, Ada R., "Parents and Teachers Appraise Grade Grouping," *Elementary School Journal,* Vol. 51 (January, 1951), pp. 271-279.

———, "Grouping Children in Primary Grades," *Elementary School Journal,* Vol. 50 (May, 1950), pp. 502-508.

POLLEY, John W., and others, *Community Action for Education* (New York, Bureau of Publications, Teachers College, Columbia University, 1953).

POTTER, Gladys L., "Making Continuity Possible," *Childhood Education,* Vol. 25 (November, 1948), pp. 128-131.

PRATT, Caroline, *I Learn from Children* (New York, Simon & Schuster, Inc., 1956).

PRATT, Willis E., "A Study of the Difference in the Prediction of Reading Success of Kindergarten and Non-Kindergarten Children," *Journal of Educational Research,* Vol. 42 (March, 1949), pp. 525-533.

PRESCOTT, Daniel A., *The Child in the Educative Process* (New York, McGraw-Hill Book Company, Inc., 1957).

PRESTON, R., and REDDIN, E., "Status of the Curriculum," *Review of Educational Research,* Vol. 27 (June, 1957), pp. 250-261.

PRINDLE, Frances, "Education's Stake in the Nursery School," *Elementary Journal,* Vol. 56 (March, 1956), pp. 291-297.

RAGAN, William B., *Modern Elementary Curriculum* (New York, Henry Holt & Company, Inc., 1953).

RAND, Winifred, SWEENEY, Mary E., and VINCENT, E. Lee, *Growth and Development of the Young Child* (Philadelphia, W. B. Saunders Company, 1953).

READ, C. H., and ROBERTS, D. D., "What Parents Like in the Kindergarten Interpretation Program," *Nation's Schools,* Vol. 59 (April, 1957), pp. 50-52.

READ, Katherine, *The Nursery School: A Human Relations Laboratory* (Philadelphia, W. B. Saunders Company, 1950).

REDDING, Frank, "T is for Textbooks," *National Education Association Journal,* Vol. 46 (March, 1957), pp. 156-159.

REDL, Fritz, *Understanding Children's Behavior* (New York, Bureau of Publications, Teachers College, Columbia University, 1954).

————, *Teachers Study Their Children* (Washington, D.C., American Council on Education, 1940).

REEDER, Ward, *An Introduction to Public School Relations* (New York, The Macmillan Company, 1953).

REHWOLT, Walter, and HAMILTON, Warren W., *An Analysis of Some of the Effects of Interage and Intergrade Grouping in an Elementary School,* thesis (Los Angeles, University of Southern California, 1956).

RIBBLE, Margaret, M. D., *The Personality of the Young Child* (New York, The Columbia University Press, 1955).

RICHARDSON, S. K., and others, "How Good School-Home-Community Relations Aid the Kindergarten Program," *California Journal of Elementary Education,* Vol. 24 (August, 1955), pp. 46-61.

RICKARD, Garett E., "Establishment of the Graded Schools in American Cities," *Elementary School Journal,* Vol. 48 (February, 1949), pp. 326-335.

RILEY, Fay C., "Grouping Gives Each Child a Chance," *Nation's Schools,* Vol. 56 (August, 1956), pp. 51-53.

ROFF, R., "Grouping and Individualizing in the Elementary Classroom," *Educational Leadership,* Vol. 15 (December, 1957), p. 171.

ROTHNEY, John W. M., *Evaluating and Reporting Pupil Progress,* What Research Says to the Teacher Series, No. 7 (Washington, D.C., National Education Association, 1955).

RUDOLPH, Marguerite, *Living and Learning in the Nursery School* (New York, Harper & Brothers, 1954).

RUSSELL, David H., *Children's Thinking* (Boston, Ginn and Company, 1956).

SANDIN, Adolph A., *Social and Emotional Adjustments of Regularly Promoted and Non-Promoted Pupils* (New York, Bureau of Publications, Teachers College, Columbia University, 1944).

SAUCIER, W. A., *Theory and Practice in the Elementary School* (New York, The Macmillan Company, 1951).

SAYLOR, J. Galen, and ALEXANDER, William M., *Curriculum Planning: For Better Teaching and Learning* (New York, Rinehart & Company, Inc., 1954).

SCHEIFELE, Marion, *The Gifted Child in the Regular Classroom* (New York, Bureau of Publications, Teachers College, Columbia University, 1954).

SCHERER, Lorraine, and others, *How Good Is Our Kindergarten?* Bulletin (Washington, D.C., Association for Childhood Education International, 1958).

School Library Association of California, *Recommended Standards: Elementary School Library,* reprint, Bulletin (March, 1955).

Secretary-General of the United Nations, and others, *Teaching International Understanding,* reprint, *School Life,* Vol. 39 (March, 1957).

SEEDS, Corrine, "Dramatic Play as a Means to Dramatic Social Living," *Childhood Education,* Vol. 19 (January, 1943), pp. 218-221.

SEIDMAN, J., *Readings in Educational Psychology* (Boston, Houghton Mifflin Company, 1955).

SEIPT, Irene S., *Your Child's Happiness* (Yonkers, N.Y., World Book Co., 1955).

SHANE, Harold G., *The American Elementary School,* 13th Yearbook, John Dewey Society (New York, Harper & Brothers, 1953).

———, "Recent Developments in Elementary School Evaluation," *Journal of Educational Research,* Vol. 44 (March, 1951), pp. 491-506.

SHARPE, D. Louise, ed., *Why Teach?* (New York, Henry Holt & Company, Inc., 1957).

SHEEHY, Emma D., *The Fives and Sixes Go to School* (New York, Henry Holt & Company, Inc., 1954).

SHULKEY, S. C., "Fort Worth Has a Middle-of-the-Road Organization," *Childhood Education,* Vol. 28 (December, 1952), pp. 175-178.

SINCLAIR, Thomas J., *An Analysis of Certain Factors Relating to Business Sponsored Teaching Aids,* thesis (Evanston, Northwestern University, 1948).

SLATER, Eva May, *The Primary Unit,* Curriculum Bulletin No. 3 (Storrs, University of Connecticut, 1955).

SMITH, Hyrum Mack, "Studying the Child in the Kindergarten," *National Education Association Journal,* Vol. 45 (February, 1956), pp. 80-81.

SMITH, B. Othanel, STANLEY, William O., and SHORES, J. Harlan, *Fundamentals of Curriculum Development* (Yonkers, N.Y., World Book Company, 1957).

SMITH, Norvel L., "Primary Schools and Home-School Relationships," *Educational Administration and Supervision,* Vol. 42 (March, 1956), pp. 129-133.

SMITTER, Faith, "What is a Primary School?" *California Journal of Elementary Education,* Vol. 17 (February, 1949), pp. 139-145.

SNIDER, D. J., *Froebel's Mother-Play Songs* (Chicago, Sigma Publishing Company, 1895).

SPEARS, Harold, *Some Principles of Teaching* (Englewood Cliffs, N.J., Prentice-Hall, Inc., 1949).

———, *The Teacher and Curriculum Planning* (Englewood Cliffs, N.J., Prentice-Hall, Inc., 1953).

STEARNS, Harry, *Community Relations and the Public Schools* (Englewood Cliffs, N.J., Prentice-Hall, Inc., 1955).

STEIN, D. A., and MUKERJI, R., "Creating with Words in the Kindergarten," *Educational Leadership,* Vol. 15 (January, 1958), pp. 221-227.

STEINER, Arch K., "A Report on State Laws, Early Elementary Education," *School Life,* Vol. 39 (May, 1957), pp. 7-9.

STENDLER, Celia Burns, "Wanted: More Emotional Security for Children," *National Education Association Journal,* Vol. 42 (March, 1952), pp. 139-140.

———, and YOUNG, Norman, "The Impact of Beginning First Grade upon Socialization as Reported by Mothers," *Child Development,* Vol. 21 (December, 1950), pp. 241-260.

STEPHANS, Ada Dawson, *Providing Developmental Experiences for Young Children* (New York, Bureau of Publications, Teachers College, Columbia University, 1952).

STERN, C., and GOULD, T., *Early Years of Childhood* (New York, Harper & Brothers, 1955).

STEVER, Dorothy V., "The Kindergarten Environment," *California Journal of Elementary Education,* Vol. 17 (February, 1949), p. 3.

STILES, C. L., "Creative Use of Space, Time, and Materials," *Educational Leadership,* Vol. 15 (December, 1957), pp. 165-170.

STILES, Lindley J., ed., *The Teacher's Role in American Society,* 14th Yearbook, John Dewey Society (New York, Harper & Brothers, 1957).

STODDARD, Alexander, J., *Schools for Tomorrow: An Educational Blueprint* (New York, The Fund for the Advancement of Education, 655 Madison Ave., January, 1957).

STONE, Joseph, and CHURCH, Joseph, *Childhood and Adolescence* (New York, Random House, Inc., 1957).

STRANG, Ruth, *An Invitation to Child Study* (New York, The Macmillan Company, 1951).

———, *Reporting to Parents* (New York, Bureau of Publications, Teachers College, Columbia University, 1954).

STRATEMEYER, Florence, and others, *Developing a Curriculum for Modern Living* (New York, Bureau of Publications, Teachers College, Columbia University, 1957).

———, *Guides to a Curriculum for Modern Living* (New York, Bureau of Publications, Teachers College, Columbia University, 1952).

STRAUSS, A. L., "The Development of Conceptions of Rules in Children," *Child Development,* Vol. 25 (1954), pp. 193-208.

SUMPTION, Merle, and LANDES, Jack, *Planning Functional School Buildings* (New York, Harper & Brothers, 1957).

Swedish Institute, *Education in Sweden* (Stockholm, The Institute, 1950).

SYMONDS, Percival M., *Dynamics of Parent Child Relationships* (New York, Bureau of Publications, Teachers College, Columbia University, 1955).

TABA, Hilda, and others, *Diagnosing Human Relations and Needs* (Washington, D.C., American Council on Education, 1955).

TAYLOR, E. R., "Is the Kindergarten a Learning Situation?" *American Childhood,* Vol. 38 (April, 1953), pp. 23-25.

GENERAL BIBLIOGRAPHY

TEMPLE, Alice, *Unified Kindergarten and First Grade Teaching* (Boston, Ginn and Company, 1925).

TILLMAN, Viola, *A Good School Day* (New York, Bureau of Publications, Teachers College, Columbia University, 1950),

————, "Continuous Progress in School," *Childhood Education,* Vol. 18 (September, 1941), pp. 21-23.

THIMBLIN, L. M., "Adapting the School and Class Organization to the Varying Needs in Kindergarten and Through Grade Three," in *Proceedings of the Annual Conference on Reading* held at the University of Chicago, Vol. 16 (December, 1954), pp. 51-54.

THOMAS, Edith M., "Grouping in the Classroom," *Childhood Education,* Vol. 30 (October, 1953), pp. 69-71.

THOMAS, Maurice J., *Climate for Learning* (Pittsburgh, University of Pittsburgh Press, 1953).

————, *Improving Public Education Through Citizen Participation* (Pittsburgh, University of Pittsburgh Press, 1954).

THOMAS, R. Murray, *Ways of Teaching in Elementary Schools* (New York, Longmans, Green & Company, 1955).

THOMPSON, Ethel, "The Ungraded Plan," *National Education Association Journal,* Vol. 47 (January, 1958), pp. 16-17.

THOMPSON, George, *Child Psychology* (Boston, Houghton Mifflin Company, 1952).

THORPE, Louis P., *Child Psychology and Development* (New York, The Ronald Press Company, 1955).

TODD, M. N., "Kindergarten Report Card," *American School Board Journal,* Vol. 112 (February, 1946), pp. 82-84.

TORGENSON, Theodore L., *Studying Children* (New York, The Dryden Press, Inc., 1947).

TRAGER, Helen G., and YARROW, Marion R., *They Learn What They Live* (New York, Harper & Brothers, 1952).

TROW, William Clark, *The Learning Process,* What Research Says to the Teacher Series, No. 6 (Washington, D.C., National Education Association, 1954).

TYLER, Ralph, *Basic Principles of Curriculum and Instruction* (Chicago, University of Chicago Press, 1950).

ULICH, Robert, *Three Thousand Years of Educational Wisdom* (Cambridge, Mass., Harvard University Press, 1950).

————, *History of Educational Thought* (New York, American Book Company, 1945).

UNESCO, *Mental Hygiene in the Nursery School* (Paris, UNESCO, 1933). (United States distribution through UNESCO Publications Center, U.S.A., 801 Third Avenue, New York 22, N.Y.).

United States Office of Education, *Basic Body Measurements of School Age Children: Handbook for Planning School Buildings, Furniture, and Equipment* (Washington, D.C., Government Printing Office, 1955).

————, *Designing Elementary Classrooms,* Special Bulletin No. 1 (Washington, D.C., Government Printing Office, 1953).

————, Division of International Education, *Education in the U.S.S.R.,* Bulletin 1957, No. 14 (Washington, D.C., Government Printing Office, 1957).

————, *Education in the United States of America,* Special Series No. 1, rev. ed. (Washington, D.C., Government Printing Office, 1955).

————, *Good and Bad School Plants,* Special Publication No. 2 (Washington, D.C., Government Printing Office, 1954).

————, *Lighting Schoolrooms,* Pamphlet No. 104 (Washington, D.C., Government Printing Office, 1948).

————, *Planning and Designing the Multipurpose Room in Elementary Schools,* Special Publication No. 3 (Washington, D.C., Government Printing Office, 1955).

————, *Reporting Pupil Progress to Parents,* Brief No. 34 (Washington, D.C., Office of Education, 1956).

————, *School Buildings,* Bulletin No. 17 (Washington, D.C., Government Printing Office, 1950).

VANDEWALKER, Nina C., *The Kindergarten in American Education* (New York, The Macmillan Company, 1908).

WAECHTER, Heinrich H., and WAECHTER, Elizabeth, *Schools for the Very Young* (New York, F. W. Dodge Corporation, 1951).

WALDROP, M., and SPIEGEL, R., Group Processes in a Community Nursery," *Understanding the Child,* Vol. 25 (January, 1956), pp. 14-15.

WALLIHAN, Robert A., *A Comparative Study of Retardation in the Primary Grades of San Diego, California,* thesis (Boulder, University of Colorado, 1951).

WASHBURN, Ruth W., *Children Have Their Reasons* (New York, Appleton-Century-Crofts, Inc., 1942).

WESLEY, Edgar B., *NEA: The First Hundred Years* (New York, Harper & Brothers, 1957).

WHITING, J. W. M., and CHILD, I. L., *Child Training and Personality: A Cross-Cultural Study* (New Haven, Yale University Press, 1953).

WIGGIN, Kate Douglas, and SMITH, Nora Archibald, *Froebel's Gifts* (Boston, Houghton Mifflin Company, 1895).

WILES, Kimball, *Teaching for Better Schools* (Englewood Cliffs, N.J., Prentice-Hall, Inc., 1952).

————, "When Is a Teacher Mature?" *Educational Leadership,* Vol. 8 (May, 1951), pp. 493-496.

WILLCOCKSON, Mary, ed., *Social Education for Young Children* (Washington, D.C., National Council for the Social Studies, NEA, 1956).

WILLIAMS, Catherine M., "Sources of Teaching Materials," *Educational Research Bulletin,* Vol. 34 (May, 1955), pp. 113-140.

————, "Pictures with a Purpose," *National Education Association Journal,* Vol. 46 (March, 1957), pp. 197-198.

WILLIAMS, Margaret, "What Are Children Learning Through Independent Work Periods?" *Childhood Education,* Vol. 30 (December, 1954), pp. 183-190.

WILLS, Clarice D., and STEGEMAN, William H., *Living in the Kindergarten* (Chicago, Follett Publishing Company, 1956).

————, *Living in the Primary Grades* (Chicago, Follett Publishing Company, 1956).

WISLOCKI, Florence Clothier, "Teachers as Human Beings," *Vassar Alumnae Magazine* (December, 1956), pp. 19-21.

WOLF, Anna, and SZASZ, Suzanne, *Your Child's Emotional Growth* (New York, Doubleday & Company, Inc., 1954).

WOLFF, Werner, *The Personality of the Preschool Child* (New York, Grune & Stratton, Inc., 1946).

WRIGHTSTONE, J. Wayne, *Class Organization for Instruction*, What Research Says to the Teacher Series, No. 13 (Washington, D.C., National Education Association, 1957).

————, "Trends in Evaluation," *Educational Leadership,* Vol. 8 (November, 1950), pp. 91-95.

————, "What Research Says About Class Organization," *National Education Association Journal,* Vol. 46 (April 1957), pp. 254-255.

YEAGER, W., *School-Community Relations* (New York, Henry Holt & Company, Inc., 1954).

ZIESS, E. C., "The Kindergarten Teacher's Role in Guidance," *Childhood Education,* Vol. 38 (February, 1953), p. 12.

ZIRBES, Laura, "Teachers for Today's Schools: A Symposium," *Educational Leadership,* Vol. 10 (December, 1952), pp. 152-156.

Audio-Visual Aids

All descriptions have been taken from *The Educational Film Guide* and *The Filmstrip Guide,* both published by the H. W. Wilson Co., New York.

Film descriptions include: title, source, year of release, running time (min.), sound (sd.) or silent (sil.), and black and white (b & w) or color (c).

Filmstrip descriptions include: title, source, year of release, number of frames (fr.), sound (sd.) or silent (sil.), and black and white (b & w) or color (c).

Following is a key to abbreviations used for sources. Films and filmstrips may be secured from other than the direct source. Users will find the following reference of help in determining the closest source of purchase or rental if their school does not maintain its own audio-visual library:

REID, Seerley, and others, *A Directory of 3,300 16MM Film Libraries* (Office of Education, U. S. Department of Health, Education, and Welfare, Government Printing Office, Washington, D.C., 1956).

Abbreviations	*Complete Name of Source*
ACEI	Association for Childhood Education International, Washington, D.C.
AmCouncilEd	American Council on Education, 744 Jackson Pl., Washington, D.C.
BaileyFI	Bailey Films Inc., 6509 De Longpre Avenue, Los Angeles, California.
Brandon	Brandon Films Inc., 200 W. 57th St., New York, N.Y.
CACE	California Association for Childhood Education, Mrs. Sadye Lewis, 1755 Bel Air Avenue, San Jose, Calif.

CEF .... Child Education Foundation, 535 E. 84th St., New York, N.Y.

ColUPress .... Columbia University Press, Communications Materials Center, New York, N.Y.

Coronet .... Coronet Films, Coronet Building, Chicago, Illinois.

EBF .... Encyclopedia Britannica Films, Inc., 1123 Central Avenue, Wilmette, Ill.

EyeGate .... Eye Gate House, Inc., 2716 41st Ave., Long Island City, New York

EF .... Educator Films, 7934 Santa Monica Blvd., Hollywood, Calif.

ImpcoInc .... Impco Inc., 1050 Boulevard, New Milford, New Jersey

IndU and EdFlmLibAssn ...... Indiana University, Audio-Visual Center, 1800 E. 10th St., Bloomington, Ind.

IntFlmBur .... International Film Bureau, Suite 308-16, 57 East Jackson Blvd., Chicago, Ill.

IowaStU .... State University of Iowa, Bureau of Visual Instruction, Iowa City, Iowa

JamHandyOrgn .... The Jam Handy Organization, 2821 E. Grand Blvd., Detroit, Mich.

McG-H .... McGraw-Hill Book Company, Inc., Text-Film Dept., 330 W. 42nd St., New York, N.Y.

Moulin&Assoc .... Moulin & Associates, 621 S. Lebanon, Los Angeles, California

MSTA .... Missouri State Teachers Association, Columbia, Missouri

NEA .... National Education Association, Washington, D.C.

NEA-PublicRelations .... National Education Association, Dept. of Public Relations, Washington, D.C.

NEA-PublicationsSales .... National Education Association, Publications Sales, Washington, D.C.

NEA-Press&RadioSection ..... National Education Association, Press and Radio Section, Washington, D.C.

NEA-Rural .... National Education Association, Dept. of Rural Education, Washington, D.C.

NET .... Film Service, Indiana University, Audio Visual Center, Bloomington, Ind.

329

NYMetropStudy .... Metropolitan School Study Council, 525 W. 120th St., New York, N. Y.

NYU .... New York University Film Library, 26 Washington Place, New York, N.Y.

PennStateCol .... Pennsylvania State University, Audio-Visual Aids Library, State College, Pa.

SchExec .... School Executive, 470 Fourth Avenue, New York, N.Y.

SeminarFlms .... Seminar Films, Inc., 347 Madison Avenue, New York, N.Y.

SVE .... Society for Visual Education, Inc., 1345 W. Diversey Parkway, Chicago, Illinois

TchrsCol .... Teachers College, Columbia University, Bureau of Publications, 525 W. 120th St., New York, N.Y.

UW .... United World Films, Inc., 1445 Park Avenue, New York, N.Y.

UW-Educ .... Educational Film Dept., United World Films, Inc., 1445 Park Avenue, New York, N.Y.

UW-Govt .... Government Films Dept., United World Films, Inc., 1445 Park Avenue, New York, N.Y.

VaStBofE .... Commonwealth of Virginia, State Board of Education, Richmond, Virginia

VEC,Inc .... Visual Education Consultants, Inc., 2066 Helena St., Madison, Wisconsin

VirEdDpt .... Commonwealth of Virginia, State Board of Education, Richmond, Virginia

WayneU .... Wayne University, Audio-Visual Materials Consultation Bureau, 5272 Second Blvd., Detroit, Michigan

YoungAmerica .... Young America Films, Inc., 18 E. 41st St., New York, N.Y.

FILMS

A Day in the Life of a Five-Year-Old
Tchrs Col., 1949, 20 min., sd., b & w.

Portrays young children interpreting the world about them in a spacious, well-planned and equipped kindergarten setting. The role of the teacher in guiding these children through a happy, meaningful, and satisfying day is shown.

A Child Went Forth
Brandon, 1942, 20 min., sd., b & w.

Shows the experiences of children, ages two to seven, at a summer camp where they are allowed freedom to explore their new environment and to make their own social adjustment in a program designed to encourage physical health, mental alertness, and the courage to attack new problems.

A Child's World
E.F., 1952, 19 min., sd., b & w.

Points out the importance of nursery school to preschool children; documents the functions, limitations, and purposes of the Buckley Schools of Los Angeles. The training is shown to produce self-control, orderliness, obedience, and a capacity for co-operation with an emphasis on sound academic training.

A Long Time to Grow: (Part 1) Two and Three-Year-Olds in Nursery Schools
NYU, 1951, 35 min., sd., b & w.

Concerns two- and three-year-old children in a nursery school. Shows their learning behavior and activities throughout the day, and throughout the various seasons of the year.

Answering the Child's Why
EBF, 1951, 13 min., sd., b & w.

Dramatizes actual situations in which youngsters meet with positive or negative attitudes toward their questions; suggests the resulting effect on their personalities.

At Home with Your Child Series
NET, 1956, sd., b & w.
No. 10. *The Toddler* (29 min.)

> Describes the child in his second and third year. Stresses the importance of play, the development of possessiveness and self assertion, vocabulary development, and the nap and bed-time ritual. Shows some of the activities of children of this age.

No. 11. *Playmates* (29 min.)

> Presents some of the aspects of behavior and needs of the three-to five-year-olds. Discusses physical growth, play, likes and dislikes in foods, the acting out of roles, and the free flow of the imagination.

No. 12. *Getting Johnny Ready for School* (29 min.)

> Surveys the difficult year from five-and-a-half to six-and-a-half. Discusses physical development, points out the desirability of the preschool visit, and considers tests of readiness, hearing, and vision.

Baby Meets His Parents
EBF, 1948, 11 min., sd., b & w.

Points out how differences in personalities can be accounted for, not only by heredity, but also by the human relationships and environmental factors experienced during the first years of life.

Belonging to the Group
EBF, 1952, 16 min., sd., b & w.

Examines the idea of respect and explains its essential relation to living in a democracy.

Child Development Series, I
McG-H, 1950, sd., b & w.
   Children's Emotions (22 min.)

   Discusses the major emotions of childhood—fear, anger, jealousy, curiosity, and joy. Points out what the parent can do to lessen fears and promote the child's happiness and natural development.

   Principles of Development (17 min.)

   Outlines the fundamentals of child growth and development from the point of early infancy. After defining the principles of development, the film considers the variables which make each child different from every other one.

   Social Development (16 min.)

   An analysis of social behavior at different age levels and the reasons underlying the changes in behavior patterns as the child develops. Points out development from the stage where the sexes and ages are mixed indiscriminately to the point where children begin to pick members of their own sex as playmates, and to seek out the natural leader for their groups.

Child Development Series, II
McG-H, 1956, sd., b & w.
No. 1. *Children's Play* (27 min.)

   Points up the changing form of children's recreation, portraying play at each age level. Demonstrates the important contributions parents can and should make in order to give their children the best possible chance for healthy play.

No. 3. *Sibling Relations and Personality* (22 min.)

   Demonstrates the relationships a child has with his brothers and sisters throughout developmental years—an important factor in personality shaping. Emphasizes the importance of understanding complex personality influences in helping youngsters through childhood and adolescence.

No. 4. *Sibling Rivalries and Parents* (11 min.)

> Describes the reasons for a certain amount of rivalry among brothers and sisters, the varied manifestations of it, and means of holding natural friction to a minimum. Shows that friction is a normal human trait.

Children Are Creative
Bailey F I. 1953, 10 min., sd., c.

Contrasts old and new methods of teaching art. Reveals a classroom scene in which an instructor encourages observation of a mother hen and her chicks. Children assemble media of their own choice and work creatively with a minimum of direction from the teacher.

Children Growing Up with Other People
UW-Educ., 1948, 30 min., sd., b & w.

Illustrates the stages of growth in children, showing by example the constant adaptation to the world around them. Tact, discernment, and patience are, we learn, required of the adult who assists the child, especially as he moves closer to adulthood. The significance of the child's awakening to the responsibilities of social behavior after the self-centered individuality of childhood is clarified.

Children Learning by Experience
UW-Educ., 1948, 40 min., sd., b & w.

Develops the theme that all children want to learn, they enjoy practicing simple skills, they strive ever to understand the world around them, they learn some things at second hand, and a great many things by play and imagination.

Children Must Learn
NYU, 1940, 15 min., sd., b & w.

Designed to illustrate the unsatisfactory relationship between education and the local necessities of life which characterizes American education in many parts of this country.

Community Resources in Teaching
IowaStU, 1950, 20 min., sd., b & w.

Seeks to show how the community and its resources, and the school and its functions can be woven together into a "pattern" of education by bringing the students into the community to use its resources as laboratory studies, and inviting the community into the school as lecturers or demonstrators.

Curriculum Based on Child Development
McG-H, 1954, 12 min., sd., b & w.

Describes various techniques and procedures which can be used effectively in gearing a curriculum to the needs and behavior characteristics of specific age groups.

Democracy
EBF, 1946, 11 min., sd., b & w.

The nature and meaning of democracy.

Design of American Education
McG-H, 1952, 16 min., sd., b & w.

The organizational structure of American public education, first as it might be if it were an 'assembly line' educational process controlled centrally, and as it actually is in a democratic society—constitutional delegation of education to the various states with decentralization and state supervision, a system that develops responsible citizens in a democratic society.

Discussion in Democracy
Coronet, 1949, 10 min., sd., b & w.

A typical group of students learn, through expert advice and through their own experiences, the relationship of organized discussion to a democratic society.

Early Play
EBF, 1947, 15 min., sil., b & w.

Stresses the importance of determining each youngster's preferences in play and play objects. Illustrates the simple play situations enjoyed by most children at different ages.

Early Social Behavior
EBF, 1934, 11 min., sd., b & w.

The observer sees the manifestations of infant personality in a variety of social settings. Ten different children from eight weeks to seven years of age are studied. Individual differences are emphasized. The social significance of the household is conveyed by scenes which reflect parent-child relationships, and interaction between brothers, sisters, and adults.

Education for Democracy
MSTA, 1948, 22 min., sd., c.

Attempts to depict with actual classroom situations the manner in which Missouri schools achieve the purposes of education in our American democracy, as outlined by the Educational Policies Commission of the National Education Association.

Elementary School Children
McG-H, 1954, sd., b & w.
Part 1. *Each Child Is Different* (17 min.)

> A glimpse into the lives of five children in the fifth grade on the first day of a new school year. Shows that each is a complex and unique pattern, shaped by many influences in his home and community. Indi-

cates that the teacher, facing this new group of children for the first time, knows that it is one of her most important tasks to discover what these influences are so that she can adjust her educational program to fit the needs and characteristics of each child.

Part 2. *Discovering Individual Differences* (25 min.)

Shows how a fifth grade teacher systematically studies the differences in background, abilities, and needs of children in her room. In this process she utilizes the following techniques: observation, cumulative records, behavior journal, discussion with other teachers, interviews with parents, and staff conferences.

Emergence of Personality
EBF, 30 min., sd., b & w.

A combined forum version of the three films: *Baby Meets His Parents; Helping the Child to Face the Dont's;* and *Helping the Child to Accept the Do's.*

Experimental Studies in Social Climates of Groups
IowaStU, 1940, 30 min., sd., b & w.

Shows behavior of groups of boys organized into clubs, one run on democratic principles, one organized as an autocracy, and one as a laissez-faire group. Shows responses when groups are changed from one type to another. Graphs and charts give statistics as to group actions and reactions.

Family Circles
McG-H, 1949, 31 min., sd., b & w.

Shows how the interplay of home and school influences affect the development of today's youngsters. The experiences of three children illustrate how parental indifference, lack of imagination, and emotional conflict at home can destroy the confidence and the enthusiasm necessary for a child's success at school. On the positive side we see the parents of Jimmy, who co-operate with his teacher, encourage his interests and help build constructive social attitudes.

Family Life
UW-Educ., 1957, 20 min., sd. b & w.

Each member of the family in his own way participates in the tasks of providing food, clothing, shelter, and creating an atmosphere of co-operation and mutual concern.

Fears of Children
IntFlmBur, 1951, 30 min., sd., b & w.

A parent-child situation is presented in which the mother tends to coddle her five-year-old son while the father advocates sterner discipline and encouraging the child to do things for himself. The resulting conflict confuses the boy and magnifies his rudimentary fears. Through the advice of a friend the parents make a greater effort to understand the situation and a happy solution is indicated at the end of the film.

Field Trip
VaSt. B of E., 1949, 10 min., sd., b & w.

Instructions on how to plan and take a field trip, using a trip to Dismal Swamp as an example.

Frustrating Fours and Fascinating Fives
McG-H, 1952, 22 min., sd., b & w.

At home at the age of four we see a boy's behavior deviate from childish help-lessness to vigorous self-assertion, and at kindergarten, from imaginative crafts-manship to inconsistent destructiveness. Although the change is gradual, at five Roddy appears more independent of adult support with an insatiable curiosity about everything around him.

From Sociable Six to Noisy Nine
McG-H, 1954, 22 min., sd., b & w.

Shows the typical behavior and sensible parental guidance of several children of six to nine years of age.

Frustration Play Techniques
NYU, 1942, 35 min., sd., b & w.

Study of normal personality development in young children, and a demon-stration of special techniques in the diagnosis of normal personality.

Growth: A Study of Johnny and Jimmy
IntFlmBur, 1941, 43 min., sil., b & w.

Illustrates the influence of exercise on the development of each motor func-tion at each level. Comparative behavior is shown during the first two years, when the twins were the subject of special investigation, and during the follow-ing six years.

Growth of Adaptive Behavior
EBF, 1946, 15 min., sil., b & w.

Finer motor co-ordinations are traced through their development during the child's first five years. Shows the growth of discrimination in action and in selection as the child meets the world.

He Who Dares to Teach
Moulin&Assoc, 1955, 18 min., sd., c.

This film on the operation of one of California's parent-nursery classes shows the nursery school and the one-a-week evening classes for parents.

Helping Teachers to Understand Children
UW-Govt, 1953, sd., b & w.

Part 1. (21 min.) The story of the work of the Institute for Child Study at the University of Maryland. Shows how a school faculty may set up a local child study program and receive guidance and aid from the Institute.

Helping Your Child Feel Emotionally Secure
SeminarFlms, 30 min., sd., c.

Consists of three separate reels, each 10 min. Each reel contains five short incidents which show the right and wrong way for parents to handle a situation.

Homes
UW, 1957, 18 min., sd., b & w.

Shows that home life of children around the world is strikingly similar though climate and economic levels may differ widely.

Individual Differences
McG-H, 1950, 23 min., sd., b & w.

The case study of a shy, slow child who is different from his classmates and from his older, socially-adept brother. Points out that individual differences must be met in terms of individual interests and capacities, that it is the job of the school to shape education to individual needs.

It's a Small World
ColUPress, 1951, 38 min., sd., b & w.

By means of hidden cameras the film shows spontaneous actions and reactions of children in a full day of nursery school life.

Learning is Searching
NYU, 1955, 30 min., sd., b & w.

A third grade in the new Lincoln School studies tools and their origins. The process of search is stressed. Shows the relationship of these studies to the group's other school activities. Presents the enthusiasm as well as the limitations of the children.

Learning Through Cooperative Planning
Tchrs Col, 1948, 20 min., sd., b & w.

Shows how elementary school children can learn to plan co-operatively.

Linda and Roy Go Fishing
ImpcoInc, 1953, 11 min., sd., c.

A discussion film introducing the private thought world of children. Photography of children with a sound track of adult voices predicting the thoughts of the children. Focus of film is around the co-operation, ingenuity, self-reliance, respect, and understanding required of the two children working together.

Making Learning More Meaningful
McG-H, 1954, 12 min., sd., b & w.

Demonstrates a typical third grade classroom situation in which there is a definite need for learning experiences related to everyday living which help in the understanding of abstract concepts in the counting and use of money. The class then proceeds with a project showing the use and flow of money in a community; the various stages of the project and the post-project follow-up are described.

Meeting Emotional Needs in Childhood: The Groundwork of Democracy
NYU, 1947, 33 min., sd., b & w.

Concerned with the kind of attitude toward people and the sense of community responsibility the child is developing as he grows to adulthood.

Near Home
IntFlmBur, 1946, 25 min., sd., b & w.

Tells the story of 31 children and their teacher starting local studies. Methods and materials are drawn from everyday educational practice in various parts of England and Wales and molded into one concrete example set by the Bishop Auckland School.

Our Shrinking World
Young America, 1946, 11 min., sd., b & w.

The development of many phases of transportation and communication through the ages. Develops an appreciation of the relative values of the factors stimulating progress. Emphasizes the necessity of appreciating the problems of all the peoples of the world as they live more and more closely together.

Planning for Personal and Professional Growth
McG-H, 1956, 18 min., sd., b & w.

Dramatizes case studies of the personalities and careers of four typical teachers to show how a teacher can avoid failure and frustration, and how she can make her teaching experiences rewarding by planning for her own personal and professional growth.

Practicing Democracy in the Classroom
EBF, 1953, 22 min., sd., b & w.

Shows how a teacher, along with fellow members of her faculty, some parents, and students worked out a satisfactory approach to the problem of teaching a course in American history by using methods that give students a chance to develop the knowledge, skills, and attitudes of a desirable citizen of a democracy.

Preface to a Life
UW-Govt, 1950, 29 min., sd., b & w.

Portrays the influence parents have on a child's developing personality.

School Children
UW, 1957, 20 min., sd., b & w.

Shows children, through school relationships, learning the skills which help them to live better with themselves, with each other, and with people all over the world.

School and the Community
McG H, 14 min., sd., b & w.

Addresses itself to the problem of the wall of separation between many schools and their community, and the losses which both suffer thereby. Argues that everyone—teachers, parents, school officials, and the citizenry at large—shares responsibility for these poor conditions. Shows the benefits which both the school and the community obtain when they co-operate.

School in Centreville

NEA-Rural, 1950, 20 min., sd., b & w.
Shows how education in rural schools can be geared to the problems of learning to live in the community.

Skippy and the Three R's
NEA, 1955, 29 min., sd., b & w/c.

Shows how a first grade boy is taught reading, writing, and arithmetic by a teacher who utilizes the boy's interest to help him to realize his own need for learning.

Studies in Human Development Series
PennStCol-PCR, 1946, sil., b & w.
Part 4. *Three Years to Five Years* (18 min.)

> At third year, socially interdependent play, development of skills in drawing, and typical motor-co-ordination demonstrated. Fourth year brings finer co-ordination, greater ability in drawing, and rudimentary musical skill; application of performance tests for intelligence shown at this level. During fifth year boy enrolls in kindergarten and begins characteristic social play activities.

The Child at Play
TchrsCol, 1952, 18 min., sd., b & w.

Shows the nature of children's spontaneous play as reviewed in a one-way vision room.

The Elementary School
VirEdDpt, 1952, sd., b & w.

Part 1. (25 min.) Emphasizes aspects of good school environment, such as plant and equipment, pupil and teacher welfare, and school relationships. Shows provisions for physical and mental health of all pupils.
Part 2. (25 min.) Shows experiences through which children acquire the communicative and number skills and develop their interests in the practical and fine arts.
Part 3. (20 min.) Shows opportunities for children to develop a knowledge of the physical world and an understanding of their country and the relationship of peoples.

The School—The Child's Community
WayneU, 1952, 16 min., sd., b & w.

The many ways a school can encourage children to accept responsibilities and share in the making of decisions that concern them are pictured by showing student participation in the community activities of an elementary school.

The Teacher
CEF, 1953, 25 min., sd., c.

Shows the process by which a student is prepared to teach the child from two to eight in a modern professional college.

The Teacher as Observer and Guide
TchrsCol, 1946, 20 min., sd., b & w.

Six sequences, presenting actual classroom practice, direct attention to the importance of the teacher as an observer and guide of pupil growth. Teachers are guiding pupils to better ways of solving their problems; providing needed assistance to slow learners; promoting the growth of character and citizenship; and observing and stimulating the development of artistic talent.

This Is Robert
NYU, 1942, 1 hr. 20 min., sd., b & w.

Traces the development of an aggressive, "difficult" yet thoroughly appealing child from his early nursery school days to his first year in a fine public school.

Understanding the Child Series
NET, 1955, ea. 30 min., sd., b & w.
Part 1. *How Children Grow*

> Discusses the concepts of maturation and nurture, and examines their relation to physical, intellectual, social, and emotional growth. Two girls, five and eight, are used to demonstrate intellectual achievement.

Part 2. *Physical Development*

> Discusses the physical growth of children, emphasizing that the parents should realize that each child grows at his own rate.

Part 3. *Mental Growth and Achievement*

> Discusses intelligence and achievement and the methods of testing intelligence. Points out the necessity for appreciating the differences between intelligence and achievement.

Part 4. *The Child as a Whole*

> Discusses the importance of measuring a child's capacities by his organismic age rather than his calendar age. Explains how organismic age is figured.

Part 5. *Social Relations*

Discusses how growth can be looked upon as a process which enables the infant to move away from the home. Emphasizes the importance of encouraging this kind of growth which takes him from the crib to his whole home, to the neighborhood, to the town, and to the world.

Part 6. *Emotional Development*

Discusses the aspects of emotional development. Explains the origin of many children's fears, and discusses frustrations, temper tantrums, and ways of testing children for emotional disturbance.

Part 7. *Child Rearing Practices*

Summary discussion of previous "Understanding the Child" films dealing with the patterns and measurement of growth in children. Indicates the need for scientific knowledge in child rearing practices and how the knowledge is constantly changing.

Using the Scientific Method
Coronet, 1952, 11 min., sd., b & w.

Presents the scientific method in the context of an everyday problem.

What Greater Gift
NEA-Press&RadioSection, 1953, 28 min., sd., b & w.

A high school girl, contemplating teaching as a career, sees classroom scenes which show what teaching is like today, and learns of the professional preparation, understanding, and skills essential to good teaching.

Your Children's Play
McG-H, 1952, 21 min., sd., b & w.

Illustrates how children learn by playing—how they acquire knowledge, physical dexterity and an understanding of the world about them, and how play activities channel their emotional states. Throughout the film are offered suggestions on what parents can do to aid their children's development, with instances given of how parents, seeing only the adult point of view, can cramp the child's growth by unwise interference.

FILMSTRIPS

Bringing the Community to the Classroom
WayneU, 1952, 45 fr., sil. with captions, b & w.

Shows the many ways in which one teacher calls upon the community to teach a specific unit of work. Also illustrates how other teachers in various curriculum areas may bring community resources to the school so that instruction may be of maximum effectiveness.

Child Cooperation and Self Discipline
SVE, 1954, sil. with captions, b & w.

Drawings. The resulting effects of co-operation and non-co-operation are compared in common everyday activities. Intended to impress children with the general idea and satisfaction of sharing, to teach elementary factors of democracy, to motivate discussion of attitudes, and to present an approach to self discipline.

Children in the Primary School
ACEI, 1952, 51 fr., sil. with captions, b & w.

Describes and illustrates good school experiences for children six, seven, and eight years of age.

Contemporary School Design in 1952
SchExec, 1953, 50 fr., sil. with captions.

Materials developed from the 1952 Annual Competition for Better School Design, sponsored by School Executive Magazine. Photographs, plans, and sketches are included.

Titles are:
  Sites and Building Exteriors
  Interiors and Instructional Spaces
  Interiors and Large Group Spaces
  Technical Features of Buildings
  Outstanding Design Solutions

Cooperative School Plant Planning
IndU and EdFlmLibAssn, 1952, 100 fr., sil. with captions, c.

Presents a functional approach to dynamic group action as applied to the community planning of school buildings. Outlines the roles of the board of education, the superintendent of schools, the educational consultant, the architect, the engineer, other experts, as well as children, teachers, and citizens of the community as they take part in a co-operative school plant planning procedure. Many details of administration are covered, as well as ways in which co-operating groups and individuals can benefit.

David and His Family
YoungAmerica, 1949, 30 fr., sil. with captions, b & w.

The story of David's life at home with a new baby brother, and how he adjusts himself to the situation.

Democracy Builds a School
VEC,Inc., 1954, 39 fr., sil. with captions, b & w.

Shows the steps taken by the citizens of Park Forest, Illinois, to establish a new school and plan its facilities.

Good Day Series
CACE, ea. Kg.-grade 8 60 slides on filmstrip, c, script, accompanying records; ed., Helen Heffernan, Chief, Elem. Ed., State Department.

Titles include:
Good Day in the Kindergarten
Good Day in the First Grade
Good Day in the Second Grade
Good Day in the Third Grade

Group Life for the Pre-School Child
NYU, 1949, 36 fr., sil., b & w.

Scenes of group activities at the Harriet Johnson Nursery School, known as the Bank Street school, in New York City.

Living and Working Together
JamHandyOrgn, 1954, sil. with captions, c.

Series includes:
Family Begins the Day
Safe Way to School
A Busy Morning in School
Lunch and Play at School
A Birthday Party at School
Family at Home

N.E.A. in Action
NEA-Publications Sales, 1954, 50 fr., sil., c., script, tape recording.

Highlights of the report on activities of the National Education Association.

Report Card Comes Home
WayneU, 1951, 38 fr., sil. with captions, b & w.

Shows the part parents can play in making the school's reporting system a contribution to the child's classroom progress.

Responsibility Can Be Taught
NY-MetropStudy, 1954, 34 fr., sil., c.

Designed to establish better understanding between parents and teachers as to how they may consistently work to develop better feelings of responsibility in young people. Assigning reasonable jobs to children, adults and children doing real jobs together, teaching by example and precept, reasoning with children, and giving rewards and punishments are suggested.

School Buildings and Equipment
AmCouncilEd, 1952, sil., b & w.
Part 1. *Modern Elementary School* (55 fr.)

> Shows current trends (1952) in school buildings and equipment, and indicates how these support the educational programs of the elementary school.

Teacher and Public Relations
NEAPubRel, 1952, 50 fr., sil. with captions, b & w.

How to build an appreciation of the professional skills and achievements of teachers, why we teach, what we teach, how we teach, homework assignments, reports to parents, public relations, values of co-curricular activities, making parents partners, and working with community groups.

Trips Here and There
EyeGate, 1954 es. 25-30 fr., sil. with captions, c.

Photographs. A boy and his mother take trips ranging from his immediate neighborhood to more distant places. Intended to introduce children to a variety of places and experiences.

Titles include:
  Our Neighborhood Stores
  Crossing a Bridge
  People of Other Neighborhoods
  People at Work
  Visiting a Town
  Visiting a Village
  Visiting a Large City
  Trip to the Mountains
  Having Fun in the City

We Plan Together

YoungAmerica, 1952, 27 fr., sil. with captions, b & w.
Presents several typical problems that may arise in primary grade classes. Solutions to the problems are offered and agreed upon by the children.

What Has the Nursery School to Offer?
ACEI, 1944, 69 fr., sil. with captions, b & w.

Designed to help parents, teachers, administrators, students in teacher education, and the public understand the program of the nursery school.

Working and Playing Together
McG-H, 1953, 45 fr., sil. with captions, c.

Stresses the values to be gained from playing and working together with other children and with other members of one's family. Shows how helping others is a means of building happiness.

Your Educational Philosophy—Does It Matter?
Wayne U, 1952, 40 fr., sil. with captions, b & w.

Begins with pictures illustrating the idea that "Philosophy is like the wind—you can't see it; you see only its effects." Then presents a number of views of the classrooms of two teachers, both of whom are considered by their principal to be among the best members of his staff. Ends with a series of photographs that compare similar situations in the two classrooms concerned. No interpretation of the classroom scenes is given.

RECORDINGS

Characteristics of a Good Teacher
Educational Recording Services, Los Angeles, California.

Part 1. Dr. A. S. Barr—*Personal Qualties and Competencies of the Good Teacher.*

Parent-Teacher Conferences, Vol. I.

Wayne University, Detroit, Michigan (Audio Visual Consultation Bureau).
Subject is school conferences: three records.

Report Forms

MILWAUKEE PUBLIC SCHOOLS
PROGRESS REPORT
Primary School

To the Parents:

The educational welfare of children and youth is best served when there is complete understanding and cooperation between the home and the school. As a basis for such understanding and cooperation, the school prepares this report on your child's progress. It will be sent to you three times each semester.

This report records pupil achievement. It also presents the best judgment of the school as to the growth that has taken place in those personal characteristics that make for good citizenship in the school and community.

It is hoped that parents will find time to study this report carefully. They are invited to confer with principals and teachers at any time the need arises. The school will appreciate any comments from parents that will assist in meeting the needs of individual children.

H. S. Vincent

Superintendent of Schools

_____
Principal

_____
Teacher

_____
School

School Year 19_____ 19_____ Semester_____

Classification Next Semester_____

PERSONAL AND SOCIAL GROWTH

Meaning of Marks:

    C—Is making good progress.

    D—Needs to improve.

Report Period

1   2   3 **HEALTHFUL LIVING**

___ ___ ___ Practices good health habits

___ ___ ___ Observes safety rules

PERSONAL DEVELOPMENT

___ ___ ___ Plays well with others

___ ___ ___ Respects rights of others

___ ___ ___ Observes rules and regulations

___ ___ ___ Shows growth in self-control

___ ___ ___ Accepts responsibility

WORK HABITS AND ATTITUDES

___ ___ ___ Follows directions

___ ___ ___ Completes work begun

___ ___ ___ Works well independently

___ ___ ___ Works well with others

ATTENDANCE

	1	2	3		1	2	3
Days ABSENT				Times TARDY			

Name _____

SEMESTER ABOVE KINDERGARTEN							
1	2	3	4	5	6	7	8

GROWTH IN LEARNING AND SKILLS

Meaning of Marks:

C—Is making good progress.
D—Needs to improve.

This form of progress report covers a period of at least three years in the primary school. It takes time to recognize the learning power of each child. **In these early years,** growth may be rapid during one period and slow during another. Therefore, it seems wise to use a narrow marking system — 2 symbols — until the growth and power can be more definitely determined. In the beginning each child will be marked in some areas but not in others.

Report Period

1   2   3   **READING (See Progress Chart on Back of Card)**

___ ___ ___ Shows readiness for reading
___ ___ ___ Reads with understanding
___ ___ ___ Is acquiring needed reading skills
___ ___ ___ Reads independently for pleasure
___ ___ ___ Reads independently for information

LANGUAGE (Speaking, Writing, Listening)

___ ___ ___ Shares ideas and experiences with others
___ ___ ___ Expresses ideas clearly
___ ___ ___ Is a good listener
___ ___ ___ Is acquiring skill in handwriting
___ ___ ___ Is acquiring skill in spelling
___ ___ ___ Writes his own stories and letters

ARITHMETIC

___ ___ ___ Uses numbers with understanding
___ ___ ___ Reasons well in solving problems
___ ___ ___ Is acquiring number facts

Your child shows special interest in areas marked (X).

___ ___ ___ Arts and Crafts   ___ ___ ___ Science
___ ___ ___ Music   ___ ___ ___ Social Studies
___ ___ ___ Stories and Poetry   ___ ___ ___ Physical Activities

READING PROGRESS	
LEVEL	DATE
1	
2	
3	
4	
5	
6	
7	
8	
9	
10	
11	
12	

1. As children progress from Level 1 to Level 12 the reading material becomes increasingly more difficult.

2. The latest date indicates the level on which the child is reading.

3. A conference between the parent and the teacher is desirable.

Remarks:

Date

have studied this report.

1._____

2._____

3._____

Parent's Signature

10RP—9-54

MINNEAPOLIS PUBLIC SCHOOLS

MINNEAPOLIS   MINNESOTA

Progress Report

School Year_____

for KINDERGARTEN

The family, home and school are vital factors in the educational progress of your
child. We must all work together for his
best physical, mental and social growth.

We hope this card will tell you how your
child is progressing on the basis of his own
abilities. If you wish to discuss this further,
feel free to consult with his teacher. We
are always glad to plan a personal conference with you.

Rufus A. Putnam
Superintendent of Schools

A MESSAGE TO PARENTS

The kindergarten is a place where your child will learn to live, work and play with other children of his age. Day by day growth can best be accomplished by setting standards for each individual child, not by comparing him with his classmates. You, as a parent, can share his kindergarten experience by showing interest in his progress.

Some of the experiences, in addition to his social, physical and emotional development in which he will show progress are:

Enjoying stories, poems and books
Retelling stories
Dramatizing
Repeating rhymes
Singing in tune
Recognizing colors

Enjoying drawing
Showing interest in numbers
Handling scissors well
Tying shoe laces
Putting on wraps
Knowing address

Showing curiosity and interest in things about him

NAME _____

	1			2			3		
	O	S	N	O	S	N	O	S	N

SOCIAL DEVELOPMENT

Joins happily in group play _____

Shows courtesy and consideration _____

Respects rights and property of others _____

Is dependable _____

Responds willingly and readily _____

Uses a pleasant speaking voice _____

Takes part in informal conversation _____

Listens while others are speaking _____

PHYSICAL & EMOTIONAL DEVELOPMENT

Practices good health habits in school _____

Relaxes during quiet periods _____

Is happy and well adjusted _____

Finds joy and satisfaction in work and play _____

Is developing in motor control and coordination ___

WORK HABITS

Listens to and follows directions _____

Uses time and energy well _____

Starts work and completes it on time _____

Does neat work _____

Works without bothering others _____

Works well as a member of a cooperating group ___

Thinks and solves own problems _____

Attendance record for school year

Days present _____ _____

Days absent _____ _____

Times tardy _____ _____

PARENTS' SIGNATURES

	Date	
Conference or Report Card		
Conference or Report Card		

RECOMMENDED PLACEMENT

_____is assigned

to grade_____ , room number _____

Date _____   _____

Teacher's Signature

School   Teacher   Principal

_____   _____   _____

_____   _____   _____

_____   _____   _____

19B   6M   9-51

MINNEAPOLIS PUBLIC SCHOOLS

MINNEAPOLIS　　　　　　　　　　　　　MINNESOTA

Progress Report

School Year_____

for GRADE ONE

The family, home and school are vital factors in the educational progress of your child. We must all work together for his best physical, mental and social growth.

We hope this card will tell you how your child is progressing on the basis of his own abilities. If you wish to discuss this further, feel free to consult with his teacher. We are always glad to plan a personal conference with you.

Rufus A. Putnam
Superintendent of Schools

A MESSAGE TO PARENTS

Marks for your child are based upon the child's own abilities insofar as the teacher can judge from standard tests, teacher-made tests and observation. These marks do not indicate his standing in relation to the group. If you wish to know where your child stands in his group, make arrangements to discuss this with his teacher.

HABITS AND ATTITUDES

	1			2			3		
SOCIAL DEVELOPMENT	O	S	N	O	S	N	O	S	N
Plays well with others									
Is friendly									
Assumes and carries out responsibilities in school									
Responds to rules and regulations									
Shows courtesy and consideration									
Uses good judgment									
Listens attentively to others									
Takes care of materials									
Puts on and removes wraps in reasonable time									
Respects rights and property of others									
HEALTH HABITS									
Works and plays safely									
Practices good health habits in school									
Appears to have sufficient rest									
WORK HABITS									
Works well with others									
Works well alone									
Starts work promptly and completes it									
Shows neatness in work									
Listens to and follows directions									

NAME _____

O — OUTSTANDING PROGRESS — Very good for this child, makes wholehearted effort.

S — SATISFACTORY PROGRESS — Suitable growth according to ability, tries to do what is expected.

N — NEEDS IMPROVEMENT — Not working up to capacity.

KNOWLEDGES AND SKILLS

	1			2			3		
	O	S	N	O	S	N	O	S	N

SOCIAL STUDIES & SCIENCE
Assumes responsibility of good citizenship_____

Contributes to the study of community life_____

Shows powers of observation _____

Shows interest in world around him _____

READING
Reads with understanding_____

Reads well orally_____

Shows growth in word recognition_____

Reads independently for information and pleasure____

ORAL & WRITTEN LANGUAGE
Listens attentively_____

Expresses ideas well orally_____

Expresses ideas well in writing_____

Takes part in activities _____

Shows growth in spelling_____

Writes legibly_____

ARITHMETIC
Uses numbers understandingly_____

Knows number facts (Third grade)_____

INTEREST & EFFORT IN
Art activities_____

Music experiences_____

Physical education_____

Handwork_____

Attendance record for school year

Days present _____ _____
Days absent _____ _____
Times tardy _____ _____

PARENTS' SIGNATURES

	Date	
Conference or Report Card		
Conference or Report Card		

RECOMMENDED PLACEMENT

_____is assigned

to grade_____ , room number_____

Date_____   _____
                                                  Teacher's Signature

School   Teacher   Principal

_____   _____   _____

_____   _____   _____

_____   _____   _____

19C   10M   9-51

MINNEAPOLIS PUBLIC SCHOOLS
MINNEAPOLIS   MINNESOTA

Progress Report

School Year_____

for GRADES 2 and 3

The family, home and school are vital factors in the educational progress of your child. We must all work together for his best physical, mental and social growth.

We hope this card will tell you how your child is progressing on the basis of his own abilities. If you wish to discuss this further, feel free to consult with his teacher. We are always glad to plan a personal conference with you.

Rufus A. Putnam
Superintendent of Schools

A MESSAGE TO PARENTS

Marks for your child are based upon the child's own abilities insofar as the teacher can judge from standard tests, teacher-made
tests and observation. These marks do not indicate his standing
in relation to the group. If you wish to know where your child stands
in his group, make arrangements to discuss this with his teacher.

HABITS AND ATTITUDES

	1			2			3		
	O	S	N	O	S	N	O	S	N
SOCIAL ATTITUDES									
Listens attentively when others are speaking									
Is courteous in speech and manner									
Respects authority									
Respects rights and property of others									
Plays well with other children									
HEALTH HABITS									
Practices habits of cleanliness									
Applies good health rules									
Appears to have sufficient rest									
WORK HABITS									
Is prompt in beginning and finishing work									
Follows directions									
Uses time wisely									
Uses materials carefully									
Works well in a group									
Assumes responsibilities									
Works independently without disturbing others									

NAME _____

O — OUTSTANDING PROGRESS — Very good for this child, makes wholehearted effort.

S — SATISFACTORY PROGRESS — Suitable growth according to ability, tries to do what is expected.

N — NEEDS IMPROVEMENT — Not working up to capacity.

KNOWLEDGES AND SKILLS

	1			2			3		
	O	S	N	O	S	N	O	S	N

SOCIAL STUDIES & SCIENCE
Shows background of valuable experiences_____
Shares worthwhile experiences_____
Shows interest in class activities_____

READING
Shows growth in readiness for reading_____
Shows enjoyment in reading_____
Understands what he reads_____
Shows progress_____
Reads independently_____
Reads well orally_____

ORAL & WRITTEN LANGUAGE
Express himself before a group_____
Express thoughts clearly and in sequence_____
Writes own stories independently_____
Shapes words and sentences well_____

NUMBERS
Uses numbers understandingly_____

ART
Shows interest_____
Expresses ideas clearly_____

MUSIC
Enjoys singing in group_____
Shows growth in carrying a tune_____
Is attentive_____

Attendance record, for school year

Days present _____
Days absent _____
Times tardy _____

PARENTS' SIGNATURES

	Date	
Conference or Report Card		
Conference or Report Card		

RECOMMENDED PLACEMENT

_____is assigned

to grade_____ , room number_____

Date _____   _____
                                              Teacher's Signature

School   Teacher   Principal

_____   _____   _____

_____   _____   _____

_____   _____   _____

19A   7M   9-51

Index